CW00566664

THE GREATEST

WILLIAM FOTHERINGHAM

THE GREATEST

The Times and Life of BERYL BURTON

YouCaxton Publications
Oxford & Shrewsbury

ISBN 978-1-912419-53-1
Printed and bound in Great Britain.
Published by YouCaxton Publications

YCBN: 02

To my mother, Alison Harding,
the exemplar of courage and creativity

Contents

Author's note

There are various acronyms in this book, often derived from British racing organisations running championships of various kinds, so for the sake of clarity, here is a brief explainer.

BBAR: British Best All Rounder (usually abbreviated to BAR): season-long time trial competition based, for women, on average speed of fastest rides for 25, 50 and 100 miles; for men, on 50 and 100 miles and 12 hours.

BCF: British Cycling Federation: British governing body for road and track racing, founded in 1959 after merger between BLRC and NCU. It has recently dropped the Federation and is just known as BC; it now also runs cyclo-cross, BMX and mountain biking.

BLRC: British League of Racing Cyclists: organisation set up during World War Two to promote road racing on British roads along the lines of racing in Europe.

CTC: Cyclists' Touring Club: founded in 1878 to support cyclists as they discovered British roads; it still exists today as Cycling UK, a campaigning organisation promoting cycle use.

NCU: National Cyclists' Union: also founded in 1878, the NCU was the British governing body for track and 'massed start' racing until its merger with the BLRC.

RRA: Road Records Association: UK organisation which supervises cycle record attempts on the road, founded in 1888.

RTTC: Road Time Trials Council: founded in 1922 to oversee time-trialling on British roads; it took over the running of the BBAR from *Cycling* magazine in 1944.

UCI: Union Cycliste Internationale: world governing body of cycling.

WCRA: Women's Cycle Racing Association: founded in 1949 as the Women's Track Racing Association, this was a pressure group dedicated to the cause of women in cycle racing, which ran its own British women's national championships. It was disbanded in 2007 as it was felt it had achieved its founders' objectives.

Additionally, frequent mention is made of records. Unless mentioned otherwise, these are **RTTC** women's competition records, i.e. the fastest times recorded in time trials run by the RTTC.

Chapter 1

Overtaking

57min 54sec: Beryl Burton's time for the third 25-mile sector between Widford and Rayleigh, women's national 100-mile championship, E83, August 1968.

It was a soaking wet late summer day on the A12 between Romford and Marks Tey. Misty drizzle was hanging low, spray was whipped up from the tarmac by the traffic, and garage advertising flags were stretched out by the breeze. For the 23 women who started the 1968 British 100-mile time trial championship these were far from ideal conditions. But one, Beryl Burton, was set fair for a ninth gold medal at the distance, though she had her mind focused on a far bigger target. As she tried to avoid slipping and falling at the roundabouts, Burton knew she was 'on a ride', set for yet another time-trialling breakthrough: less than four hours for 100 miles - an average speed of over 25 miles per hour.

Plumes of spray flew off Burton's wheels, rain ran down her forehead and off the end of her nose, and she had to move her hand every few minutes to wipe the droplets off the stopwatch sitting to the right of the bars of her Jacques Anquetil racing bike. She tucked down into the huge drop handlebars, her face inches from the flapping brake cables, her back flat and her legs shining with the wet. Her early times were comfortably inside the hour for the each of the first two 25-mile segments, from the start near Brentwood, up the Ingatestone, Chelmsford, Witham and Kelvedon bypasses, turning where the A12 met the A120 at Marks Tey, and back down the A12 again. She knew that the record was there for the taking.

For onlookers soaking on the roadsides of the course, shaped like a giant slantways 'L', the question was not whether Burton would win. That was a given even if she punctured or crashed, so vast was the gulf between her and her fellow women. It was simply matter of how great her margin of victory might be, and whether or not she could brake the magic four-hour barrier.

Her helpers shouted encouragement. 'Mek it crack,' yelled her training partner, boss and Morley CC clubmate, Nim Carline. When one spectator screamed something about 'Greatwood', Burton took a few minutes to register what he meant. John Greatwood was the holder of the fastest time on the course, 4 hours 2min; if she was ahead of him, the record was 'on'. She constantly calculated her speed as the miles sped by. She took particular care at each traffic island where other competitors had fallen, sustaining grazes to elbows, knees and hips. The third 25 miles – back down the A12 to Gallows Corner, then along the A127 towards Rayleigh – went by in just below 58 minutes, giving her a cushion of four minutes for the closing quarter.

In that final hour around Rayleigh and Horndon, Burton fought her gears and the weather, working hard to maintain speed, composure and concentration, one eye on the stopwatch, one eye on the road ahead. She could not afford to puncture. She had a long pump and spare tubular tyre attached to her bike, but the record would slip away if she had to change a 'tub' and pump it up. She had to make sure she stayed upright at every roundabout, gauging the speed so she lost as little momentum as possible, while not making her lightweight tyres slide on the wet tarmac – 'Straining every muscle, hammering away,' she wrote later. At the finish –

close to the crossroads where the A128 meets the A127 east of Rayleigh – she finally lifted her head from the bars and at last allowed the rain to trickle down her neck and shoulders while she looked at the steam rising off her bare arms.

The second-placed rider, Ann Horswell, had crashed on a roundabout and finished 23 minutes slower, but other times were what truly mattered to Burton. She had broken her own 100-mile record by more than six minutes, recording a time of 3hr 55min 5sec. That was faster than any of the 100 men who had entered the Essex Cycle Racing Association '100' held a couple of hours earlier. She had become the fourth fastest rider of any gender over a distance that was a regular target for the best British time-trialling men of the day. Those cyclists who had gone faster than Burton in other 100-mile events – Frank Colden, John Watson, the men's record holder Martyn Roach – were all among the star time-triallists of the day. Her time was 3min 25sec slower than the fastest time set in competition to that date, Roach's 3hr, 51min 41sec.

'It must be hard for lay folk, non-cycling or others, to appreciate what this performance means,' wrote Mal Rees in *Cycling*. He compared the 'stupefaction' at Burton's ride with what would have happened had the Olympic medallists Lillian Board or Mary Rand beaten the four-minute mile so decisively. Rand was mainly known for the long jump, but took medals in pentathlon and 4x100m relay at the Tokyo Olympics. Rees's point was that this ride placed Burton among Britain's greatest female athletes of any endurance sport. The four-minute mile was not something to be invoked lightly, given the legendary status of Roger Bannister's breaking of that magic barrier.

Burton joked to Horswell afterwards that she should not ride so fast, then she would not fall off. Privately, she was a little frustrated at not having broken the 3hr 55min barrier and gone even closer to the men's record. That was typical: Burton was never completely satisfied with any of her achievements. Even so, this was still the ride that Burton considered the best of her career. She had plenty to choose from: seven world championship gold medals, over 100 national titles and a wealth of records, meaning that this rainy day in Essex must have been as close as she got to a truly perfect race.

The way into Beryl Burton Gardens is down a wide passageway off Morley's main street, past a yellow wheelie bin lying on its side, then right and left up the back of the buildings next door to the vast Morrison's supermarket. Cast-iron letters form an archway across the gap in the south side of the shops, next door to the Yorkshire Bank and a few yards up from the town hall with its Grade I listed Italianate bell tower.

As a memorial to Morley's most famous daughter, arguably the greatest cycling champion Britain has ever produced, the gardens themselves are something of an anticlimax: three neatly kept, brick-built raised flower beds in a space that has to be less than a hundredth of that allocated to the supermarket car park. If you want to ponder the priorities of 20th and 21st century Britain there is a moral here: car parks given priority over gardens, the humdrum over epic and romantic achievement.

The size of the gardens does not reflect the vastness of Burton's achievements: the many years she competed at the top, the wealth of titles she won, the quantity of other cyclists she inspired and the number of people whose lives she touched. It is not that extraordinary for cycling memorials to be anticlimactic, whether it is the Eddy Merckx metro station in Brussels or the minuscule Tom Simpson 'museum' in the Nottinghamshire town of Harworth. Nonetheless, there is surprise and delight to be found in this relatively confined space. Turning your back on the supermarket car park – which you do with absolutely no regret – you can contemplate a vast mural of vibrant vision, epic scale and great beauty, spanning the entire 60 feet along the back of the bank building.

There, right at the centre, is Burton in her blue and white Morley Cycling Club jersey, framed by tall trees (one of the trunks is painted over the drainpipe coming down off the bank's roof) and the profile of the bell tower which stands only a few hundred metres away. She is racing through the dappled reflection of the leaves on the road, the towering, puffy clouds of an English summer's day piled up behind her. The silhouettes of two onlooking cyclists, bikes leaned up against a tree to her left, are a nod to the style of Frank Patterson, the illustrative artist whose pen and ink drawings of the first half of the 20th century capture the essence of pastoral cycling among the delights of rural England.

It is a timeless image that presses every button of the English cycling psyche: a solo cyclist in pastoral bliss, no sponsor logos to soil the jersey. It tweaks the emotions in the same way that a black and white print of Fausto Coppi in his Bianchi jersey racing solo up a mountain would tug the heartstrings of an Italian, or a photo of Jacques Anquetil and Raymond Poulidor elbow-to-elbow on the Puy de Dôme in the 1964 Tour de France would send shivers down the spine of any French cycling fan of a certain age.

Burton's stature has always been obvious to the English cycling community: she was its champion of longest standing, its most prolific record holder and its most enduring and successful medal winner, both nationally and internationally at least until the advent of the Lottery-funded track 'medal factory'. Burton began winning medals at UK level in 1957 and took her last in 1986, by which time she had won 96 national titles. At world championship level, she managed 15 medals in as many years between 1959 and 1973, including seven world titles.

As time-trialling historian Peter Whitfield put it: 'One name stands out above all others: Beryl Burton, for the way she totally dominated the women's sport over a period of 25 years and the way she achieved parity with the men… Seventy national championships and 25 successive women's BAR [Best All-Rounder] titles make up a lifetime's achievement that will surely never be equaled… After just five years in the sport she had already won everything there was to win five times over, world championships as well as every time-trialling honour, yet she persisted, constantly pushing back the boundaries of the possible.' He added: 'Her achievement was a triumph of pure amateurism, pure self-discipline. She had no coaching, no science and only the most basic equipment and machine. Everything she knew and everything she achieved she did by herself.'

When the unofficial house journal of cycling in the UK, *Cycling Weekly*, was relaunched in 1992, the editor at the time, Andrew Sutcliffe, wanted a series of interviews with the most legendary and significant cycling personalities in the UK and worldwide. The list included past and current stars of the Tour de France in Robert Millar, Barry Hoban, Greg LeMond, Laurent Fignon, Miguel Indurain, Sean Kelly and Brian Robinson. There was Reg Harris - the one British cyclist to have approached the status of national treasure ('Reg rides a Raleigh') – and there was Burton. There had to be Burton.

By then, she had long been a fixture in British cycling. She was past her best, but she had been so ubiquitously dominant in women's racing for so many years that it was almost taken for granted. Everyone assumed that she would be there forever; everyone expected her to remain the first choice as guest of honour for every cycling club dinner for a good 20 years more. No one quite understood why she was still racing in her mid-50s, given that she was nowhere near the standard she had set for herself, but then no one truly knew what drove Burton. She had spent her life in a constant search for recognition but was now content to compete for the sake of it.

She was well known, but no one truly knew her. Part of the paradox lay in the discipline in which she had specialised for much of her career. Burton had always based her racing on time trialling, and was too easily dismissed as a pure time-trialling champion. Her speciality was still the most accessible form of cycle racing in the UK but was something of a backwater, a self-contained and self-absorbed milieu. In the early 1990s racing against the watch did not lead anywhere internationally. Burton was on the less glamourous side of the fence.

British time trialling has never quite bridged that great divide, although the inception of a world title in the discipline in 1994 has changed the equation internationally. However, Burton's profile has risen. The gender politics of her sport, along with those of sport in general, have slowly evolved and are beginning to catch up with the wider world. As opportunities for women in cycling have expanded, and their voices are being increasingly heard within the cycling world, minds have been cast back to one of the greatest female exponents the sport has ever seen, and her stature as an outstanding champion has been resurrected.

Perhaps it needed someone from outside the world of bike racing to appreciate Burton's true value. Great credit is due to the actor Maxine Peake, who realised in 2012 that Burton's story was unique and worthy of retelling; that year's radio play, *Beryl: a Love Story on Two Wheels*, morphed into a stage play, *Beryl*, in 2014, and the success of its national tour in 2015 underlined the enduring fascination with the champion herself. "Criminally ignored," was Peake's view on how Burton had remained in obscurity.

Peake's play made headlines partly because it coincided with the campaign to promote world-class cycling in Yorkshire. This was led by Welcome to Yorkshire, who successfully bid for the Tour de France start in 2014 and the world road race championships – based in Burton's former home town of Harrogate – in 2019. Yorkshire is not the only cycling hotbed in the UK, but it has been marketed with unique fervour; its heroes, alive and dead, have played a key part in the campaign to build the region's profile as the UK home of cycling. The Yorkshire organisers are to be praised for their wisdom in pushing an agenda of gender equality; they have continually placed female stars such as Burton, her daughter Denise and Lizzie Deignan alongside the region's male heroes such as Brian Robinson and Barry Hoban.

In 1971, *The Times* described Burton as 'the least publicised, least rewarded great woman athlete ever to be disregarded by her own country.' And this was when she was at her peak. She is not alone unfortunately: who now remembers Dorothy Round, a double Wimbledon singles winner, Diane Leather, the first woman to beat 5min for the mile, or the soccer player Lily Parr? Burton deserves to be ranked alongside any of them, together with more recent names such as Virginia Wade, Rachel Heyhoe-Flint or Mary

Peters. In her own sport, the comparison should be made with greats such as Marianne Vos and Jeannie Longo.

Where Burton was truly exceptional, probably unique, was in setting a record distance for 12 hours in 1967 which exceeded the men's mark: the first and last time any woman cyclist broke a male record of this stature. Since the early 1960s, her fellow women cyclists have cited her as an inspiration – and they still do. But her achievements can be put into their proper context only now that people are at least prepared to discuss what equality in sport should look like.

In 1974, the chronicler of British time trialling, Bernard Thompson, described Burton's career as 'a perpetual assault upon the so-called dignity (or is it egotism?) of the stronger sex.' In a rather backhanded way, Thompson had hit the nail on the head: the sporting world was run by men and most of them did not know what to make of Beryl Burton. On the international stage, Burton was poorly served by a sport that remained resolutely unequal throughout her lengthy career, and offered limited opportunities for her to express her talent. She wanted to race in the Olympics as early as 1960, but never got the chance; when women cyclists were finally admitted in 1984, she still targetted a place in the Games even though she was long past her best.

Paradoxically, though, for a discipline seen as a backwater, British time trialling was ahead of its time – and far in advance of some mainstream sports – in offering relative parity of opportunity. Burton's performances not only inspired generations of women cyclists, they also served as a constant argument that women and men should race together; that women were worthy of equal status alongside men and should be offered equal competitive opportunities. These notions seem blindingly obvious in the 21st century, but it took decades to overturn received wisdoms.

Thompson, the writer who covered time trialling most consistently and thoroughly during the years when Burton was at her peak, wrote of his timidity at approaching her. He confessed to having a complex about Burton, built 'of awe at racing exploits which to my old-fashioned thinking seemed perfectly credible and permissible for male riders but which were almost completely beyond my comprehension when performed by a woman.' He was 'mesmerised' by Burton, who delivered a 'regular series of numbing shocks to my system'.

What threw people completely was not just that Burton won races, or that she won by such huge margins, but how her times compared to those of men. Another writer, Mike Daniell, in an open letter to Burton in spring 1968, said: 'soon you were setting new horizons in women's time trialling and instead of our being able to rest complacently (I'm talking about male "testers") in the knowledge in all forms of athletics that the best women were about 10% slower than the men… you really had us worried.' In posting times that were up there with the best men in the country, Burton continually broke new ground from the mid 1960s to the mid-1970s. Thompson described her 4hr 8min 22sec in the 1966 women's 100-mile championship as 'a man's ride', in the sense that it was a time that – in his eyes and in the eyes of all bar Burton – only a man was capable of posting; the point was rammed home when the men's title was won a few weeks later in a slower time.

However, Thompson seems not to have grasped – or certainly never explicitly mentioned – that all the championships and high-profile events (such as the 1967 12-hour in which Burton broke the men's record) were the tip of a more significant iceberg. That iceberg consisted of regular races, once or twice a week, in which Burton proved she was as good as male time triallists. Here, she was completely breaking the mould. These were men who worked for a living as she did, holding down jobs while competing at an astonishingly high level in UK time trialling; she was as good as or better than most of them. Only the very best, such as Alf Engers, remained out of her reach. That is her most dramatic achievement: there are no documented examples of a woman consistently, for well over a decade, achieving parity with men in any endurance sport.

Thompson hailed Burton as 'the woman who has done more for British cycling than anyone'. It was a valid point, echoed by team manager and official Eileen Gray, who fought hard for decades to ensure that women achieved entry to the world championships and Olympic Games. Gray felt that Burton's double gold medal at the Leipzig world championships in 1960 'persuaded the powers at home that women's racing had to be taken seriously, for which succeeding generations have [...] to be thankful'.

By maintaining her place at the top for so long, Burton became an enduring role model. There was a visible upturn in the mid to late 1970s in the number of women racing; they were the ones who had been brought up during the Burton years. All of those interviewed while researching this book – even those who did not get on with her - describe her as an inspiration, an icon, an example of what they might achieve. By the '80s, she was racing – and sometimes beating – women less than half her age; in some cases the parents of her youthful rivals had raced against her, and had usually been frustrated.

By then, she was a national institution; world championship contenders from the Swinnerton sisters in the 1970s, to the 1982 World Road Race champion Mandy Jones and her later successors Yvonne McGregor and Lizzie Deignan (née Armitstead) have all cited Burton as a role model. 'When I started cycling I got Beryl's book out of the library and read it,' said McGregor. 'I can totally identify with her way of riding to win.' When Yorkshirewoman Deignan began cycling in her teens, she was told tales of Burton by her grandmother; Deignan went on to succeed Burton and Jones as world road race champion.

Women cycle racers of the 1960s and 70s found her particularly influential. 'She was my hero. I dreamt about her as a teenager,' said Maggie Thompson, née Gordon-Smith, who was a British national champion in the 1970s. 'I had seen her picture in a *Girl* diary from 1962 – it was the first picture of a cyclist that I ever saw, alongside all the film stars, sports stars and so on.' Bernadette Malvern, née Swinnerton, who won a silver medal at the world championships in 1969, recalled, 'I absolutely idolised her, for her single-mindedness. There was an element of, 'a woman can do this'. I was behind as a teenager, always catching up, and Beryl was one thing I focussed on, 'I can do this'.'

Male cyclists also admired her: 'Burton was and still would be the world's best cyclist,' was the verdict of Alf Engers, another truly iconic champion of British time trialling. Engers continued, '[She] is the best British female cyclist of all time. Sorry to all the others. She was that bloody strong … She was head and shoulders above everyone else. She worked, she was the business. I admired her.' 'The greatest racing cyclist that ever lived,' was the verdict of the 1967 world champion Graham Webb. 'The greatest athlete of all time,' wrote Mike Daniell in *International Cycle Sport* in 1968.

Burton was also a magnificently accessible champion. 'We had first-hand experience of Beryl's awesome power when she caught us one Sunday afternoon when we were riding with the York Tandem Club near Malton,' wrote one Yorkshire cycling blogger of an episode in the late 1970s, when Burton was still at her peak. 'Beryl had been on a training run around the Wolds and was on her way back [home]. She would have done well over 100 miles. She slowed down alongside [my companion] to have a chat just as he had taken a large bite of a Mars bar. Despite having slowed down she was still half-wheeling us [riding slightly ahead] so we sped up to keep pace with her. [His] attempts to respond to Beryl's questions about where we had been and how far we were going descended into farce as he struggled to breathe, chew and talk at the same time and only managed to choke and spit out soggy lumps of Mars bar all over his arms and handlebars. Beryl waited patiently while he composed himself and his face retuned to something like its normal colour, and after a few more words and a "nice to have met you" said she had to get back to get the family's evening meal on the table. With that she pushed on her pedals and accompanied by a couple of rasps as her back tyre bit into the road surface she accelerated smoothly away.' The twist here is that the cyclists Burton had caught up were riding a tandem – in other words, they potentially had twice her horsepower.

The long-standing chair of British Cycling, Bob Howden, liked to tell the story of how he was overtaken by Burton on the road when he was a teenager, and – as teenagers frequently do when they are overtaken by a 'real' cyclist – he promptly went tearing past her. Instead of giving him an ear-bashing, the world champion recommended that with that turn of speed he had better find a cycling club to join right away. It was a similar tale to the one told by another British Cycling chair, Brian Cookson, who recalled how as a teenager he witnessed Tom Simpson's last race on British soil:

inspirational, undoubtedly, but Burton was infinitely more accessible, because of the local level at which she competed.

Burton belonged to an era when champions were generally more approachable, but her amateur status meant she was available to any fellow British cyclists who wanted to talk to her. Engers recalled seeing her at the newly opened Gosling cycle track in Welwyn Garden City, warming up 'with a lot of blokes hanging on behind her, and she was never looking round'. She would be seen at the Herne Hill velodrome in South London, making her family's lunch on a camping gas stove in the car park, or at a cyclists' café tucking into bread and butter pudding and custard. On her death, one letter-writer recalled being loaned a spare part to fix his saddle at the Fallowfield track in Manchester by someone he at first took for simply 'a lady in the crowd'. Burton then reminded him that she had ridden over from her home in Leeds that morning, and would need the part for her bike to ride home again later in the day.

Nothing could be further from the image of a Tour de France star: training in a foreign land, racing up mountain passes whose length and altitude bear no relation to anything found on British soil, wearing a jersey bearing the unfamiliar names of foreign companies. Exotic, yes, but not easy to relate to. The low-key nature of time trialling chimed with Burton's visible lack of pretension, but the sport's unique qualities only added to her legend. There is a time-honoured moment at most time trials when the participants gather at the results board to assess the day's performances over a cup of tea; here, a champion such as Burton could be addressed face to face. Since she raced over precisely the same courses as the also-rans, male and female, they could compare their far slower times to hers. It is still possible to make these comparisons, because she rode the same distances as most British cyclists have done at some point or another – 10 and 25 miles being the most popular. Some of the courses she rode are still in use, so the parallels are all the more direct. Burton's times were overtaken only once aerodynamic aids became the norm. Nowadays, a cyclist may look at Burton's time for 10 miles and marvel at how she went a minute or two faster *without* the benefit of a smoothed-out carbon-fibre bike, a skinsuit, triathlon handlebars and a disc wheel.

The times mattered to Burton and are the milestones that mark her lifetime's achievements, but there was more to her life than hours, minutes and seconds. There are challenges in reconstructing that life. She was a household name, but she and her family kept little in the way of records or photographs. That reflected a lack of time for sentiment and introspection, but also this simple fact: British working class people of the post-war years didn't feel their personal lives were of great interest. As a result, relatively little is known about Burton other than the stories that fitted the template: the liquorice allsort offered to Mike McNamara as he was overhauled in the 12-hour; the long hours worked at Nim Carline's rhubarb farm; the size of the gears she churned as she pedalled to that string of successes. There is one written account, Burton's autobiography *Personal Best*, but it emphasises the *Best* rather than the *Personal*; there is ample coverage of her myriad racing achievements, relatively little about her life, and even less about the other people in it.

Burton herself is not an entirely reliable witness. Like many champions, she liked to project a particular version of herself. This was the 'BB' seen by thousands of cyclists around the results board after a time trial or as she handed out the often vast and confusing plethora of trophies at cycling club dinners. 'BB' had a homespun image, the Yorkshire cycling lass who had got where she had by dint of hard graft and determination, with few resources. While the broad lines were certainly correct, there were plenty of hints that more was going on underneath the carapace.

The public episode that pointed to greater complexity in the Burton story was the 1975 national road race championship, in which Beryl finished second to her daughter Denise and suffered something akin to a nervous breakdown. It is a moment of great poignancy, suggesting that Burton wasn't as happy in her own skin or as confident as she seemed to be. It was also, probably, a unique situation in endurance sport: there are no other documented examples of mothers and daughters competing against each other at this level.

Burton is commemorated with a permanent display in the Manchester velodrome, where you can see some of her medals, her rainbow jerseys and more personal items such as those antique pedals and leather shoes. You can cycle the Beryl Burton cycle way from Harrogate to Knaresborough, or simply admire that mural just across from the busy, claustrophobic indoor market in the centre of Morley.

Look again at the mural. The group of local artists who created this work were selected by the memorial fund set up after Burton's premature death, aged 59, in 1996. They have clearly done their homework, capturing in the portrait the most distinctive element of Burton's aerodynamically perfect riding style: her habit of riding with her right hand higher up the drop of her handlebars than the left. This was a personal tic seen by thousands upon thousands of British cyclists, male and female, who could only look on in awe as Burton overtook and left them behind en route to one of her legions of time trial and road race victories. Every cyclist of a certain age in England must have at least one time-trialling friend who will recall being passed by Burton, usually with the accompanying words 'Come on, you're not trying hard enough.'

If Burton had a gravestone, those seven words should perhaps be her epitaph. 'Come on, you're not trying hard enough' was the maxim that she lived by – a phrase directed not only at the multitudes she overtook on her bike, but also at herself. Her constant dissatisfaction with what she had achieved drove her to the heights. Her endless striving for something – even if she was not always totally clear quite what – ruled her life in every waking hour, and dictated the destiny of those closest to her. She lived by it, and most likely died by it as well.

Chapter 2

'A Stubborn Little Mule'

60-90min: usual time taken for the 11-plus examination, Britain, 1950s.

In late 1940s Britain, the 11-plus exam was a key staging post for British schoolchildren: a decisive fork in the road between schools and between likely career paths. On the one hand was a possible place at a grammar school or technical college, both offering an obvious way 'up and out' in a country where social mobility was just awakening after the disruption of the second world war. The other way led to a secondary modern school, and most likely a life of graft in a factory or a mine.

The 11-plus could split families, with one child passing the test and going down one social path – grammar school, frequently university, then a profession – while another might 'fail' and end up at the secondary modern or technical college, then perhaps a manual job at 15. It would also divide children's peer groups: they might rub shoulders for years at primary school then never see each other again. For working-class families, a place at grammar school offered their child a way of avoiding a future of manual labour, at a time when the economic crash, mass unemployment and widespread poverty of the 1930s were still recent memories. The 11-plus exam was therefore an immense source of stress for most primary-school pupils and their families. Those who were under the most pressure were brighter children from working-class families facing financial challenges: Beryl Charnock fell firmly into this category.

The Charnock family was far from rich, and the need for hard work had been ingrained into the three children. Maureen and Beryl were born before the Second World War, in February 1935 and May 1937 respectively; Jeffrey arrived with the years of peace in 1946, although with austerity and rationing continuing into the 1950s they were far from years of plenty.

The father of the family, John Charnock, was employed in engineering companies, and later spent a long period working for a coach company, Rogers, for whom he both maintained and drove the vehicles. His wife, Jessie, held down various jobs over the years, including a spell at the tailoring company Montague Burton, then one of Yorkshire's biggest employers. Beryl clearly inherited her parents' work ethic: she would graft virtually all her adult life, slotting her jobs and her cycling together. She took great pride in this, but eventually it rankled when she came up against younger rivals who she felt had it easier.

Jeffrey paints a picture of a family which both struggled financially and endured a disrupted life. The children moved around, not always living with their parents; they spent a brief period with their grandmother in Armley; another short spell with an aunt. That may have been partly due to financial pressure, but during the war years it was probably down to logistics. John worked in a factory that produced tanks – most probably the sprawling Royal Ordnance site at Barnbow – while Jessie drove ambulances; given the hours they must have had to work at key moments in the war, it would have made sense to farm the children out to relatives.

From the mid-1950s, Jessie's health deteriorated – she was a heavy smoker – and she became progressively more and more unwell, eventually dying at only 61 years of age.

At the time of Beryl's birth the family lived in Dorset Terrace, one of ten rows of yellow-stone back-to-backs to the east of Harehills Lane, roughly halfway between Leeds city centre and the sprawling Roundhay Park. 'There was no money, it just wasn't flashed around,' recalled Jeffrey. They were not uncommon in this; the financial upheavals of the 1920s and the 1930s had seen to that, followed by the austerity of the war years. At Christmas the children received an apple and an orange; Jeffrey had rugby boots for school, but it took several years before he was given a ball to practise with. 'It was tough. The family had a tough time.'

In her autobiography, *Personal Best*, first published in 1986, Beryl Burton gave absolutely no details of her parents' work, what kind of people they were, what kind of a relationship they enjoyed with their children, or what the family background was. She said nothing about their financial circumstances – whether they were relatively well off or struggling. She did not even provide the names of her parents. This hardly points to a happy childhood; rather, it appears to be something she was happy to put behind her. She stated: 'We had a fairly strict upbringing; perhaps, by the standards of today, very strict.' However, she did not expand on this.

In an interview in 1964, she described her upbringing as 'stern': '…when I was very young my mother was out at work. I had to return from school to help to do housework, feed the family, and do all sorts of chores. It was all a fight to survive.' She and her elder sister were given a list of jobs to be done each evening; they got round the system by doing each other's tasks on alternate days, which enabled them to have every other evening free. According to Jeffrey, their father was 'a disciplinarian' who – like many parents of the time – would resort to corporal punishment. 'You had to behave yourself. It wasn't like today. In those days that's how people were. People were aware of authority. We were made very aware of values, of right and wrong. You weren't short of getting a crack or two, but we all survived.'

Beryl Charnock was a stubborn, competitive child, and, she said, 'one of those children who love school, I really did, I used to hate the holidays.' She remembered being given new exercise books at school and vowing to herself that they would never contain anything but good marks. She was obsessive about the neatness of her books, 'best writing, careful underlining with the ruler, all that sort of thing.' Yet almost on the day the new books were handed out, she got the wrong answer to a sum. 'Teacher crossed it out with her thick pencil and ruined my book. Was I mad? I went berserk! … I must have been a right big-head at school.' Indeed, one of Beryl Charnock's teachers described her to her face as 'a stubborn little mule'.

One story is well known: Beryl would throw a ball hard against a wall and catch it on the rebound, setting herself a target of doing it 20 times. 'If I failed to complete 20 without a mistake I would be filled with an inner rage […] even then I was setting myself exacting standards. After 20 would come 25 and so on, each failure resulting in an inward "ticking off". I would even bite the ball with frustration. I would then play the game with two balls, always setting myself a target that had to be beaten before I increased it.' Clearly, she judged herself harshly; but she was about to endure an even harder test: the 11-plus.

Pupils of the time talk of being at schools where 'every day [was] laced with 11-plus-ness', of classes where children were individually ranked according to how they performed, with the rankings making it clear that they would or would not pass the test. Well-connected families whose children were 'expected' to pass might pull a string or two if their offspring did not get through – or the teachers might have a quiet word on their behalf – but for those lower down the social scale the pressure was intense. For a competitive child who was expected to perform well, failure could be devastating. The scars would last. Decades afterwards, some of those who took the exam and did not pass it, still painfully – and incorrectly – brand themselves as 'not very bright'.

The precise format of the 11-plus varied from one Local Education Authority to another, but most consisted of three parts: Arithmetic, General Intelligence (also known as General Problem Solving or General Knowledge) and English – often a comprehension test or essay question. The duration of the papers was roughly one to one and a half hours each, although again this varied from one Local Education Authority to another.

Beryl Charnock had no fear going into the exam: she had worked hard, and was well prepared. But her experience on the day was one familiar to many students: 'I completely froze. Even papers which should not have caused me any great problem might as well have been printed in Urdu. I was an abject failure!' There may be those who still believe this was 'only an exam', but the weight that Beryl Burton gave those 90 minutes when she recalled her childhood is easily illustrated. Burton's youth merits a mere two pages in her autobiography. The 11-plus examination and the horrendous consequences that it had for her take up a page and a quarter of those two pages.

The tests offered a brutal, binary outcome: pupils were given either a pass or a fail. However, there was an arbitrary element to it, as the pass rate (between 10% and 35%)

depended on how many places were available in the local grammar, secondary modern and technical schools compared to the number taking the exam. Fewer places at grammar school tended to be available for girls, and there were also fewer in some towns, depending on the number of schools. So it was possible to be a talented student in a year when few places were available and competition was high and still be sent to a secondary modern, or to get a lower mark but have luck, or demography, on your side.

That mattered little to Beryl. She did not pass. Almost 40 years later, she described what resulted as 'a nervous breakdown'. The strain of the examination caused her to go down with rheumatic fever, which was still relatively common in the UK in the late 1940s, particularly among children. Typically the disease results in fever, swelling, painful joints and sometimes a rash. Beryl also developed a complication known as Sydenham's chorea, or St Vitus' Dance, in which the body develops involuntary movements, apparently flowing from one muscle to the next. The technical term is a hyperkinetic movement disorder; the twitching, twisting or writhing is not voluntary. The brain can do nothing to control it. It could last for up to three months. The condition was not uncommon in children and adolescents who developed rheumatic fever; it was seen in about 20% of cases, but has become increasingly rare in recent years.

Beryl Charnock was unable to speak, and was paralysed down one side. Eventually the fever subsided, but even then she had to hop on one leg from her hospital bed to visit the bathroom, and it was months before she could use both hands. Despite this, Beryl retained her independent spirit, even in hospital. She was supposed to remain covered at night to avoid catching a chill, which, it was believed, would cause the fever to recur. However, she would become overheated as she lay on the ward, and would hang her leg out of the blankets to relieve the sweating, whereupon the night sister would shove it back under the covers. She was prescribed sleeping pills but refused to take them – and in the end the doctors caved in and allowed her to go without.

The 11-plus failure, closely followed by this serious illness, had a massively disruptive effect on Beryl Charnock's life. She spent nine months in St James' Hospital in Leeds, followed by 15 months of convalescence, during which she was sent to a convalescent home run by nuns in Southport, on the other side of the Pennines. Again, she kicked against the system – at the convalescent home the children were taken to church each morning, but the incense would make her feel nauseous, so she was excused.

The entire experience was emotionally devastating for her family. 'Southport was a million miles away in those days,' said Jeffrey – it is 80 miles from Leeds, way over on the Irish Sea coast. It was a complicated rail journey, with a change of stations in Manchester; the few through trains took a minimum of four hours. It was possible to make the trip in a day, but not easy, and it would not have been cheap. It might seem strange in the 21st century that a child so young could be placed so far from her family, but that reflects the times: hospitals in the 1940s and 1950s discouraged parents from visiting children during lengthy stays; it was common to have only weekly or even monthly visits. This was, however, not long after the war, when families had been separated as a matter of necessity, seen as a price worth paying in the cause of keeping children safe.

'That period must have been extremely difficult,' acknowledged Jeffrey. 'The family situation was… we didn't have a settled life going on at that time.' Communication must have been virtually impossible. Beryl recalled missing her brother and sister and finding that their absence made her anxious. She would keep watch out of her window in Ward 19 of St James's Hospital, her eyes on the main gate where the family would appear at visiting time. Although she seems never to have acknowledged any long-term effects of her time in Southport, it is highly likely that there were lasting consequences from this lengthy separation from her family at such a difficult time – immediately following her illness and the immense knock to her confidence of failing the 11-plus.

One of the potential after-effects of rheumatic fever, occurring in about half of cases, is damage to the heart muscles; it is not entirely clear why this happens, but it is the cause of the bulk of deaths related to the disease, which killed over 300,000 people a single year worldwide as recently as 2015. The conventional thinking was that sufferers would not be able to exercise without restraint. Jeffrey underlined this: 'After the illness our parents were given all kinds of dos and don'ts for Beryl. We were supposed to wrap her in cotton wool, but there was no way it could be done. She wasn't like that.' Throughout her racing career, his sister liked to remind people that she had been advised by doctors not to cycle, but if she did get on a bike, that she should walk up the hills.

When Beryl Charnock was released from the convalescent home, it was to a new home and a new school: two more disruptive factors added to a cataclysm that had been completely life-changing. During 1949 the family had moved to Moortown, to the west of Roundhay Park around the city ring road, and a couple of kilometres north of the centre. Saxon Road was a new development of the type that was springing up all over the country as councils built rapidly to overcome housing shortages in the post-war years. The house was a red-brick three-bedroom semi-detached, the first in a row that faced what was then still a stream in open fields, and now is where a shopping centre stands.

'It was like moving to a palace,' recalled Jeffrey, who was three at the time. There were vast woods where the children would play, and sloping fields where they would go sledging when snow fell. There was no shop on the estate to begin with, so food was bought from a grocery van. The move marked the beginning of a time of greater stability for the Charnocks. The garden was substantial – especially after a terrace in Leeds – and the family used it to grow vegetables. Both the Charnock parents were working. 'I was a latchkey kid,' recalled Jeffrey; 'I had a key which I kept on a chain round my neck. You got independent very quickly.'

Beryl went back to school, but it was to a secondary modern, not a grammar. Stainbeck Secondary Modern for Girls was about a mile away from the Charnocks' new home. (She referred to the school in her autobiography as Stainbeck Secondary, omitting the 'modern,' possibly because of the stigma some linked to that category of school.) Stainbeck had just been opened, presumably to cater for the expansion in the population in that part of Leeds after the war. It became co-educational in the 1960s and is now – following rebuilding – Carr Manor High. In the 1950s it had Victorian buildings with steep stairs, a 'bungalow' where domestic science lessons were taken, and at least one ancillary building that had been used for storage during the second world war. In the early 1950s the curriculum was mostly vocational; secretarial skills such as typing reflected the fact that most pupils were expected to go straight out to work when they left at 15. One recalled that the choices on leaving were a biscuit factory or a clothing factory.

Despite the name, Stainbeck was not 'modern' in some ways. The head, Miss Busfield, wore a black gown and cap at assembly; there was a school song in Latin. Many of the teachers were among the generation of women who had lost partners and husbands in the war and devoted themselves to their profession. Beryl Charnock's form teacher at one time was a Miss Billington, who taught English and typing; she sat at a desk raised above her class, and would scan the pupils with her eyebrows raised over her lowered half-moon glasses. The stairs were worn with pupils' feet tramping up and down; Miss Billington's class was on the fourth floor of one of the Victorian buildings.

'I worked hard to catch up and my school reports were quite good,' Beryl wrote in her autobiography. However, she does not seem to have had a happy time at school, according to one classmate, who recalled her arriving in their class midway through their final year, after Christmas. 'She didn't mix,' recalled Pam Hodson, who coincidentally came from a cycling family and rode the 1968 world championships (her son, Jonny Clay, would go on to be a Great Britain team cyclist and Olympic medallist). 'She didn't allow herself to come down to our level. Perhaps she thought she was better than us.'

According to one source, Beryl Charnock 'alienated people' by telling tales on classmates who tried to communicate with each other behind the teacher's back. 'She'd put her hand up and say, "Miss, they're playing pass the paper again." That was her way. She had a lot to learn, and was playing catch-up.' Most probably, Beryl had yet to come to terms with the events of the previous two years, and simply resented being at this particular school.

Even so, Jeffrey Charnock believes that Beryl did derive something positive from her childhood, in spite of the traumas of the 11-plus and her lengthy illness. 'I often call it "the Charnock way". Beryl was like that, I'm like that, my daughter as well. It's about a sense of values, what's right and wrong. Being competitive and determined is a Charnock thing. Something comes up, you sort it out, you get on with it. It runs through the family.'

As a young child, Beryl Charnock had acquired a love of swimming, where she was 'modestly successful'; she was particularly good at swimming under water, implying that she already had a naturally very efficient heart and lungs. (Eileen Sheridan, the top British woman cyclist of the 1940s and 1950s, also started out as a swimmer, so too the 2018 Tour de France winner Geraint Thomas.) In 1960, after becoming a world champion on two wheels, Burton went so far as to say, 'Swimming is my real love. I always wanted to be a top swimmer. As a kid I joined the Leeds Co-op Swimming Club and in a short while won two races in a gala and was second in the breaststroke. And I loved underwater swimming and would stay submerged until my ears sang. [I] looked like a swimmer too.' Indeed, in later years, her relatively well-muscled physique had more the look of an all-round athlete than a specialist cyclist.

After Beryl was released from hospital, she suggested that she might begin cycling with her friends. Her father was not enthusiastic – possibly because of the cost of a bicycle, possibly because of the doctors' warnings – and vetoed the idea. Beryl was not having any of that, and the upshot was a compromise: she was permitted to use her elder sister's bike, but was given specific instructions that the other kids were not to borrow it. Inevitably, one of them did get hold of the machine, and promptly rode it into a wall.

Her father was not much happier when Beryl began cycling with her future husband, Charles Burton.* She met him soon after she started her first job, at the same clothing firm, Montague Burton, where her mother Jessie had once worked. John Charnock 'had pre-determined ideas for his kids', Jeffrey recalled; failing the 11-plus was presumably not among these ideas, any more than gadding about on a bike with a young man who was seven years her senior and who lived on the opposite side of Leeds.

Beryl Burton said unequivocally that in choosing to go out on club runs with Charlie and his comrades in the Morley Road Club, she was swimming against the parental tide. 'Father believed most passionately that daughters who went out early on Sundays should leave their bedrooms tidy with beds made, floors polished [!] and additionally attend to a few chores around the house. And he was wont to turn the heat on anyone who poured scorn on his beliefs…' As a result, Burton told her interviewer, 'most Sunday mornings soon after the town clock struck six I would be tiptoeing about the house, stealthy as a cat, to avoid waking the family, fiddling about with a duster. I couldn't waste time waiting for them to get up.'

In her memoirs, Burton draws an explicit link between her 'failure' at the 11-plus and the internal forces that drove

---

** Burton told Brian Johnston in a 1960 BBC interview that she took up cycling aged '15 and a half', which was presumably not long after she met Charlie. They married in April 1955, when she was nearly 18. Burton's own autobiography is not specific about when they met or exactly how long it was before they got married. Charlie told me that they were married not long after they met, but this cannot be the case; it must have been a good two years, given how much cycling she packed into the period between their meeting and her first successes in 1956.*

her to multiple world championships and national titles. 'I felt that my whole future had been placed in jeopardy by a silly examination thought up by people who had long since forgotten their own schooldays. I knew that I was quite bright and I had had good school reports before my illness. I determined there and then that somehow I would make my mark.' The rest of her life was to be dedicated to proving her worth, time and time again.

Chapter 3

A Partner for Life

33min: approximate time for Beryl Charnock's first 10-mile time trial, Morley, 1953 or 1954.

Charles Burton was given a bike on his 12th birthday. It is one of sport's *Sliding Doors* moments: who can tell what the future would have held if Abraham and Florence Burton had turned down his request, or had opted for a different present? From his early 20s, Charles was the indispensable other half of team Burton alongside Beryl, and for a spell in the 1970s the crucial third element in the Burton cycling family along with Beryl and their daughter Denise. In this role he was universally referred to as 'Charlie'.

Charles Burton was born in Moss, a hamlet near Askern, in South Yorkshire, a little way north of Doncaster. Once a small spa, it was the home of a Coalite works fed by the Askern Main colliery, which was where Charles's father, Abraham, worked. He looked after the pit ponies; the family home was about 200 yards from the mine. An injury underground eventually left Abraham Burton bedridden and confined to a room on the ground floor of their home. Charles's mother, Florence, was originally from Morley, just to the south of Leeds, and much of his extended family still lived in that neighbourhood; Florence's family were mill workers but, he told me, 'she could run a shop, she worked in various shops.'

Charles was fond of light opera as a young man; he began to act, sing and dance for local amateur dramatic clubs when he was six, playing characters such as Buttons in Cinderella.

Even late in his 80s he retains a sense of dramatic timing and irony; he mixes up the odd memory – indeed, much of what happened in the 40 years of his marriage now seems to be a blank – but he can be extremely dry in the time-honoured Yorkshire way. Tell me about yourself, I ask. The reply is brief but pithy: 'My mother made me and my father helped along the way.'

As his 12th birthday approached, Charles decided he wanted 'a proper bike, with drop handlebars'. Once he'd been given the machine and had 'really gone up in the air', as he puts it, he had to find a use for it. He joined the Morley Road Club, which used to meet in a little attic in the town's High Street – the same High Street where the entry to the Beryl Burton Memorial Gardens can now be found – 'above the Co-op, going up the steps to the top of the building'. There, in the manner of British cycling clubs to this day, the Morley would sit and natter over countless cups of tea. Charles soon became their hill-climb champion, not surprisingly given his slight build and small stature, and in 1950 was persuaded to start the national hill-climb championships in North Wales. Riding it was his biggest cycling achievement, he said.

By the time he was 14, towards the end of the Second World War, Charles had already begun working for the Montague Burton tailoring company as a runner, carrying notes and paperwork from place to place. His father had got him the job, having previously spent time at the company as a lorry driver; he was certain that he did not want his son to follow him down the pit and this was his way of making sure that did not happen. Socially, tailoring was a cut above hacking away at the coalface. Montague Burton had been in existence for 40 years, and had over 600 outlets; after the war the firm became the largest tailors in the UK, thanks partly to a government contract supplying 'demob' suits to servicemen when their time with the armed forces ended. It was a name to be reckoned with in Yorkshire, Leeds's biggest employer with a raft of art deco stores and an immense factory – Hudson Road Mills – that employed around 10,000 people at its peak.

After his two years of National Service in Germany, as a clerk in the RAF, Charles returned to work at Montague Burton. Beryl Charnock, meanwhile, seven years his junior, had left school and joined one of the company's offices, where she worked as a Hollerith operator, processing customer and accounting data with a hole punch machine; the information was retained on punch cards. One day, fate sent Charles into her office. 'She was one of the new girls, who came in after I'd been away for a week or so's holiday, and I remember saying to Bill – my colleague – "Who's that?" "A new girl," he said... That was that.'

His wife did not explain in her autobiography precisely why Charlie came into the office that day, or what his job was at this stage; his memory is hazy here, too. Beryl simply remembered, 'I eyed him from top to bottom without, I hoped, making it too obvious.' It was his cycling shoes which made the biggest impression, and which would always be cited in the Burton story. 'I always remember,' she told Marjorie Lofthouse for *Woman's Hour* in 1980, 'I looked down at his feet and he'd got these – what to me don't seem any different now to any other sort of footwear – cycling shoes, and I looked at these cycling shoes and I thought "Oh, poor lad, he must have something wrong with his feet," because they looked so strange and so odd. And now I look at cycling shoes and they don't seem odd at all to me. He started chatting to me and I started chatting to him.'

Soon after this, some time in 1953 or 1954 – the available information is not definitive – Beryl Charnock gave up swimming and began cycling with Charles Burton. She started from scratch. She had never ridden a bicycle much, apart from the abortive attempt with her sister Maureen's machine and trips on a roadster to a cleaning job. Later, she said that she had actually preferred swimming, but her future husband was afraid of water after being pushed into a swimming pool when he was young. Because she was 'going with him' she had no option but to give up all things aquatic. Swimming was her 'real love', she told *Sporting Cyclist* magazine in 1960: 'I always wanted to be a top swimmer.'

'I became a bike rider because of Charlie,' she said, although she was equally keen to point out that he wasn't a tyrannical husband who had forced her into the saddle. In no time at all, she added, she had appropriated one of his two bikes ('he parted up like a lamb and I rode it for a year'); it helped that at five foot six Charles was not significantly taller than she was. He eventually helped her find a bike of her own, 'carefully writing up the specification on a scrappy bit of paper'.

Initially Beryl rode an Armstrong Moth, an off-the-peg racing bike from one of the cycle companies that made up Birmingham-based Tube Investments. Eventually she moved up to a custom-made machine from a local shop, which cost £7 15s. This was not a sum to be spent casually when the average male weekly wage was £9 and the average for a woman was £5 (and it is likely that both Beryl and Charlie would have earned even less than that). However, it was still relatively affordable when compared with today's average wage/handmade racing bicycle correlation. Moreover, the couple had an arrangement with John Hutchins, the bike shop owner, whereby they paid him half a crown (two shillings and sixpence) a week all through the year for the run of the spare parts he kept above the shop. Over the years there would be many such arrangements, notably with Yorkshire's biggest cycle dealer, Ron Kitching. Kitching was a big supporter of Beryl Burton's – Charlie worked for him at one point – and provided subsidized kit over many years.

At a time when British cycling was split between the establishment National Cyclists' Union and the breakaway British League of Racing Cyclists, the Morley was known as a traditional club: its basis was time trialling and its members were mainly affiliated with the NCU. The BLRC clubs that formed in opposition to the NCU clubs in many towns were more purely racing oriented. The Morley also had strong connections to the Cyclists' Touring Club ('always off touring with tents', I was told by local racer Eileen Cropper, whose Bradford Elite club was firmly BLRC).

At the end of 1957, the two clubs in Morley, the Road Club and the Wheelers, merged to form the Morley Cycling Club. The Morley CC's turquoise, white and black jersey became synonymous with Burton and the club's culture shaped her attitude to the sport and pastime for the next 30 years; she would remain unshakably rooted in time trialling and cycle touring until the end of her life. Beryl, Charlie and their daughter Denise would pedal off on many cycling holidays over the years, not to mention countless outings, often in foul weather. Every winter she would get out a heavy bike, so slow-looking that 'even CTC members' (she said) would stare at the mudguards, lamps and saddlebags.

Throughout her racing years, Beryl Burton was far more eloquent when speaking about her love of cycling for its own sake than when asked about her many medals and titles. That initial sense of adventure, escape and discovery must have stayed with her, as well as the utility of cycling as a staple mode of transport. This attitude is in sharp contrast to that of other – male – cycling champions, such as Bernard Hinault, Fausto Coppi or Tom Simpson, who found cycling enjoyable and rewarding, but whose interests were very much welded to the professional, money-earning side of it.

Every Sunday morning, the Morley would meet in Leeds' City Square, outside Sir Henry Tanner's ornate General Post Office building with its central clock tower. They would proceed in a neat crocodile, two by two, out through the suburbs, taking great care not to drop their wheels down into the Corporation tram lines. Cine film footage taken by two club members, Peter and Tony Jackson – nicknamed the Morley film unit – shows a group whose bikes have a shared 'look': saddlebags on carriers, Bluemels mudguards on every bike, Ever Ready lights, and carriers on the front forks to hold the 'sprint' wheels used for racing. Among them would be Beryl Charnock, who presumably had done her housework at home in Moortown before setting out at the crack of dawn; Charles Burton would ride in from Morley, on the opposite side of the city.

The early 1950s were a high-water mark for Britain's cycling clubs. The pastime blossomed among working class people, mainly men, for myriad reasons. Car ownership had yet to become commonplace meaning that a huge number of people cycled to work, so there was a simple crossover to cycling for leisure. Disposable incomes were increasing as post-war austerity gradually eased, so better bikes were within reach of a great many people. Outdoor 'adventure' activities such as hiking and youth hostelling had already become popular in the 1930s as a way for people to escape structured days in factories and offices, and by the 1950s working hours were getting shorter, so there was more time for leisure. Club cycling was a relatively cheap way to find comradeship, adventure and fun; not surprisingly, this boom in the sport bred a wealth of other British cycling stars as well as Beryl Burton.

These were the years that produced images of bikes stacked 10-deep outside London's Herne Hill velodrome but such scenes were not exceptional: a track meeting at Welwyn Garden City might draw 10,000 on a good day, while the Cyclists' Touring Club's York rally would attract 25,000. Cycling in the 1950s had a curiously genteel side; magazines harked back to the pre-war years, running pastoral touring articles with titles like 'In Search of Beauty', 'Awheel to the Wirral' and 'Between Clee and Clun', written by correspondents with Edwardian-style pseudonyms – *Centaur*, *A Lightweight Man*, *Nimrod*, *Wayfarer*. The UK bike industry reigned supreme; the pages of *Cycling* and *Sporting Cyclist* were packed with ads for now long-defunct shops, not to mention manufacturers such as Williams (chainsets), Elswick and Hercules (bikes), Bluemels, Aurelia (lights), Perry (chains). A minority, including Brooks, Reynolds and Raleigh, are still going.

Industrial Yorkshire was a hotbed of cycling. This was a sport and pastime of the urban working class, who pedalled to factories and rail depots during the week, then used the same bikes to ride with cycling clubs at weekends. The area produced Britain's first Tour de France finisher, Brian Robinson, a joiner from Ravensthorpe, and went on to spawn a wealth of champions: other Tour de France riders such as Victor Sutton, a boatbuilder from Doncaster, Barry Hoban, a mine electrician who lived close to Wakefield, and Albert Hitchen, a railway fitter from Mirfield. Further down the sport's hierarchy, Yorkshire produced a wealth of time trial and road race champions.

Across Britain, the armies of cyclists marched on their stomachs, seeking the maximum amount of calories for the minimum of expenditure. Lunch would be sandwiches carried in the saddle bag, eaten in a village pub or tea room chosen beforehand because the owners would be happy to provide a pot of tea with unlimited extra hot water for cycling clubs, costing about four pence a person.*

Industry stalwart and racer Ron Kitching captured the novelty, eccentricity and adventure of cycling in these years in his autobiography *A Wheel in Two Worlds*: 'Each place we stopped for tea had its own atmosphere. Mrs Stables' place at Grassington – Ashfield House – had great hot pasties. And old Mr Stables was a Dalesman storyteller. He used to puff on his pipe and then get out his fiddle. "Come on, Sam," we used to encourage him, "play us a tune and tell us a story" [...] while Mrs Stables and her daughters were feeding us.' There were japes: horseshoes might be purloined from a roadside smithy and sneaked into a saddle bag to slow a rider down, and there might be roadside 'drum-ups' to make tea over a campfire using a billy can.

The tea venues varied widely by menu and reputation, which was all part of the great process of discovery. In Yorkshire, Fearby was known for Mrs Ingram's ham and eggs, but Mrs I. could cook for only two customers at a time. Approaching the village there would be an almighty burn-up to avoid being one of the unfortunates who were kept waiting for the fry-up. Mrs Ambler's at Thirsk was legendary for rabbit pie. Sometimes Yorkshire clubs would venture as far as

---

* *Until relatively recently, some cycle touring guides listed cafés with the suffix OS, standing for 'own sandwiches', meaning they had no issue with guests bringing their own food.*

the Lake District for overnight stays at guest houses such as Waithwaite Farm, with 'a big log fire blazing in the kitchen and a long table [with] 13 big bowls of different puddings … we just went on and on eating.' There was romance in discovering new parts of the country, or even the county, and it was best done on two wheels: barely anyone had a car, the roads were relatively quiet, and the rail network, albeit far more extensive than today, did not cover all destinations or offer the same flexibility.

In an era when few houses had televisions, and families made their own evening entertainment, cycling clubs were about far more than merely racing: they were a little world of raffles, cake baking and special occasions such as Christmas parties. The activities sound redolent of a merry Famous Five or Swallows and Amazons tale – scavenger hunts, treasure hunts, quizzes, talent evenings, tea dances and so on. The clubs were genuinely social institutions. Some, particularly those in London, had club huts built on waste ground on the edge of town, so that members could ride out on a Friday evening or Saturday morning after work, sleep over in bunk beds, cook in basic kitchens and then either race or put in marathon touring rides. 'Cycling clubs were a hive of activity,' one rider of the time, Mary Horsnell, told me. 'At a club night you'd have riders everywhere: someone would be getting a massage, others roaring away on the rollers.'

There must have been a wealth of potential in the new world that Charles Burton showed Beryl Charnock once he had explained precisely what those curious shoes were. That age gap would have amounted to a lot in terms of life experience; Charles would have seemed almost like a father figure, a man who had spent time abroad on National Service and who had seen something of the world. Beryl came from a family background that lacked structure and stability. She did not get on well with her parents. She had spent two years getting over illness and she had not fitted in at secondary school. She was driven to 'make her mark', but until now she had lacked a means of doing this.

In Europe, cycle racing was a means of escape from rural or urban poverty; in the UK it also offered a point of entry to an entire social structure. For an independent-minded, 'stubborn' girl who had already had to butt up against her father's obstructiveness, the idea that cycling did not meet with his approval may have been an additional spur. It is no surprise that Beryl Charnock threw herself into cycling, body and soul, even before racing provided an outlet for her competitive nature.

Burton needed more competitive drive than her male counterparts. She did not face overt sex discrimination within the club; most women who cycled at the time were not actively discouraged, but might not be taken seriously, because there was absolutely no template that suggested to men that they should show respect to women cyclists. One rider of the time told me she had bricks put in her saddle-bag to slow her down, and that men would hold her back as they rode uphill. When Britain's greatest woman cyclist of the post-war years, Eileen Sheridan, began riding, she was frequently told by men that the distances they rode would be too great for her and the pace on club runs would be too fast. They were wrong.

Beryl Charnock's early days in this new world of possibility were a struggle, but she was not alone in that. 'From Moortown into the centre of Leeds it was mostly downhill, and that part of the day was easy,' Beryl recalled of early club runs. 'The rest of the day usually remained a blank. I would return home absolutely whacked. For weeks mother would ask me on my return home where I had been and usually I had no idea.' She would also ride to Morley for evening training sessions once she had finished her working day at the Hollerith machine. 'I'd be sold out in five miles. Two of them would have to push me up the hills. Charlie was always one [...] on some of those runs I've actually been in tears through exhaustion. I didn't let the lads know though. Not me. Anything lads can do, I can do.'

When Beryl began riding with the Morley she frequently fell off, as Charlie recalled: 'We thought, "We'll never make a cyclist of her." She was always blinding along and putting the brakes on too late.' Because she had come to cycling only in her teenage years, she had not had the chance to learn the automatic reflexes that many pick up by riding a bike when very young; the sense of how fast is too fast and when you need to slow down. This now had to be learnt. She would never be a totally confident bike handler, which had a decisive impact on her cycling career.

The Morley Road Club had – as most cycling clubs did – an unwritten code that they would not leave anyone behind on a club run. It was more of a guideline with an unwritten codicil – again common to most clubs – that a novice who proved repeatedly weaker and unable to hold the pace would eventually have to either improve or give up. So Beryl Charnock turned up and suffered, week after week, as those with ambition do at that stage of their cycling lives. 'Whether I actually enjoyed myself I can't recall,' she said later. 'What I do remember is that I was not going to be beaten by anything.'

That film footage by Peter and Tony Jackson of one of those early morning club runs shows Beryl sitting very confidently on the front of the string in an electric orange jersey. The destination is Bolton Abbey, via the climb of Strines, a long, draggy ascent near Sheffield where the Morley hill-climb championship was held, although that was for men only. Charles Burton is seen smoking a pipe; there is horseplay at the café stop, where Beryl gets a couple of the lads to help her wind her knitting wool. Filmed from behind, the riders tackle one steep climb; Beryl can be seen sitting in the saddle, looking strong and smooth at the front of the little group, while the men are struggling, all over their bikes, arms and legs working hard.

Beryl Charnock did not want to be seen making an effort: when she began cycling, she always rode with her hands firmly on the top of the handlebars rather than using the more aerodynamic position lower down the bend. Many novices do this because they feel less safe 'on the drops', but she had a particular reason of her own. 'I hate people seeing me "trying",' she said. 'It embarrasses me. If anybody is about I pretend to be completely unconcerned. I put on this air of calmness. I fancy I couldn't make the effort if I thought people were watching.' The lads on the club run would shout at her that she wasn't working hard, so she would yell back, '"What do you expect to happen? Want to see me swaying all over the road?" I wouldn't have them pushing me around. I continued to sit still and let my legs do the work and the lads, whatever they said, had no effect on me. I never let them know that I had to "try" to stay with them.'

One irony was never, ever lost on her: when she had applied for the job at Montague Burton, she had had to go through a medical. She told Yorkshire TV in 1986 of how the doctor had looked at her medical record, and said, 'You won't do any sport at all will you?' She had replied that she did a little cycling: '"Oh," – eyebrows went up to the ceiling sort of thing – "you take it very steady".' Did she get out of breath, the doctor asked? 'Occasionally,' she replied. 'Well,' he said, 'if the hills get too hard you must get off and walk. I'm sure the boys will wait for you.' As Burton liked to tell, she and 'the boys' had had many laughs about that.

It's safe to assume that by the time that cine film was shot, Beryl Charnock had become, literally and figuratively, Beryl Burton. She is clearly not a novice who is struggling to stay with the club, but exudes confidence. Charlie famously said, 'We pushed her for the first year. She rode with us for the second. And she rode away from us in the third.' The cine footage looks as if it was taken in year three. Here is a woman who has found her place.

Charles and Beryl were married in April 1955, the month before her eighteenth birthday; not yet legally an adult, she had to ask her father's permission. There are hints that the family were not entirely happy with the gap in age between the two of them. 'I think it was something to do with her mum,' Charlie told me. 'She wasn't right happy with her mum, at the time she wasn't… so I said come and live with me then. It wasn't a forced marriage, but it was only ten months until Denise came along.' Beryl was, she recalled later, considered very young to be married; her sister Maureen – 'Belle' – also married early. The wedding was in the church at Moortown, not far from her parents' home (it is now next to a massive roundabout on the A61). Her brother Jeffrey was a 'groomsman', or usher.

According to one friend of the time, Shirley Robinson, on the afternoon of her wedding, Beryl Burton was riding a 10-mile time trial near Hull. The wedding night was spent in a youth hostel near the race, where Beryl and Charlie had to sleep in segregated rooms as was customary in YHA accomodation. The honeymoon was a break in a caravan on Yorkshire's East Coast. After initially moving in with Charlie's parents in Fountain Street in Morley, the young couple decamped to a one-up, one-down back-to-back in Cross Street, just round the corner, in June 1955; they would stay there for about four years. The street has now disappeared under an industrial estate.

Charlie and Beryl Burton were to remain married until Beryl's death in 1996. These days, though, he prefers to be addressed as Charles. It seems like a formal reversion to his original identity after almost 40 years of being 'Charlie', the one-man support team who tweaked the family bikes to ensure that they were just so, who handed up bottle after bottle from the roadside, first to Beryl and later on to Denise as well. It was said that he sewed raw steaks into Beryl's shorts, to prevent her becoming saddle sore. Beryl never had a coach, and, she was adamant, never wanted any coaching.

'Charlie is my only adviser,' she said, 'all I get is lots of encouragement and the occasional comment. This is all I need or want, and this is one reason why he comes [everywhere] with me.' She was not lacking in approaches from the men who looked after the male stars of the time. One, Eddie Soens, wrote of how he found her less than receptive. 'She had lots of opportunities to get help, lots of chances for coaching,' said one rival, Bernadette Malvern. 'But she was very set in her ways. If she thought something worked for her, she didn't want to change it.'

Beryl described her husband as 'chief mechanic, schedule organiser, babysitter, house decorator and general factotum'. He looked after all their bikes, which at one point numbered nine or 10. Every week, she said, 'he checks the bicycle and tubulars [tyres] so I am sure of [them] being in perfect condition.' In a Yorkshire TV interview with Burton at a

10-mile time trial between Pickering and Malton in 1986, Charlie can be seen pumping up Beryl's tyres seconds before she goes to the start line. He can also be spotted near the turn, having pedalled out on his bike with a pair of spare wheels. By then he was in his late 50s and had been her right-hand man for 30 years. 'He was lovely,' said Malvern, '"Buurrrlll," he used to call her. Everything was geared around her, I don't think that ever changed.'

Charlie attended myriad club dinners where Beryl was topping the bill – shaking hands, handing out trophy after trophy and talking politely to chairman and secretary. At one such dinner in Essex, the organisers were mortified when they realised that the 'top table', where the speakers and club officials would sit, had been laid two places short. 'It doesn't matter,' Charlie replied. 'I will have a kip in the van outside, as we are driving home tonight.' Charlie's gender-reversed role was not to the taste of all the males within Yorkshire cycling. One of Beryl Burton's fellow cyclists asked her father for help one day, and was told, 'I'm not chasing about after you like that Charlie Burton.'

Both Beryl and Denise Burton acknowledged that Charlie was completely indispensable to the success they enjoyed. 'I know she wouldn't have been as successful without my father there,' Denise told Hugh Gladstone. 'He cycled to work and back, but he gave up everything else. He did the bikes, drove her about and did a lot for me too when I was at home. He's as much a champion as her, really.' After winning one of her world titles, Beryl paid him this tribute: 'When Charlie's not there I feel as if half of me has been left at home. When he has prepared my bike I know it's well done, with my riding in mind – it's not that I don't trust the mechanics, but there's nothing like real personal interest.'

At the Sports Writers' Association dinner in December 1967, at the height of her success, Beryl quipped that, 'at five feet six, and eight and a half stone, Charlie has decided to let Henry Cooper off for kissing me the other week,' adding that, 'after almost 13 years of marriage I still think I got a bargain; mind you, I think he got one as well!' She added: 'It has become quite a giggle at events because if I win or do a record time, some of the lads go and congratulate Charlie. On the Continent it requires a flotilla of helpers to keep a rider at the top, whereas I've got my hubby.'

As in many successful double acts, the main reward Charlie received for his devotion to his other half was to have his identity largely subsumed into his partner's. He became Beryl's husband, the bloke who would come along on trips with the Great Britain team and sort the bikes, and who might get a post-race embrace from his wife if the team manager told her to kiss him for the photographers. But it was not all plain sailing. The impression of a perfect partnership over 40 years hid any rifts and tensions. 'She can be fairly hard to live with, but if she wasn't she wouldn't have got where she has,' was Charlie's diplomatic view in 1984. There are consistent accounts of difficult moments between the pair over their 40-year partnership. This is hardly surprising, but nonetheless tends to be overlooked amidst the medals and the plaudits.

Eileen Sheridan recalled one such episode at the world championships in Milan in 1962. 'Charlie was bringing Beryl's bike overland on the back of a motorbike; I think the bike was strapped to his back or something. He punctured and had a terrible time getting there. When we got to the track with the riders, Beryl's bike hadn't arrived. When Charlie got there, he was so tired and dirty from travelling through that summer heat... They were both a bit upset. They were both stressed out and worried; I can see it from both sides, and I knew if she wasn't happy, she wouldn't ride well. Charlie turned away and was going off; I caught his arm and said, "Come back at six o'clock" – then they looked at each other and made it up.'

Chapter 4

A Kind of Freemasonry

17sec: Beryl Burton's winning margin in her first national 25-mile time trial title, Redhill, Surrey, June 15 1958.

In the 21st century, it is impossible to imagine anyone riding a time trial along what the locals once called the 'top road' in Morley. Where the A650 heads north-west from Wakefield to Bradford and skirts the south-east side of the town, it runs along a ridge which is now lined with traffic lights, business parks, garages and all the paraphernalia of any suburban road. The Morley Road Club Wednesday evening 10-mile time trials started outside a pub on this road and ran past what used to be the crossroads on Tingley Common, now a gargantuan roundabout where the M62 meets the Dewsbury Road. Five miles up the road, the riders did a U-turn and retraced their route to the start.

In 1953 or 1954, this was where Beryl Charnock started racing. At first she rode out from her work in Leeds to spectate, but it was inevitable she would eventually race herself. She said later, 'Charlie used to say to me, "You should ride on a Wednesday night," and I'd say, "Ooh, I'm not fast enough, not good enough to race."' Although she doubted whether she was really cut out for competition, she had one other thought in the back of her mind: she still didn't want the gaggle of guys with whom she rode up into the Dales on Sundays to notice that she was actually trying.

For her first time trial Beryl managed just below 33 minutes, which she would later describe as 'terribly slow' and cite as evidence that she did not have natural cycling talent. 'It's the same in other sports, when you get to the top people think you're a natural, they don't realise you've spent years and years getting there from nothing.' In fact, in the context of the equipment and roads of the time, a 33-minute '10' was not 'terribly' slow for a beginner. Five years earlier and 40 miles to the south-east, the future Tour de France hero Tom Simpson – a pocket-sized 13-year-old – rode his first time trial, a 5-miler, in 17 minutes, while a few miles to the west, around the same time, Barry Hoban rode his first '10' with the Calder Clarion in 27min 40sec.

Burton, Simpson and Hoban all came into cycling the same way, via a route that was organic, unstructured and utterly familiar to thousands of British cyclists in the 20th century: struggling to keep up with older and more experienced riders on club runs, then trying out a local 10-mile time trial. You turned up, paid the minimal entry fee, rode the race, then looked at the hand-written result sheet to compare times. The world of the club '10' was – and remains – gloriously non-judgmental and accessible: all you need is a racing bike.

Beryl Burton did not take to it immediately. Charlie recalled: 'I had to get her to use drop handlebars, then I had to get her to use the position.' 'Get off the tops,' he would tell her. 'Get down to it and bray.' His wife's response was: 'Not likely. I wasn't accustomed to taking orders. And I stayed on the tops. Just cussedness of course [... and] afraid that I might make a spectacle of myself.' Beryl was determined that anyone watching should get the impression she was not trying. She was effectively taking out insurance against being told she was not good enough, which was hardly surprising given her experience of painful failure, and the fact that even riding her bike was against doctors' orders.

'It was an ordinary ride,' she said of that first time trial. 'The club members kidded me that it was much better. Then I had a second go and got second place, which did me no end of good. But I was still no cyclist.' Gradually she realised that she could compete, and eventually she allowed Charlie to persuade her to become more aerodynamic. Her husband's back-up was crucial: he would time her in training, and explained to her how to negotiate the U-turn in the middle of the road which the course marker had decreed was the turn point. (This practice, possible only when traffic levels were light, is now outlawed on obvious safety grounds.)

Denise Burton arrived on 24 January 1956, when Beryl was still three months short of her 19th birthday and was yet to venture deep into the competitive side of cycling. She had ridden a few 10-mile time trials and had progressed to the inter-club races organised by the gloriously named Heavy Woollen Combine, an association of the clubs in the cloth-producing districts of Yorkshire's West Riding. She had ridden just one 25-mile time trial. Burton recalled feeling happy at the thought of becoming a mother, but tinged with an element of regret at the break she had to take from racing her bike. For the next few years, she would mention in interviews that she and Charlie expected to have at least one more child, and that would require more time out from competition. That moment never came.

Even this break from racing was short. Burton was not clear how soon she got back into the saddle after having Denise, but one friend recalled her riding a time trial six weeks afterwards. In any case, it did not take long before Charlie put a sidecar for Denise on his wife's bike and off they went. (Naturally the Burtons did not have a car; relatively few people did.) They created something of a stir around Morley, which had seen nothing like it before: one nervous neighbour gave Florence Burton conniptions when she speculated that being bumped up and down in the sidecar might affect Denise's spine. Beryl, on the other hand, believed Denise was better in the fresh air with her parents, and in any case she slept for much of the time in the sidecar. Over the winter, the entire family would go out on club runs if the weather was mild enough for Denise to avoid hypothermia. Burton recalled one occasion on which the toddler stood up in the sidecar as they passed Leeds town hall, and began whooping at the top of her voice. She was firmly strapped in after that.

Burton was not unique in combining cycling and motherhood. In 1958, a letter in *Cycling* magazine written by Wynne Wrightson of Gloucester described how she clocked up almost 6,000 miles in the nine months before giving birth to her first child, and another 5,000 before the birth of her second; the reduction was caused not by spending less time in the saddle, but by having to cycle more slowly owing to the weight of the older child in a sidecar.

Similarly, Eileen Sheridan managed to come back to cycling soon after the birth of her son by caesarean section in April 1946; within seven weeks she set out on an 80-mile ride, in spite of doctors' orders that she was to rest for a year. Like Denise Burton, Clive Sheridan accompanied his parents on their bikes, first in a trailer and later on a child seat. Sheridan raced six months after the birth, and by the spring of 1947 she was competing full-time again after a winter's training.

This is not to say that combining racing and motherhood was simple. An article in *Cycling* late in 1958 detailed Beryl Burton's life: 'cooking, washing, shopping and chasing around after Denise from 7.30am to 7.30pm', after which she would go out for an evening's training on her bike. Eventually, she settled into what would become her routine: training every evening from Monday to Thursday, covering anywhere between ten and 40 miles using a medium-sized fixed gear, on different out and home circuits. The length of ride depended on the available daylight, her state of fatigue and her commitments at home. Friday was the club night at the Morley's HQ above the Co-op.

At weekends, Charlie dealt with childcare while Beryl got on with racing; Beryl recalled that her first race outside Yorkshire was in Lancashire, so she rode there and back, and Charlie rode out with Denise in the sidecar to meet her on the way home. Charlie was not the only one involved in looking after Denise while Beryl raced; they also received help from the Burton family. Beryl acknowledged this in her autobiography, but there was no mention of her own mother. It was partly down to the fact that the Charnocks lived on the other side of Leeds, but Denise also hints at the rift her father had previously mentioned: 'I stayed with them occasionally, they were a bit more… I didn't know them as well, probably because I didn't get taken there as often – my grandma wouldn't take me as often. You go back to what my dad said about my mother marrying young, you can probably see the whole picture.'

By the end of the 1956 season, after Denise's birth, Burton had become the 14th fastest woman in the country at 10 and 50 miles, and 13th fastest at 25 miles, so she recorded. She had begun to present serious competition to her fellow Yorkshirewoman Iris Miles, who rode for the same South Yorkshire club as Tom Simpson: the Scala Wheelers. She was also acquiring a reputation locally. 'We used to look at the entry list,' said Shirley Robinson. 'If Beryl had entered, we knew we'd be riding for second.' The exception, apparently, was one race about six weeks after Denise was born – 'a few of us bragged about that, as it was the only time we got to beat her.'

Burton and Miles shared digs the night before the White Rose Ladies' 25-mile time trial close to York, one of Burton's first racing trips away from husband and baby. The following day Burton beat Miles by a mere two seconds. This was a remarkable scalp for a 19-year-old novice, given that the Doncaster woman, three years Burton's senior, was the dominant time triallist of 1956 and 1957: women's Best All Rounder in both those seasons, national champion at 50 and 100 miles and competition record-breaker at 25, 50 and 100 miles. Burton was progressing very, very rapidly indeed.

In 1957, she moved on to national time trial championships. For the 25-mile title near Grantham, she and Charlie rode down on the Saturday, stayed in the house of a member of the organising club, then pedalled north again after she had taken her sixth place: they did not have sufficient cash for the rail fare. Such excursions would become the norm for the Burtons, who slept in the houses of countless cycling friends over the years prior to races. It was also typical of a time when, as one writer put it, 'races more than 20 miles away represented a complete weekend away from home'. In his autobiography, Barry Hoban wrote of riding 90 miles across the Pennines to compete in the national junior '25', then 90 miles home after the event; similarly he recalled riding with his clubmates to catch the ferry to the Isle of Man. These trips would often involve groups of cyclists travelling through the night, those without lights riding on the inside of the group to keep out of view of the police.

As well as other cyclists' spare rooms, a huge variety of 'digs' were used by bike riders across the country. At one lodging house near Southend an old track racer and his wife kept a massive visitors' book; on the A10 at Quendon in Essex, a

Mrs O'Brien might end up with 80 racing lads sleeping on camp beds. A Norfolk landlady was nicknamed the Saggy Stocking, and a nearby barmaid would arrange dates with her friends for the riders. The great short-distance specialist Alf Engers recalled climbing up a vertical ladder to a bedroom in a cottage with no running water, and being warned not to linger on the outside toilet perched over a stream because the proprietor kept bad-natured bees. As with the tea places, the myriad 'digs' were all part of the great adventure.

The sparseness of the women's time-trialling calendar meant that long trips to races were the norm, by train and bike if it was too far to ride. 'There was a small number of events for us,' Mary Horsnell told me. 'If you wanted any kind of racing programme you had to travel – from Essex, in my case, to Shropshire, Wales, all over England. It was vexing because there would be weekends with three races you could get to, then nothing for three weeks. There was no co-ordination.' Until the end of the 1970s the numbers involved in women's racing were relatively small in every discipline. 'Wherever you went, it was always the same crowd that went everywhere, plus whatever local girls,' Horsnell recalled. 'Even before Beryl's time, first, second and third would usually be predetermined because the fields were so small.'

Burton backed up that sixth in the 1957 25-mile championship with eighth in the 50-mile title and her first medal at national level, the silver in the '100' championship, where Miles was among the victims, along with the other star woman of the day, the Isle of Man's Millie Robinson. She combined this with a job – she had moved from Montague Burton to clubmate Nim Carline's market garden – and looking after a young infant. What's more, she was not yet riding the fastest racing wheels and tyres available (she was using Michelin 'high pressures', at a time when 'pressures' were heavy in weight and 'feel' so serious racers used tubular tyres): she promised herself a pair of faster racing wheels when she pushed her time for 25 miles down to 1hr 5min. That goal was achieved at the end of the season – although she was still two minutes slower than Miles's competition record – and after changing to 16-ounce tubular tyres she saw an immediate improvement. She was beginning to be noticed: Eileen Sheridan, no less, described her as a 'formidable' competitor.

Time trialling was not the only option available to a young woman with a bike and strong competitive instincts. There were a handful of women's road races, usually referred to as 'massed start', which were mostly run by BLRC affiliated clubs. Sometimes, when Beryl rode these, she, Charlie and Denise would hitch a lift with another West Yorkshire road racer, Eileen Cropper, in the van driven by Eileen's husband Sidney. There was a far more extensive calendar of track races than today; Miles won a South Yorkshire Track League for women and was a force to be reckoned with in the grass-track events which were often held at colliery sports days. Burton took to track racing – especially the individual pursuit– a few years later, but time trialling was where the Morley culture guided her.

The appeal is obvious. This is the most measurable cycling discipline: you always end up with a time, which can be compared to those of others, and to your own previous performances. Having an exact result to look at and place on record must have drawn a woman who had been deprived of control at key moments in her young life. Burton's view was that 'time trialling is the true side of the sport. One is solo, not relying on anyone else, and therefore the result is up to the individual and the individual only.' Riding alone would have felt safer for a rider who had come relatively late to the sport and who was never enthusiastic about racing in a bunch. A few years later, Charlie told *Cycling*, '[Beryl] has never really taken to road racing. She is an individualist and when racing doesn't like to be hemmed in or even in company.'

'Testing' appealed to the puritan in Burton: she was at pains to underline how hard she worked in every area of life, and her sport was no exception. She wrote in her autobiography: 'I think that as a nation we are basically rather lazy, and who wants to spend hours training after work in all weathers to improve in a time trial by 10 seconds and still finish 61st in a field of 120? Well, some do, and they are the salt of the earth. An untold number come into the sport each year and I would hazard about one in 10 stick it out. Those who do find a way of life which transcends everything else – a kind of freemasonry.'

Now largely viewed as a homespun, somewhat geeky side of the sport, in the 1940s and 1950s time trialling had its sparkling side: glitzy celebrations at the Albert Hall, where the discipline's governing body, the Road Time Trials Council, had held its Champions' Night at the end of every season since 1931. Champions' Night featured guests of honour from the highest level of European professional cycling, such as Fausto Coppi and Jacques Anquetil, and would draw audiences of up to 7,000 club folk during the post-war boom, when it was moved to Olympia. The evening was a music-hall extravaganza with a cyclists' prize-giving attached. One compère was the popular entertainer Tommy Trinder (catch phrase – 'you lucky people'); an evening's line-up might include scantily clad Crazy Horse style high-kicking dancers such as the Cavalcade Girls, jugglers, fire-eaters, a soprano, knife-throwers, limbo dancers and a steel band. In 1947 it took place in conjunction with Bertram Mills' circus.

Roy Green in *Sporting Cyclist* described a raucous scene after the dinner moved to Derby's Rainbow Rooms in the late 1960s. 'Keith Stacey had a big Seamons [Cycling Club] crowd cheering him with a huge banner... And chants of Liv-er-pool, World Cup style, greeted the six Liverpool Eagle prize-winners... The cheers, chants, applause, swelled up every time a Yorkshire lad or lass went up – often enough... The exuberant pride of the Yorkies finally erupted in a takeover bid from the dance band for a mass singing of the anthem 'Ilkley Moor b'aht 'at".'

This was a big, boisterous night out, one that time triallists would travel from the other end of the country to attend. For a woman cyclist, this was as glamorous as it got at this time; women were not permitted to ride world championships – although this was about to change — and national title races in all disciplines were relatively low-key events. Both Sheridan and Burton clearly appreciated the glitz: dressing up to the nines, the dancing, the stars, the recognition from both the men who ran the sport and those who dominated it on the road. At their first Champions' Night Beryl and Charlie turned up in informal outfits, realised everyone was dressed up formally and rushed back to their hotel to change, only to find everyone had by now switched to informal evening wear. It was a long way from a one-up and one-down in Morley.

The principal joy of time trialling is its accessible nature; it is the two-wheeled equivalent of the parkrun. 'The only qualification required is the ability to ride a bicycle,' wrote Bernard Thompson. 'During the Second World War coal miners worked their Saturday shift, rode to their event and slept in a hedge near the start. Factory workers rode straight from work early on Sunday morning… After the war riders would think it perfectly normal to ride 80 miles on Saturday afternoon to a race, ride a 100-mile time trial on Sunday morning, then ride the 80 miles home again.'

Time trialling is a uniquely British form of bike racing, which came into being around the end of the 19th century as racing on the roads – and the mere act of cycling – came under pressure due to incidents involving cyclists, their pacers – usually tandems or solo cycles – and other users. The first time trial was run by the North Road Cycling Club on 5 October 1895, under the leadership of Frank Bidlake, known widely as the 'father of time trialling'. Bidlake's conviction was that the sport had to remain underground and purely amateur in order to survive, so he devised a method of racing that did away with pacers, and made the events as inconspicuous as possible.

Thus, a time trial was devised specifically to look completely different from a group of 'scorchers'. The riders started at one, two or three-minute intervals and rode alone and unpaced (this was the key distinction between time trialling and the road events ridden with pacers, either solo or on tandems). Being 'confidential' was partly about avoiding the attentions of the traffic police, but amateurism in the purest sense would also avoid issues such as betting, race fixing and doping. Bidlake's motto was, 'to be too successful is to be suicidal'; this philosophy was to define the sport for the next century.

The conventions of time trialling from 1905 included: dark cycling attire; events run on deserted byways; riders separated by two or three minutes to avoid bunching; no pacing or company riding; no publicity as to time or place of events; no racing through villages; all appearance of racing to be avoided. To keep speeds down, races to be no shorter than

25 or ideally 50 miles (for this reason the 10-mile time trial championship was not instigated until 1994).

For additional secrecy, the courses were referred to by codes, a practice that still exists today. Take a classic course in North Devon: S1/25, known as 'Copp'. It was in the Southern District Association ('S'), course No1, in its 25-mile variant. It was on the main A377 road, running northwest from a field gate near the handful of houses at Morchard Road station to a dead turn as the road went through the middle of a wood. Even its nickname was misleading: the village of Copplestone was several miles from the start point, but you had to be in the 'freemasonry' to know that. The S1/50 and '100' courses used other variants on the main road and its neighbours.

The need for accuracy in course measurement and timing made the sport a natural home for perfectionists; course directions could be fiendishly complex. For example: 'Start at the second post of the first gateway on the left approximately 120 yards south-west of Farndon Cross Roads, two miles south-west of Newark on the A46 Fosse Way... Turn left on A52 to small bridge over stream approximately 300 yards before railway bridge...'

Courses often acquired nicknames. 'Boro' referred to the legendary set of courses using the A1's bypass of the village of Boroughbridge; it was where Burton and others broke record after record in the 1960s and 1970s. 'Brock' was on the A6 between Preston and Lancaster, named after a nearby village. The '32nd', near Bishop's Stortford, took its name from its start at the 32nd milestone from central London up the A11; its code was E1. Other famous courses include the Bridgewater Flats, the Bath Road (H5, H35, H51) and the P2 based on Ringwood. There were 'float' courses – flat, sheltered and generally out into the prevailing wind, which would help a rider home from the dead turn – and, later, 'dragstrips' such as the dual carriageway Tonbridge and Southend bypasses.

By the time Burton began racing, the original conventions had been eroded. Wearing black had given way to cycling club clothing, although officials had been disqualifying riders for wearing 'light-coloured' clothing as late as 1942. Competitors still carried bells on their handlebars, but they had actual race numbers, which had been barred as they suggested a race was occurring. The cyclists still rode alone and unpaced; they still rode – mostly – early in the morning, and were pushed off at one-minute intervals. Race programmes still bore the heading 'private and confidential.'

In 1929, *Cycling* magazine had instigated the British Best All Rounder competition, for men, based on a cyclist's best rides for a given season over 50 and 100 miles and 12 hours; the RTTC took it over in 1944. A women's Best All Rounder was begun in 1948, over 25, 50 and 100 miles. It took another 20 years for a junior BAR to appear, and a junior women's BAR did not start until 1980.

Time trialling remained a strictly amateur sport, a status which the Road Time Trials Council guarded fiercely according to Bidlake's founding principles. It had taken the National Cyclists' Union's side when the British League of Racing Cyclists broke away to launch road racing on public roads after the Second World War. An RTTC statement on 'The Menace of Mass Start Racing' described this as 'an utterly selfish and irresponsible use of roads; all such racing should be stopped. BLRC road races violate every one of the principles of clean amateurism, authenticity and regard for public safety.'

In international terms, British time trialling was out on a limb; its titles – the national time trial championships and BBAR, all run by the RTTC – carried weight in UK cycling but meant nothing beyond the Channel. In the cycling heartland of Europe, setting aside a handful of classic races (all of which are now defunct), the *contre la montre* was seen mainly as one element of a stage race, rather than as an end in itself. At most levels within the UK up to the 1970s, plenty of cyclists competed both in time trialling and track racing, and road racing and time trials – the British Best All Rounder of 1966, Arthur Metcalfe, was also the national road race champion and turned professional to finish the following year's Tour de France – but those who specialised solely in 'testing' the British way ran the risk of directing their talent down a dead-end street.

Time trialling's top male riders were a disparate bunch. The happy-go-lucky Ray Booty, the first man to break four hours for 100 miles, was talented at pretty much everything; the infernally driven Frank Colden went so hard to win the BAR and two national titles in his magic year of 1962 that he never raced again. Martyn Roach was an outspoken tax inspector; Clifton CC's 50-miler John Watson was a rugby league player who had turned down a professional deal with York. At the top of the tree was Alf Engers, who emerged not long after Burton; 'the king' of 25-miling wore fur coats over his tracksuit bottoms, sported impeccable shades, lurid shirts and flares, and had a knack for falling out with the men in blazers. This was the little world that Burton was to make her own for 30 years.

1958 was Burton's third full season of racing; it was a measure of how rapidly she had progressed that this year was dominated by her duel with Millie Robinson, the leading British woman cyclist of the day. Robinson, who had been brought up in Ireland and the Isle of Man, was an all-round talent who had won the five-day *Grande Boucle Féminine* stage race in Normandy in 1955, and had become the first British women's road race champion the following year. She was also the British women's Hour Record holder and took the world record in Milan in September 1958, pushing the distance close to the 40km (25 mile) mark with 39.719km.

The pair first met in a 25-mile time trial in East Yorkshire in April, where Robinson beat Burton by three minutes, but on 15 June, on the A23 running past Gatwick Airport in Surrey, came a landmark: Burton's first national title, over 25 miles, by 17 seconds from the Manxwoman. 'After three years of absolute superiority at the distance, [Robinson] capitulated to one of the wonder girls Yorkshire seems to be producing in all phases of the game,' wrote *Cycling*. The reporter described Burton as 'a truly deserving and welcome successor to the title, in that she competes with Millie not only against the watch but also in personal popularity… On a morning of early cold and dead stillness it was an exceptional performance on a far from easy course (five traffic islands each way and a dead turn).'

Burton was explicit about the link between this triumph and her disastrous experience in the 11-plus: 'My private vow to succeed after the cruel circumstances of my failure had at last come true. But I was determined to achieve even more.' She had, she said a couple of years later, always wanted 'a silver cup… Right from [being] a tiny girl... Illness' – the chorea after the 11-plus failure – 'spoiled my big dream of winning one from swimming. But the desire for a silver cup lingered on. It wasn't the honour of winning one that seemed to be so important, even though I did want to be the best at whatever I was doing, it was just that I liked silver cups. There was something about the shape of them and the way they gleamed in the light. […] My first racing prize was a voucher. So I bought myself a cup – a miniature! It made me very happy. It's around [my house] somewhere. If you asked me about my greatest moment I would tell you it was the day I won my first "open" cup.'

A week after the '25' triumph came Burton's first British time trial record, 4hr 33min 26sec for 100 miles – which would still be a more than acceptable time for a cyclist of any gender 40 years later. Three weeks later, on the roads north of Oxford, she added the national 50-mile title, only the second time the two titles had been won by the same woman in the same year. Again it was a battle with Robinson, this time on 'a savage morning of howling south-west wind and heavy intermittent showers', the report said: 'a staggering achievement, proving her the undisputed master [*sic*] of women's unpaced road riding this year.' Their rivalry pushed both Burton and Robinson to new heights, for example in the Clifton CC '50' in Yorkshire, where Robinson finished in a record 2hr 9min 17sec and then Burton clipped a second off that when she finished a few minutes later. Both were targeting not only the Best All Rounder, but also the first ride under 4hr 30min by a woman for a '100'.

Amidst all this racing, the Burton family went cycle touring from Yorkshire to Ireland, pedalling through the rain in the vast capes of the time which resembled tents on two wheels. The way home was packed with incident: Beryl crashed heavily in North Wales, and the trio survived an epic cloudburst in the Peak District, after which little Denise was stripped of her wet clothes in a roadside shed and put into dry kit.

While the Burtons were holidaying, Robinson had broken her rival's 100-mile record, and now had the world Hour Record in her sights. She landed the British record at Manchester in a world best distance which was not registered because she had not filed the attempt beforehand. On 21 August, Burton beat her for the national 100-mile title, on a morning of cold drizzle and rain. The time mattered as much as the medal: Burton won in 4hr 29min 21sec, which she described as 'the women's bike-racing equivalent of Bannister's four-minute mile [set four years earlier]'.

Astonishingly, given her past success in road races in France, Robinson was not selected for the British team that contested the first world road race for women in Rheims that August. But her rivalry with Burton had created an increasing awareness of just how fast women could ride on a bike, and this in turn prompted *Cycling* magazine to announce on 2 July 1958 that it would award a gold medal for the first woman to beat 60 minutes for 25 miles. (Denoting landmarks in this way was a tradition that went back to 1910, when Leon Meredith broke five hours for the '100'.) *Cycling*'s reasoning was obvious: spurred on by her duel with Burton, Robinson had taken her own record for the distance below 1hr 2min, beating 24mph for the first time. That high-speed ride in the De Montfort Ladies' event near Leicester gave her a third British Best All Rounder title. It was the last time anyone other than Burton would take that particular trophy for a quarter of a century.

Chapter 5

Brass and Muck

0.2sec: winning margin, first world pursuit title, Rocourt, Liège, late July 1959.

Beryl Burton and Millie Robinson spent the last few months of the 1958 season scrapping over national time trial titles and the British Best All Rounder award, but this was parochial stuff compared to the landmark event of that summer: the first ever world championships for women in Rheims. It was understandable that Burton did not make the British team – she was a novice – but Robinson's absence remains a mystery, as she had raced brilliantly in France in 1955 and was also the reigning British road race champion.

Even without Robinson and Burton, the British women were right in the mix. Women like Eileen Cropper, now in her 80s, one of the 29 women who made history on 30 August 1958, a formidable, unsentimental Yorkshirewoman, who has a decidedly unromantic memory of that first world championship: 'A shambles. I would never go to race in France again.' Sixty years on, Cropper is still angry at the fact that the blue jerseys of the six British women were confused with those of the French team, which were the same colour; in her view this makes the result unreliable. 'I was disgusted. Some of the girls named in the front bunch were never there.'

Cropper is listed as finishing 11th, solidly in the 15-rider main group behind the runaway winner Elsy Jacobs of Luxembourg – although her name is misspelt in the official result. For Great Britain, the women's team rode strongly across the board. All six of the women's road race team – Molly Swann, Sheila Clarke, Barbara Harris, Dot Whitwham, Jean Poole and Cropper – finished in the first 16. On the track there was silver in the pursuit for Stella Ball and bronze for Kay Ray, with Jean Dunn managing another bronze in the match sprint. Dunn was to take that medal home five years running.

After the 2012 Olympic Games in London, Lizzie Armitstead – a Yorkshirewoman like most of her predecessors in that GB team more than half a century earlier – complained with good reason that the GB men's team were better looked after. The 1958 women's squad faced discrimination as well. It was not so much a matter of resources: none of the team, male or female, were particularly well kitted out. Opinions were divided as to whether the women should be at the World's at all, with the long-standing Great Britain team manager Benny Foster firmly opposed. He devoted a lengthy section of his autobiography to explaining why he was against the inclusion of women, not troubling to tell his readers the names of the women in the team, or how they fared.

Foster did not want the women to share a hotel with the GB men and was concerned that the men might be 'unbalanced' by feeling they had to provide assistance to the women: looking after their equipment, carrying their bags, pumping their tyres up or supplying coffee during training. At both the road races in Rheims and the track championships in Paris, the women were kept well away from the men. Ball should have won the pursuit, as she qualified fastest by seven seconds and was quickest in the next two rounds; but in the final her usual helpers were pushed aside by the GB men's team officials, wrecking her start routine and probably costing her the chance to be Britain's first women's gold medallist at this level.

Relations between the men and women's teams were completely derailed. Foster could not refuse to help the British women, but did not want to be seen doing so, and race officials had no idea whether to deal with him or with the women's manager, Eileen Gray. When Gray invited the men's team to join the women for a post-race party at their hotel, Foster refused point blank, but his 'lads' went anyway, to his immense annoyance.

This was the minefield that Beryl Burton entered when she decided to target the 1959 world championships. In spite of the obvious strength of the country's women compared to the men, the newly formed British Cycling Federation – a merger between the National Cyclists' Union and the 'rebel' British League of Racing Cyclists – was unwilling to invest much money in its best chance of winning medals. For 1959, the BCF offered the Women's Cycle Racing Association a £100 grant to take a 'team' of only two riders, Robinson and Dunn. This set the tone for future years: Burton and others would continually complain of being short of resources.

The funding gap was pure sexism: it would be years before women's racing was truly taken seriously, even at this highest level. There were issues in 1959 and 1960 between the BCF, which received a fee from the World's organisers, and the Women's Cycle Racing Association, which dealt with the team's travel. The BCF gave the WCRA a budget, then kept any difference when the fees were paid; on one occasion the disparity was £100, which the BCF paid only after the WCRA took the matter to an appeals panel.

The lack of interest from the governing body stemmed more from conservatism among officials than a blanket lack of enlightenment across the sport in Britain. The BLRC had in fact been ahead of its time in setting up road races for women, and in the late 1950s there were enough events on the British calendar for Cropper and her mates to race around the country. Although the fields were small, consisting of between 20 and 25 riders, the women were racing, and compared to the rest of the world they were strong. That was partly thanks to the BLRC's policy of supporting trips to women's races in countries such as France, where Robinson had shone so brightly.

For the 1959 world championships, Burton was initially named as a non-travelling reserve. She had good reason to be miffed about this. By now, she was probably the strongest female racer in the country, having won the national '25' championship by 1min 17sec from Robinson that spring and added the '50' title again in a competition record of 2hr 6min 38sec. She had proved her credentials in the 3,000m individual pursuit the previous season, when she had beaten the experienced Val Garrett at Herne Hill. She was also becoming a more than competent road racer, capable of taking a solo win by up to four minutes and, on occasion, of dominating a sprint. In spring 1959, she notched up a spectacular win in a two-day race in Nottinghamshire where she snatched all three stages, one on her own, one in a bunch gallop and one in a two-up sprint, and in July she took the British national road race championship from a six-woman break, avoiding a bus which 'to some extent baulked the finish'. On occasion, she was tactically naive – for example, Robinson outwitted her in a race at Loughborough that spring by letting her make the pace then nipping past her at the death – but such mistakes were understandable given how new all this was.

Even when the racing committee finally came round to the idea of permitting Burton to travel with the team — after she had broken the national record at the pursuit distance of three kilometres – no further funding was forthcoming; and there was no guarantee that she would ride. It was hardly the ideal way to encourage an up and coming champion. Burton and company were given £2 per day *towards* their board and lodging; they paid their own way to and from London (from where the WCRA provided transport).

In 1959, the team drove to Belgium and Holland in an old army staff car belonging to the mechanic Tom Feargrieve,* who recalled Burton sitting in the back of the vehicle knitting as he drove. The car, nicknamed Britannia, had space for eight to ten bikes on the roof, and racked seats inside for the riders. Charlie travelled as well, but at his own expense. (Apart from their previous year's holiday in Ireland the couple had never been abroad, but that was typical of the time.) Burton described this as a rare opportunity to focus solely on her cycling, leaving behind her work, the 'domestic chores' and Denise at home in Morley.

The 1959 World's were in Holland, but the organisers refused to run women's track events, so these were put on just over the border, in the Belgian city of Liège. Women were not allowed at the official banquet; two British journalists, Jonny Dennis and Peter Bryan, boycotted the dinner and took the GB women's manager Eileen Gray out for a meal instead. The lack of resources created problems for the Burtons: in Liège, Charlie had to go out and find shellac, the glue used to fix tubular tyres to the rims of racing wheels. On race day, Beryl was loaned a pair of wheels by Millie Robinson, as she was still not using the fastest kit.

---

* *Feargrieve's son Ernie went on to be the Great Britain team mechanic in the 21st century. He believes that only one British woman – Mandy Jones in 1982 – has won a world title without one of the Feargrieve family being present.*

The Burtons' lack of cash was dire enough that Beryl could not afford to buy a proper tracksuit; at the track side she wore a pair of plaid trousers and a green cycling jacket – quite possibly the same outfit seen in the film of that early Morley club run. The trousers were eventually cut down to make use of the material, presumably when the back had worn out from contact with the saddle. Burton had a 'make do and mend' attitude: among the items she produced was a shoe bag for Denise.

Three world championship events were contested by women in the early years, the road race, the match sprint and the pursuit; of the three, the pursuit suited Burton best. Britons have always competed well at the discipline, largely because so many British cyclists get a grounding in riding 'alone and unpaced against the watch' thanks to the country's time trialling tradition. Combining pursuiting and time trialling is a strategy that has endured until the 21st century, with British stars such as Chris Boardman, Yvonne McGregor, Joanna Rowsell and Bradley Wiggins all in that same mould.

Burton was a relative novice at the individual pursuit but made an immediate impression: in the first round she overcame Marie-Thérèse Naessens of Belgium by 9.4sec, and in the second she took a notable scalp, Yvonne Reynders of Belgium, with a margin of 5sec, before beating the Russian Schogina to go through to the final against Elsy Jacobs of Luxembourg. Jacobs was a daunting opponent for an adversary who had begun pursuiting only the year before; she was four years older than Burton, had already made history by becoming the first woman to win a world road race title and had taken the world Hour Record from Robinson in 1958. She had also been the first woman to take out a racing licence in her native country, having previously had to compete on

Burton in her prime, at a race start in the 1960s with her Jacques Anquetil bike.

Captured from the side, Burton's aerodynamic style is obvious, although the vast number on her back is probably slowing her down as she attacks in the Pennine Road Race in 1967; she was also an adept track rider, as this image, right, of her win in the point to point at an unidentified velodrome in the 1960s shows. The start sheets from the writer Bernard Thompson's collection show the homespun nature of British time trialling, including a map of the course where Burton set her 100-mile record in 1968, and a written footnote showing a Burton competition record at 30 miles – "minus 29 seconds".

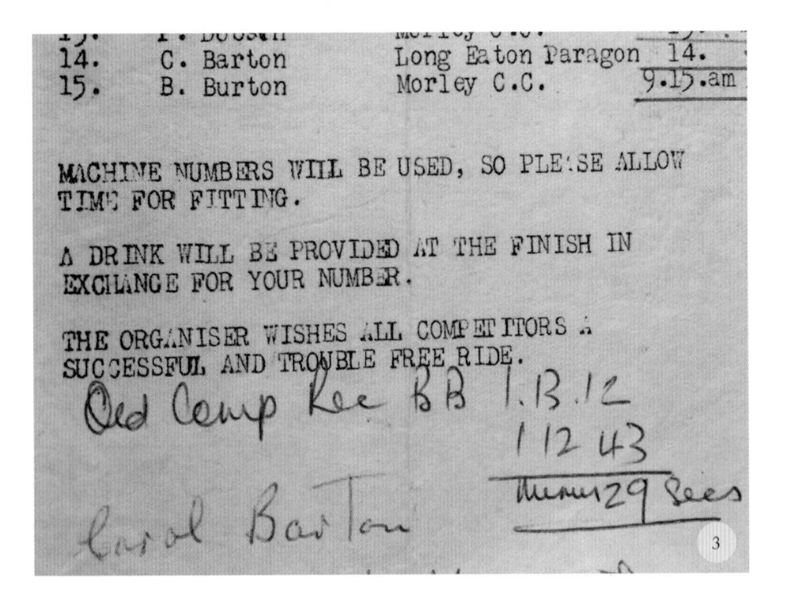

14.	C. Barton	Long Eaton Paragon	14.
15.	B. Burton	Morley C.C.	9.15.am

MACHINE NUMBERS WILL BE USED, SO PLEASE ALLOW TIME FOR FITTING.

A DRINK WILL BE PROVIDED AT THE FINISH IN EXCHANGE FOR YOUR NUMBER.

THE ORGANISER WISHES ALL COMPETITORS A SUCCESSFUL AND TROUBLE FREE RIDE.

Old Comp Rec BB 1.13.12
1 12 43
minus 29 secs

Carol Barton

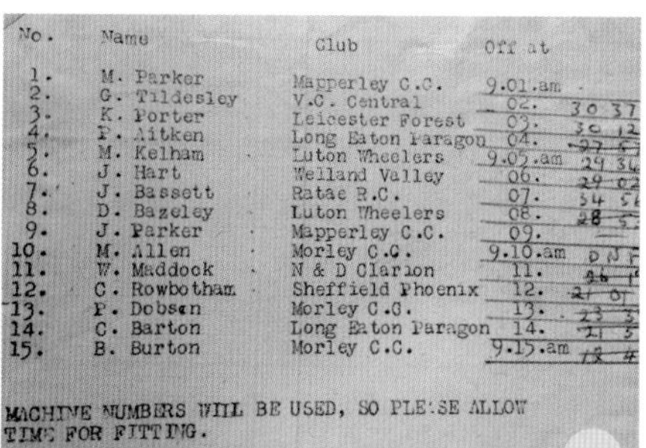

No.	Name	Club	Off at
1.	M. Parker	Mapperley C.C.	9.01.am
2.	G. Tildesley	V.C. Central	02.
3.	K. Porter	Leicester Forest	03.
4.	P. Aitken	Long Eaton Paragon	04.
5.	M. Kelham	Luton Wheelers	9.05.am
6.	J. Hart	Welland Valley	06.
7.	J. Bassett	Ratae R.C.	07.
8.	D. Bazeley	Luton Wheelers	08.
9.	J. Parker	Mapperley C.C.	09.
10.	M. Allen	Morley C.C.	9.10.am
11.	W. Maddock	N & D Clarion	11.
12.	C. Rowbotham	Sheffield Phoenix	12.
13.	P. Dobson	Morley C.C.	13.
14.	C. Barton	Long Eaton Paragon	14.
15.	B. Burton	Morley C.C.	9.15.am

MACHINE NUMBERS WILL BE USED, SO PLEASE ALLOW TIME FOR FITTING.

A DRINK WILL BE PROVIDED AT THE FINISH IN EXCHANGE FOR YOUR NUMBER.

4

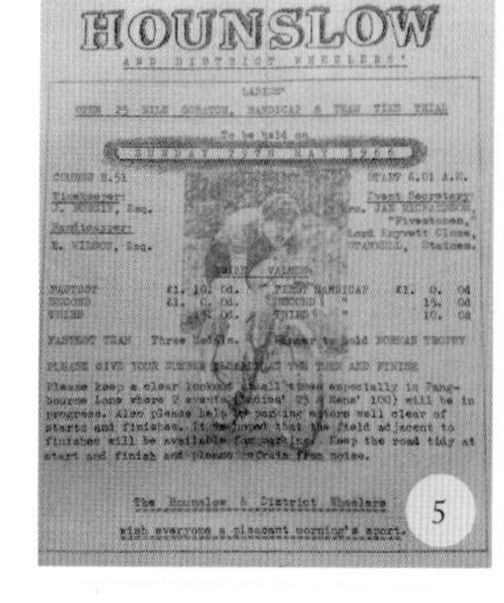

HOUNSLOW

AND DISTRICT WHEELERS'

To be held on

FASTEST TEAM Three Medals.

Please keep a clear lookout at all times especially in Pangbourne Lane where 2 events (Ladies' 25 & Mens' 100) will be in progress. Also please help by parking motors well clear of starts and finishes. It is hoped that the field adjacent to finishes will be available for parking. Keep the road tidy at start and finish and please refrain from noise.

The Hounslow & District Wheelers

wish everyone a pleasant morning's sport.

5

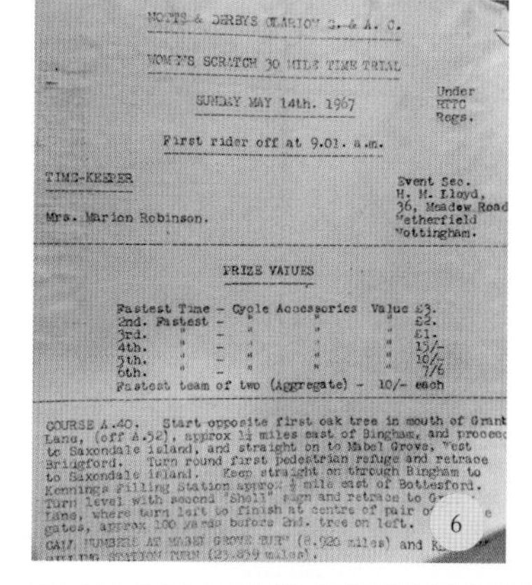

NOTTS & DERBYS CLARION C. & A. C.

WOMEN'S SCRATCH 30 MILE TIME TRIAL

SUNDAY MAY 14th. 1967

Under RTTC Regs.

First rider off at 9.01. a.m.

TIME-KEEPER

Mrs. Marion Robinson.

Event Sec.
H. M. Lloyd,
36, Meadow Road
Netherfield
Nottingham.

PRIZE VALUES

Fastest Time – Cycle Accessories Value £3.
2nd. Fastest – " " " £2.
3rd. " – " " " £1.
4th. " – " " " 15/-
5th. " – " " " 10/-
6th. " – " " " 7/6
Fastest team of two (Aggregate) – 10/- each

COURSE A.40. Start opposite first oak tree in mouth of Grant Lane, (off A.52), approx 1¼ miles east of Bingham, and proceed to Saxondale island, and straight on to Mabel Grove, West Bridgford. Turn round first pedestrian refuge and retrace to Saxondale island. Keep straight on through Bingham to Kennings Filling Station approx ½ mile east of Bottesford. Turn level with second "Shell" sign and retrace to Grant Lane, where turn left to finish at centre of pair of [illegible] gates, approx 100 yards before 2nd. tree on left.

6

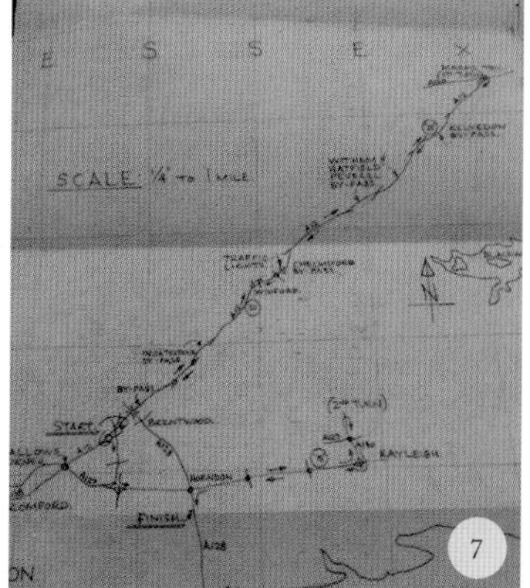

7

8

Celebrations and sadness. Top left: with the Sportswoman of the Year trophy at the Savoy Hotel in 1967; below left: at Tom Simpson's funeral earlier that year, with Eddy Merckx looking at the camera; top right: with the national pursuit champion's jersey in the Burton battlebus; below right: a kiss from Charlie after winning the 1966 world pursuit title.

1965
11

12

The final world title: top left, crossing the finish line in Heerlen, Holland on 2 September, 1967; below left, parading the rainbow jersey, with the GB team manager Chas Messenger carrying the bouquet, medal case and sash; right, Burton depicted in the pages of *International Cycle Sport* magazine during her solo break to victory.

INTERNATIONAL CYCLE SPORT

'There is a timekeeper, they say 5-4-3-2-1 go and you are on your own!' Note the stopwatch on the bars, and the frame fitting pump.

a French license because women in Luxembourg were not permitted to race.*

Burton had already shown she was faster than Jacobs over 3,000m in an international meeting at London's Herne Hill four weeks earlier, when she had come within a second of beating the national record for the distance. Even so, she was hugely nervous. The mechanic, Tom Feargrieve, tried to keep her calm by giving her an orange; her hands were shaking so much she could hardly get it in her mouth. Charlie even had to tie her shoelaces for her, and was given an earful for not doing them up just right. Indeed, he was banished from the track centre by his wife, and went through almost a whole packet of cigarettes while sitting in the stands, barely able to get each one into his mouth.

The final was 'a real hair raiser,' *Cycling* reported, 'with very little between these two outstanding girls until Beryl managed to pull away over the final 500 metres.' Burton's final margin was infinitesimal: a fifth of a second. At the Hotel Duc d'Anjou, where the team was staying, the newly won world champion's rainbow jersey was pinned to the wall above her seat at the head of the table as the team celebrated. Her rise had been meteoric, her need for recognition was acute, and this was the ultimate prize. As she wrote, it was 'some kind of retribution against the gods for that damned 11-plus and the childhood ill-health'.

The victory over Jacobs was followed by the road race championship, in which Burton finished fifth after being caught up behind a crash that delayed all six British women, four of whom also finished in the first 17. She then set out

---

**Jacobs continued racing until the mid-1970s, winning her national championship 15 times in a row; she died in 1998 aged 64.*

on a tour of races in Luxembourg and France with Millie Robinson and Kay Ray. Here she found some of the adulation she wanted, but it was sadly missing in her homeland. Her return to Leeds, wholly without fanfare, is another Burton legend: she arrived late at night at the central station, bikes and luggage, rainbow jersey and medal and all, and set off to walk up the hill to Morley, eventually managing to hitch a lift on a lorry.

That gold medal heralded a rich spate of form. Two weeks after coming home, she slashed the women's '25' record to 1hr 1min 27sec; there was excited speculation that it would soon fall below the magic 'hour', but Burton quashed that – it would take two years, she said. On the following Wednesday, she set off for the 100-mile time trial championships on the E11 '32nd' course in Essex, riding down in stages over four days. Charlie had prepared her a schedule for the 100 miles; before she left, she tucked it in her purse without asking him what it was for. She had no idea what time she might be aiming at; she simply followed his guidance.

Her victory was a performance that *Cycling's* reporter Ken Bowden described as 'the most perfect combination of style and power in a woman that I've ever seen'. Burton rode the final 25 miles faster than any of the previous 'quarters' – her times for each of the 25-mile segments would have been enough to win most women's events at the distance – and then ran back down the finish straight to cheer in Robinson. She had caught her great rival for a massive 15 minutes, no doubt letting slip a word or two of encouragement as she passed by. 'When she passed me I thought I'd stopped,' said Robinson. 'Send her to Russia!' Burton's 4hr 20min 4sec was nine minutes faster than her previous competition record, a 'dizzying, dazzling, dumbfounding time,' wrote Bowden, adding, 'Think of it, you male speed merchants. Think, most of you, that no matter how you try, you'll never equal it. Think how many men would dance for joy at such a time.'

Finally, Burton rode her first 12-hour, the Yorkshire Cycling Federation women's event, where she managed 250.37 miles (including a five-minute loss of time, equivalent to about 1.5 miles, due to a puncture). That took her 13 miles further than the previous women's record, held by Chris Watts of Addiscombe Cycling Club. 'Brilliant', 'superlative' and 'stupendous' were just some of the adjectives rightly used in the race report. The distance would have given her third place among the men in the concurrent event; among those who were slower was future Tour de France professional Barry Hoban, who managed only 248 miles on a day which he described as 'very cold for the first few hours in the early morning and a strengthening wind made conditions tough for the final miles'.

This victory gave Burton a clean sweep of all Britain's women's championships – road race, pursuit and the three time trials – and the country's four main time trial records: 25, 50, 100 miles and 12 hours. She had excelled at all distances, from the 3000-metre pursuit, lasting four minutes, right up to 250 miles over 12 hours; in athletic terms it was like a middle-distance athlete dominating every race up to ultra-distance (taking the pursuit as roughly equivalent to a 1,500m). That demonstrated astounding all-round ability.

At the end of the year Burton also had the women's Best All Rounder in her pocket, at record speed. Hyperbolically, she was described as 'the greatest woman rider cycling has ever known' at the RTTC Champions' Night at the Albert Hall: she was certainly moving rapidly towards the stature Eileen Sheridan had enjoyed in the UK. She was invited to the Pedal Club in London and the Sportswriters' Association; closer to home there was a civic reception in Morley's Town

Hall and presentation of the plaque commemorating the father of time trialling, FT Bidlake, at the Heavy Woollen Combine dinner.

Early in 1960 Burton was asked to sign the Golden Book of cycling, a massive illuminated tome kept by *Cycling* magazine under the custodianship of its then editor George Pearson, in which were inscribed the greatest feats of Britain's cyclists from 1932 until 1972. Burton was only the sixth woman to be asked to sign the book. (She was later given an inscription in a second Golden Book, founded by the Pedal Club in 1991.) At the age of 22, and in the space of 18 months, she had become the dominant force in women's racing in Britain. Golden years lay ahead.

A world away from the glitz of the Albert Hall, the gleam of medals and trophies, and the glitter of the Golden Book, inside a huddle of roughly built huts on the north side of Morley, there was an eerie crinkling noise in the gloom. Norman Carline's rhubarb was on the move. Returning to her job there, Burton came back down to earth, literally. 'Market garden' was a rather optimistic description for her clubmate's small farm off King George Avenue, a road which ran along the side of Daisy Hill, a small triangle of open ground hemmed in by the railway to the south and a main road to the north. Carline, always known as 'Nim', his farm and the boxes of rhubarb he produced played central roles in the Burton story, and in the persona that she constructed for herself over the years. She began working for Carline after Denise was born in 1956, and although she occasionally switched jobs, she could be seen toiling away at the farm until the late-1970s.

Carline's place sat at the end of rows of semi-detached houses newly built on the adjoining fields; there was a small tractor, a broken-down fence, a row of corrugated iron sheds. He also grew cabbages, broccoli and cauliflowers, and at one point tried raising pigs. Morley had a couple of other farms like this, all part of West Yorkshire's 'Rhubarb Triangle', an area surrounding Leeds from Pontefract and Garforth in the east to Brian Robinson's home town of Mirfield in the west. The area was later given EU Protected Designation of Origin status – like Champagne or Cornish pasties – for its production of Yorkshire Forced Rhubarb.

In this process, rhubarb plants are grown outdoors for a couple of years. They absorb energy in their roots from whatever sun there may be in West Yorkshire and store it as carbohydrate. The roots are then taken indoors to be 'forced' in heated buildings, in complete darkness. The warmth stimulates shoots, and these grow pale greeny-yellow due to the dark. They turn the energy in their roots into sugar, which gives the rhubarb its acidly sweet taste. A ready source of sweet energy, the anaemic-looking shoots are softer and more appetising than those grown in daylight.

The rhubarb grows with such power that there can be an eerie sensation in the dark of the sheds: think Day of the Triffids by candlelight. 'I used to think there were things running around,' said one worker. 'It was the rhubarb leaves coming out and splitting. It was sort of magical. They light the candles, and they're flickering, and then you hear all this crinkling, and it's the rhubarb actually growing.' At least the process had moved on since the 19th century, when 'night soil' from the local urban areas was used as a fertiliser.

The process is labour intensive. The roots have to be planted, dug up and re-planted, and the shoots harvested, all by hand. That calls for a casual labour force; critically for the Burton story, the bulk of the work takes place in cycling's off-season. Carline produced up to five tons of rhubarb per week from November to the end of February, and at times Burton would need to work until 10pm. There was steady labour in the summer on the mushrooms and broccoli, but not at quite the same intensity.

It was perfect for Burton mainly due to the timing: the peak rhubarb season coincided precisely with the point in the year when there was least training to be done. Shifting the rhubarb was tough physical work, which she realised would complement her training on two wheels. Carline was a fellow cyclist and club member, who would give her time off when she needed it – or when he wanted it in order to train up for the 24-hour championships which were his obsession. He was the hardest taskmaster she would ever find in cycling, as a training partner and as a boss.

Over the years, Burton tried other jobs, including at the Electricity Board, the civil service and the Post Office, which recorded in its in-house magazine in 1962 that she was a telephone accounting machine operator at the Leeds GPO (in other words, working on the same Hollerith machine she had used at Montague Burton). Farm work was the job that stuck; later in her life, after moving to Harrogate, she worked on an outdoor fruit farm near Knaresborough. She liked working outdoors – she said she would happily stay outdoors 24 hours a day if she could – and she liked the process of growing plants, feeling she had 'green fingers'.

Work, especially physical work, was always part of Burton's life. When she visited East Germany and made friends with her fellow cyclist Andrea Elle, she was clearly envious of the state support Elle received, with her daughter accommodated five days a week in a state nursery, so that Elle had only to train and race. Later in life Burton would sound slightly bitter about how much she had had to work; it was to become a source of resentment, as she realised that work was a drain on her physical resources that her younger rivals did not suffer. By 1980, she could say that 'out of 25 years I've been cycling I've worked for 23 years full time', and in a January 1985 interview she commented, 'After all, I work nine to four or 4.30, plus some Sundays. The last five weeks it's been seven days a week.'

Beryl would take Denise across Morley to the farm in her pushchair, except on days when she was going to be working on a tractor, when she would drop off Denise at Charlie's parents' house and then head for the farm on her bike. There was a variety of jobs to be done: splitting the rhubarb roots, planting them out, picking and packing the rhubarb and the mushrooms which Nim grew in the buildings when the rhubarb was outside; the rhubarb was laid 'head to tail' in long wooden boxes. Burton worked alongside the men, receiving no preferential treatment in spite of the fact that she was a woman and a cycling champion. 'Beryl was a lot stronger than me. She was stronger than anyone really, apart from Nim,' said one former worker, Sheila Broadbent. 'The planting out was particularly backbreaking. I think it's the hardest job I've ever done.' They moved boxes of vegetables on and off the lorries and dug holes to plant the plants out, hurrying to get them in the ground before the lorry returned with a new load. 'Carrying, lifting, bending, digging, all day long in all weathers until my back ached, my arms ached, my shoulders ached, my legs ached,' Burton wrote. But as in all elements of her life, she would not let up.

Carline hired people he knew, often from the local cycling fraternity, so Burton was not the only cyclist to work in what was clearly a competitive environment. When one bike racer, Laurie Morse, was working with Nim in 1967, the pair aimed to set a personal record for putting rhubarb roots into the soil, achieving a figure of 1400 per hour. In a typical afternoon, Carline and Morse might shift 300 boxes of earth and mushroom spoors. Showing that she could be their equal was another way for Burton to prove herself.

Carline, who died in 2007, was eight years older than Burton. He was not a farmer by birth, but the son of a railwayman, who had gone through grammar school and left at 16 to attend agricultural college. As well as a cyclist he was a climber, whose conquests had included the Matterhorn and the Eiger. In the 1960s, he rode to Delhi across Turkey, Iran, Iraq and Afghanistan – exotic stuff for the time. He was also one of the toughest of the Yorkshire hard men: 'Hardly the most stylish rider but one of the most determined,' wrote Mike Duffield in *Cycling*. It was a persona he liked to play up to, and one that Burton appears to have emulated.

A compact man with an ideal cyclist's body – short torso, long legs and a neat aerodynamic tuck on his bike – he specialised in the most extreme form of time trialling: the marathon events, 12 and 24 hours. In 2018, Carline was still the man who had won the most RTTC 24-hour titles, a total of six, five between 1962 and 1967. There has always been debate over whether the 12-hour is truly an appropriate element in the British Best All Rounder; Carline took this further by campaigning for the BAR to include the ludicrously tough and relatively unpopular all-day event. When he took his fourth gold medal in 1966, he nudged the competition record towards the magic total of 500 miles with a distance of 496 miles, at an average speed of almost 21mph.

His tactic in a long-distance time trial was to start as fast as he could and save nothing for later. He would have no schedule, saying 'It's just a case of keeping on hammering. Way I look at it you're bound to take a packet some time, and you don't know where it will come, so why take it easy early on?' His philosophy was simple: 'Start out to demoralise the opposition… you ride along with a big grin and a wave for everyone, make it look as though it's easy. I always take a fiendish delight in passing people – that's why I start fast, because they're all there to pass when you start.'

When he won the title in 1966, he started so quickly that he overtook the entire field in the first 70 miles. 'He started "like a bomb", was ignored by his rivals who were sure he could not last and despite a howling gale he lasted,' wrote Mal Rees of that 1966 title. 'A particularly aggressive rider, strong and a trundler of a solid man-size gear, he starts like a sprinter out of the blocks… While some riders make a leisurely stop to don warmer garb for the night, Nim puts on a cap…'

With his blond quiff and upward look through screwed-up eyes in a craggy face, Carline was a well-known local character as well as a mainstay of the Morley CC. 'So broad Yorkshire that you couldn't believe anyone could be more Yorkshire,' said one former Morley member. 'A rough diamond,' recalled Eileen Cropper, '[who] looked like a tramp, but was very rich'. He would blag second-hand clothes and shoes off his friends to avoid spending money, but when the cycling club were down the pub or in the café, he'd be the first to get out his wallet. When he went on his travels, every bike he had would be locked to the floor in the kitchen of his council house. 'Nim always had lady friends, never got married,' Charlie Burton told me. When the Morley held dances, they would put him on the door: 'He would just stand there and anyone trying to gatecrash would back off or pay the money.' At one dance, Cropper recalled, she turned up 'dolled up to the nines' and met Carline at the door: 'He asked three questions: "Who are you? What club do you ride for? And where have they been hiding you?"' Carline worked a 72-hour week most of the year, but cut back to around 40 hours in the summer, when he would knock out 500 miles a week for a couple of months to prepare for the national 12- and 24-hour championships. The farm took precedence at times: he did not race at Whitsun, because that was the height of the broccoli-cutting season. His training workload in the run up to a '24' was massive: Tuesday 80 miles; Wednesday – his afternoon off – 140-160 miles; Saturday, another morning off, 200 miles to the Lakes or Wharfedale; Sunday 140 miles on the club run.

However, his tales of how much he rode should perhaps be taken with a pinch of salt, as he clearly loved to play up to the Yorkshire hard man image. When asked by Bernard Thompson in 1973 if he suffered from back pain or aches from the cold in a '24', he replied, 'I suppose the aches and pains are there but everything hurts so much that I haven't got time to notice things like cold or backache.' His diet in a '24' would include lamb cutlets straight out of the frying pan.

Burton's training was described in an article in *Cycling* in 1959, which looked back at the winter before she won her first world title. She barely rode her bike between November and January, but would get onto the rollers once a week in December purely to loosen up her muscles. In January she began some club runs and a one-hour ride in the evenings; all her training and club riding was done on a heavy bike with a saddle-bag and a relatively high fixed gear, 70 inches,* which

* *Gear ratios are described in various ways. One is to note the number of teeth on the chainring and sprocket, another to calculate the distance each pedal revolution will move the bike forwards. A third one is to envisage the gear as a putative drive wheel for a penny farthing, expressing that in inches. A 70-inch fixed wheel would be a penny farthing wheel nearly six feet high. However, an aficionado would note that it's quite hard to find a gear of precisely 70 inches due to the way the ratios fall. Burton is more likely to have used 72" or 48x18, moving the bike over 16ft forwards for each pedal revolution.*

she admitted would test her strength when she hit a hill in the Dales at the end of a ride. From the beginning of March she picked up training more seriously, with two or three midweek outings of between 25 and 30 miles, usually in the evening, at as fast a pace as she felt she could comfortably sustain; she also included three or four 200-yard sprints. From April onwards she would compete at least once a week, as she believed racing was the best form of training; on Saturday she rode to wherever she was racing on the Sunday, if that was not too far away.

Burton had already become aware of the benefits of training with men during the season: she could drive herself harder, a technique she called 'wheel pushing' or 'half wheeling'. The sessions with Carline took that up another notch. Burton wrote: 'He was such a hard taskmaster that I would wait in the house before a training run wishing there was some way I could avoid it. I was in and out of the lavatory and perspiring even before I sat on the bike. There was no question of simply following him. I had to match him side by side, although towards the end of the stint I just had to follow his wheel, tears in my eyes but determined I would not drop behind.'

As Carline's protégée in the Morley, Burton eventually followed his 'mile-eating' approach to cycling, which she clearly adopted in an attempt to both emulate and rival him, and the pair appear to have strongly influenced the culture within the club. 'They just did huge miles, both of them,' said former member Barbara Penrice. 'The club would ride 50 miles to a pub at Huggett in the Wolds for Christmas lunch, and then come back 50 miles in the dark. It was absolutely crazy. Miles and miles and miles we'd go – it was a lot even by the standard of the time. They said they never left anyone behind, and they didn't, but you had to be good to keep up.' Another former member, Ann Battersby (née Pallister) said, 'it was meet at nine, stay out all day, take a flask, sandwiches and lights, out for dinner and tea and back in the dark.'

Both Burton and Carline were extremely direct in manner, 'a right pair' recalled Penrice. Another well-known Yorkshire racer, Keith Lambert, agreed: 'He was the same as Beryl, very direct, one who would crack the whip. There was a strong little group in the Morley who were like that. You'd be at the café in Knaresborough after a Sunday morning time trial, and Beryl would say, "Right, come on, I'm off now, I've got another 50 miles to do." Other people might wait for someone else to make a move, have another cup of tea or wait another half hour.'

The intense physical labour and the desperately hard training sessions with Carline paid obvious dividends for Burton's fitness, at least in the short term while her body was young and supple enough to deal with the workload. Her rival and later national coach Val Rushworth recalled an argument she had with Burton in which Burton queried Rushworth's use of weight training, which at the time was far from the norm. 'I said, "Burton, when you're digging rhubarb roots out of the ground and lifting them onto a low loader and lifting them off and putting them in the shed, what do you think *you're* doing?"'

There must be some myth-making in the tales of the market garden and both Carline and Burton's hardcore working and training methods. According to Burton herself, Carline actually took a break from work when he had to get the miles in for the distance championships, which sounds far more realistic than the more macho version he gave a magazine journalist. Similarly, Denise Burton-Cole suspected her mother was often out riding when she was supposed to be at work. Even when that is taken into account, however, it is clear that Carline provided something very different in Burton's life to the obvious nurturing role played by Charlie.

Nim was the one who would push her, who would treat her as an equal rather than as a superior.

The pattern was to endure down the years. Burton wanted to prove herself through physical challenges, against both genders. Lugging heavy boxes of rhubarb and mushrooms alongside men was quite a feat for a woman who had branded herself a 'failure' at school, who was one of the 'weaker sex' (i.e. expected to eschew physical effort), and who had been told by her doctor that she should take things easy. Burton probably also knew that the tales of her and Carline's methods would work on her rivals' minds. The cycling magazines made much of the way the pair trained and worked, and she would have known that that would have been talked about, adding to her fearsome reputation.

Merely riding with Carline was a way for Burton to prove, publicly, that she was stronger than most women and many men, few of whom would have dared to take up the gauntlet either on his farm or on a bike. 'She had to fight like hell to stay with him,' Burton-Cole said. 'There would be no concessions made for the fact that she was a woman. If she didn't keep up, tough.'

Chapter 6

A Woman's Place

3min 37sec: winning margin for world road race title, Sachsenring, East Germany, 13 August 1960.

Women who wanted to race bikes in the 1950s and 1960s were by turns fêted and frustrated, their achievements hailed even as their opportunities were restricted. Burton's experiences in the first years of her career had shown this: she was made welcome at the Morley, and had trophies lavished on her within time trialling, yet British officials weren't happy to splash out to support her in winning world titles. She found a measure of fame, but frustratingly little fortune to go with it. She had won a gold medal, then had had to hitch a lift home.

She was not the first woman to navigate this world of mixed messages. Once the toast of British cycling, nicknamed the 'Pocket Rocket', in early 2019 Eileen Sheridan was 93 years old, and still living in the house by the Thames that she bought in the early 1950s with her earnings from a spell as one of the first British professional cyclists of either gender. By the time Burton's career had started, Sheridan's was already over, partly because the opportunities offered to her within cycling were even more limited than when Burton was racing. Sheridan won a raft of time trial titles in the years after the war and set a series of competition records, then signed a contract with the Hercules cycle company to chase place-to-place records, including the Blue Riband: Lands

End to John O'Groats. She earned a bonus for every mile of every record she broke.

Like Burton, Sheridan faced obstacles, including parents who weren't sure she should be out on her bike. She had a full-time job, as did Burton, and showed similar commitment to the housework, baking cakes before she went to the office in the morning. She encountered hostility from male cyclists. Soon after she started cycling, some of the men she was riding with questioned whether she might slow them down – but by the end of the 140 miles she had proved herself stronger than many of them. Second time out, the men deliberately tried to burn her off, in spite of the fact that the club had a 'ride at the pace of the slowest' policy. Sheridan also faced problems with the cliquey nature of the sport – she turned up at her first time trial in red jersey and green shorts, not realising that black was *de rigueur*.

The appeal of cycling for her, as it was for Burton, was in the freedom and the process of discovery – of the wider world, and of her own potential. Also like Burton, she had a husband, Ken, who recognised early on that his wife was more talented and motivated on two wheels than he was. She too would catch slower men, and sometimes do so with a pithy comment: she recalled going past one and saying 'Golly, isn't it tough?' (His reply was a short and hollow laugh.)

Naturally gifted, with superlative skills of endurance that made her a standout star at a time when women's sport was in its infancy, the 'Pocket Rocket' became a face of cycling in Britain in the austerity years (the other being Reg Harris). When she turned professional for Hercules in 1951, having dominated domestic time trialling, she broke every record there was – including a legendary attack on the 1000-mile record which turned into an exercise as much in sleep deprivation as in cycling – and then hung up her wheels to have a second child and followed that with a second career in glass engraving. She concluded her autobiography with these words: 'Where is a woman's place? Is it … in the home? Is it in industry or in sport? If I have shown in my life that it can be – and successfully so – in all three, then I am happy.'

Sheridan feels that what held her and other women back was embedded institutional and cultural discrimination. There were not even trophies for the RTTC women's national championships early in her career – one year she shared a trophy, another time there was a whip-round among the clubs to have one made. Some men didn't believe her achievements could be genuine: 'After the 12 [hour record] I rode they asked me if I'd cut the course because I'd gone so far – but I wasn't even flogging myself at the end.'

The astonishment among male commentators about Sheridan's performances, as later about Burton's, had its roots in the 19th-century attitude that women were physically unsuited to athletic endeavour. *Young Woman* magazine in 1898 wrote of 'wheelwomen with a pronounced bicycle stoop…' regretting that this was 'fatal to dignity and good looks' and indicated 'a desire to use the bicycle for speed which is likely to turn it from an instrument of health to a means of peril. Scorching is bad enough for men but any good doctor will agree it is worse for women. The temptation arises from the thoughtlessness of men who fail to remember that woman is the physically weaker vessel.'

That belief was not limited to cycling; nor did it die out in the 20th century. In the 1920s, women's soccer was banned from British League and Association grounds – in spite of (or perhaps in fear of) its immense popularity – on the grounds that physicians believed it was damaging to the female body. Women's middle distance running events didn't make it onto the Olympic schedule until 1960, and women were told that they were physically incapable of running marathons (the women's marathon didn't figure in the Olympics until 1984).

Disapproval of women's cycling may also have derived from the fear that women would discover on the bike a freedom that was denied to them elsewhere. The American civil rights leader Susan B Anthony wrote in 1896: 'I think [the bicycle] has done more to emancipate women than any one thing in the world. I rejoice every time I see a woman ride by on a bike. It gives her a feeling of self-reliance and independence the moment she takes her seat; and away she goes, the picture of untrammelled womanhood.'

Nevertheless, women had begun to race bikes back in the 19th century. In those pioneering years there were women's races, but it is hard to tell whether they were *bona fide* competitions, or – more likely – attempts by promoters to draw crowds to novelty events in which male spectators might feast on a glimpse or two of female leg. Since women raced for money, many were effectively professionals. There was a semi-official 'world championship' in 1896, won by the Frenchwoman Amélie le Gall, nicknamed *Lisette*.

FT Bidlake, the 'father' of British time trialling in the 1890s, believed 'cycle racing for women is generally acknowledged to be undesirable', but by the time Burton came along women had been time trialling, if not in large numbers, for almost half a century. In 1908 Kate Green rode the Leeds RC '50', narrowly failing to break three hours; she also set a 12-hour distance. In 1922 the Rosslyn Ladies' CC was founded by six women, and began to promote women-only races – a 10-mile time trial that year, a 12-hour in 1924, and a '100' in 1933.

In Britain, the time triallists were the first to organise women's national championships, beginning in 1944 with the most popular distance, 25 miles, won by Susie Rimmington. That was followed by the '50' in 1948, and the '100' in 1950.

It would take time for 10 miles, 12 hours and 24 hours to be included, but compared to cycling organisations internationally, the RTTC has to be seen as an early adopter of women's racing. The BLRC began organising a national women's road race championship in 1947, and the NCU followed suit in 1956.

Cyclists such as Sheridan and Burton owed a huge debt to early pioneers such as Marguerite Wilson, the first real female star of British time trialling in the years just before the second world war: her End-to-End record in 1939 famously began in peacetime and ended after war had been declared on Germany. (Typically for the time, she was described in the press as a 'blonde bombshell'.) Another was Lilian Dredge, the first British woman to ride a road race in Europe, in 1934: a 100-kilometre (63-mile) circuit race in Brussels. (This makes the 30-mile world road race championships that Burton had to ride in the 1960s look ridiculously short). Dredge, who was ably supported by her husband Freddie, a cycling champion himself, set an End-to-End record in spite of the fact that it was not on the Road Records Association record books, and against 'strong opposition from cycling males and even from the press… regarding the possibility of a girl straining herself unduly'.

By the 1950s, that attitude was still prevalent, as the experiences of women who rode for Great Britain in the 1958 and 1959 World's showed. It took a long while to die out: the late Tom Pinnington, a BCF racing committee member, told an interviewer in 1965, 'I draw the line when it comes to women's racing. I much prefer to have my women looking feminine and this is something they are not when they are trying hard in a road race or a time trial.'

The 1950s cycling establishment was made up of men like Pinnington and the GB manager Benny Foster (who opposed the inclusion of women in the 1959 World's, as we saw in Chapter 5). Another member was the biggest British cycling star of the post-war years, Harris, who wrote, 'for a long time I have been opposed to women racing on the track in any shape or form… the thought of a women's series being included in the world championship made me shudder.' He castigated the entry of women into the world championships, which he claimed was due to 'militancy' and 'browbeating'. He claimed that women's back muscles were 'notoriously weak', that 'the smallness of their feet tends to decrease leverage', and that women were incapable of explosive effort. He also believed that 'the first thing a woman has to do is to lay aside her feminine indecision and her natural "backwardness in coming forward".'

However, such attitudes were being challenged. The shift in mood can be seen in the work of Dr CR Woodard, writer of a popular training manual, *Scientific Training for Cycling* (1951). Woodard was a big fan of Sheridan's and a major proponent of equality within the sport. 'Cycling is a sport that encourages participation by women but there is still a lot of prejudice against women taking part in strenuous exercise of any sort,' he wrote in the opening to the chapter entitled *Women In Cycling*. He noted that: 'the general standard of fitness amongst women cyclists is lower than that of men' and 'at present most women have no serious idea of how vigorous training should be.'

Where Woodard ran against the received thinking of previous years, however, was that he was adamant that women were physically capable of doing sport. He believed that women should train as hard as men, but that few did, although he was fulsome in his praise of the 'almost supreme state of fitness that Eileen Sheridan has attained'. He did not agree that athletic women found child-bearing harder than normal, and that menstruation might inhibit their performance at times other than what he delicately called 'the period of indisposition'. He also challenged the claim that women should not compete because the efforts they put in made them look 'unfeminine'; his view was that if women looked out of sorts after racing, it was because they were being advised to race before they were fit enough.

Woodard considered that many women were held back by a lack of confidence. (This is hardly surprising, given the attitudes of men such as Harris and Foster, and it still holds true today.) The doctor found this counter-intuitive given that – in his view – even though the numbers competing were 'comparatively small', a relatively high number of women such as Sheridan were posting times that compared favourably with those of the men.

He concluded, 'when women start training for cycling as seriously as men, there will be very little difference in the performances between male and female… When training is done scientifically, male and female performances will come very close together.' Six years before Burton reached her peak, Woodard was convinced that women could take on men, observing that in tennis and swimming they attained high standards – which he put down to tennis players and swimmers having better training and technical knowledge than their cycling sisters. The doctor's crystal ball was in good working order.

The belief that women were physically unsuited to sport meant that the few who were truly successful ran the risk of being described as somehow unnatural – as remorseless winning machines. Sheridan did not experience this, because her peak was brief and she was carefully marketed by Hercules, but it was a problem that would beset Burton as the years went on, and it began within a couple of seasons of her rise. 'Beryl the Unbeatable' read the headline over a report of a victory in the Isle of Man in the summer of 1960. The writer lauded her calm and competence, but added that she had won, 'with the ruthless unemotional efficiency that is becoming associated with her every performance.' That image persisted for many years, and it was as incorrect as it usually is about an athlete: Burton might have looked completely in control, but there are numerous accounts of her displays of nerves. As with most top athletes, male and female, the swan analogy applied: serene on the surface, paddling frenetically under the water.

The world championships in East Germany in the summer of 1960 came at a golden moment in Burton's career, at the end of another spectacular season of domination and self-discovery. Her spring campaign began with a two-week trip to race with a Great Britain selection at the Werner Seelenbinder indoor track in East Berlin. There, Burton was shown by the top British sprinter Lloyd Binch how to ride the 60-degree 'wall of death' bankings – a far cry from the gentle slopes of outdoor tracks such as Herne Hill. 'A wonderful trip,' she wrote, 'with a big reception [every night] where tables groaned under the weight of beautifully presented food.' Not to mention secret service 'heavies' who kept tabs on her and the sprinter Jean Dunn whenever they ventured into the city.

Two weeks' intense track racing in Berlin set Burton up for a rapid spring: she broke the 10-mile record with 24min 35sec, added the 25-mile title and the national 3000m pursuit gold medal, and notched up several wins during the series of races that made up Isle of Man Week. She then added a second 50-mile title with a new record, 2hr 5min 45sec. As in 1959, she was exhibiting supreme versatility across four disciplines, winning road races solo and competing strongly in the national grass track championship at Tom Simpson's home town of Harworth. Six hours before flying out to East Germany for the World's, she defended her RTTC 100-mile championship, in a new record time of 4hr 18min 19sec, and with an 11-minute victory margin.

There had been some debate with the British Cycling Federation over her participation in this 100-mile title race – it clashed with the team's scheduled travel to Leipzig – but eventually Burton was given special dispensation to fly out to East Berlin and join the rest of the team immediately afterwards, at her own expense. The upshot was another mini-saga; Charlie came to meet her at the airport, but her plane was late and they had no way of travelling on to Leipzig that night. Eventually, after wandering East Berlin looking for somewhere to stay, they entered a police station, more in hope than expectation; fortunately, strings were pulled and they were found a hotel paid for by the East German state.

The pursuit series on the Leipzig velodrome did not go entirely smoothly. The racing was disrupted by rain, and Burton was fortunate not to escape injury when the cone in one of her wheels broke. The British were poorly equipped as usual, and she had to accept the loan of rollers from the Russians. For the final, the GB women's coach Eileen Gray, who knew that Burton appreciated encouragement, rounded up 'practically every English journalist and rider present' with instructions to spread around the track and yell at her as she rode. 'I couldn't help giggling,' said Burton, 'as I came within earshot of each one and heard their frantic shouts.' Not that hearing can have been easy, with the velodrome packed with 25,000 spectators. Gray also delegated *Daily Express* journalist Ron White and his wife Cath to shield Burton from autograph hunters, photographers and interviewers as she prepared for her events in the track's centre; she knew that Burton suffered from anxiety and she needed to be protected.

That pursuit series was one of Burton's finest, prompting the editor of *Cycling*, George Pearson, to compare her with the French ace Roger Rivière: 'Nothing can have been more stimulating than the opening assault of Beryl in her defence of her pursuit championship,' wrote Pearson. 'She tore into last year's finalist Elsy Jacobs with a power that completely demoralised this very competent performer, beating all known standards in the west with a time of 4min 12.9sec.' That time was a world record, a huge eight seconds faster than her best opponent; she then cut that to 4min 10sec in the quarter-final, and improved again to 4min 6.1sec in beating Marie-Thérèse Naessens in the final.

In the road race, Burton went almost unchallenged on the tough five-mile Sachsenring circuit, this time in front of a crowd of 65,000. Pearson's report described her as 'immeasurably superior to any other woman cyclist on the road…' Having responded to an attack from Elsy Jacobs on the fourth lap, Burton then set a pace that suited her. She turned round and looked at the 1958 champion, who simply shook her head; she could not follow. With Jacobs back in the peloton, and Burton's team-mates shadowing counter-attacks, the race turned into a replica of the time trials she rode every weekend in the UK.

Burton said later that she did not particularly like road racing, but felt she had no option but to ride road races because there was a chance for a world title; had there been a time trial world championship, she probably would not have bothered. Charlie's take on her tactical approach is amusing: 'She had no more tactics than that Christmas tree. If she road raced she'd get to the front, get stuck in and drop them on the first stretch; if someone sat on her wheel she'd just get on with it. She just went. And when she went, she went.' Burton had a simple strategy: wait for a hill, ride up it as quick as possible, and hope to end up on her own at the top.

Under the headline, 'Beryl Toyed with Them', Pearson gave a breakdown of the times for each lap, which showed that after Burton broke away around half distance she was consistently riding faster than the bunch: her fastest lap time of 15min 32sec was around a minute quicker than the entire peloton could manage. Pearson described it as 'a world championship field that was permitted to look effective only until the champion was ready to take command.' Her winning margin was a massive 3min 37sec, carved out in just 20 miles.

Leipzig gave Burton two of the three world titles available to women, crowning her as the strongest in the world. She did not, however, rest on her laurels. According to one urban myth, when the team bikes returned to the UK after the two-day drive on top of Feargrieve's 'Britannia', Burton was waiting on the doorstep of a team official to receive her machine so she could go out training. There were track meetings and time trials in the UK, and finally a trip to Milan – financed by a hurried fundraising drive in Morley – for an attempt at Jacobs' Hour Record on the mythical Vigorelli velodrome.

The Vigorelli, at the time reputed to be the fastest track in the world, is a partly covered velodrome, open to the elements, which means that warm, dry weather is needed for any record attempt. The Burtons endured continual heavy rain and wind, and even snow. The first attempt, on 5 October, fell flat after half an hour; a second bid shortly afterwards saw Burton break Jacobs's 20km record but come up 500 metres short after the 60 minutes, a significant margin in an Hour Record. She and Charlie went home, looked at the remaining money from the donations, and decided there was just enough for a second trip if Beryl went solo. But the weather remained against her, and she spent another frustrating spell sitting in a hotel waiting for it to clear: she did not turn a pedal in earnest. It was the first major setback of her career.

The 1960 world championships in East Germany contrasted favourably to the half-hearted efforts of the West in previous and later years, but that reflected the fact that much of the agitation for the wider adoption of women's sport had come from the Eastern bloc. There were obvious political reasons for this: east of the Iron Curtain, women were seen as a truly significant element in the workforce, and thus enjoyed wider job opportunities and better childcare than in the West. Opening up women's sport was part of creating a confident, healthy female workforce, and supporting women who would win medals tapped into the greater drive to portray Communism in a positive way through sporting success. This was light years from unblemished feminism however: the East German coaches 'asked' their female cyclists to have a child – just one, whether or not they were married – as they believed it would strengthen their hearts.

The movement to have women's racing recognised internationally began after the Second World War. Marguerite Wilson had made the argument in an interview in 1946: why, she asked, should women not be represented in cycling at the Olympics when they were present in 'all types of sport and athleticism'? It was a point that the International Olympic Committee would – lamentably – take 30 more years to act upon. When Burton won her double world titles in 1960, she did so in the year of the Rome Olympics, where women cyclists were not permitted to race. It was a lost opportunity that she always resented.

Much of the pressure on the UCI to hold women's world championships came from Britain, through the Women's

Cycle Racing Association, which had been founded by GB women's team manager Eileen Gray, a South West London official who later became British Cycling's president. She set out her stall in 1957 when she organised an international race meeting in London which was clearly intended to be a pilot for a possible world championship independent of the world governing body. This was a threat Gray would continue to make over the next 20 years as she pushed further for equality in women's racing.

Following a UCI vote against women's recognition in 1956, her arguments were put forward in a double-page article in *Cycling and Mopeds* in October 1957, in which she wrote that whatever a man's ethnicity 'there is no barrier of prejudice, and if ability permits you may appear as your country's representative at either world championships or Olympic Games'. This did not apply to women, she pointed out. Gray argued that in Britain and France women were racing at a level which approached the male standard of 25 years earlier. While France, Britain and the Iron Curtain countries were pioneers, she said, otherwise 'there remains much hostility for women's sport and the sport of cycling [for women] in particular'. She underlined two 'absurdities': nations which allowed female track and field athletes to compete internationally were voting against women cyclists doing the same, and there were still nations which refused to issue women's racing licences – such as Elsy Jacobs' Luxembourg – meaning that their athletes had to apply personally to the UCI to race.

Gray's article included an explicit threat to take women's cycling outside the aegis of the UCI; that prospect was enough for the UCI to cave in and include women at the 1958 World's, with guarantees from Great Britain, France, Belgium and the USSR that they would field strong teams.

It was not done with good grace or total commitment, however – as seen in 1959, when the Dutch simply refused to run women's track racing. It would take until well into the 21st century for the UCI to engage seriously with women's equality issues within the sport; throughout Burton's career she had to contend with indifference at the highest level, with the women racers repeatedly on the receiving end of cavalier organisation. Back home in Britain, debate over a 'woman's place' in cycling would go on into the 1970s, and as recently as the 1990s the governing body British Cycling was still behind in delivering equal racing opportunities.

Going back to those images of Burton on the Morley CC club run, she looks completely at ease among the men; she leads the string of riders, she relaxes when they reach the tea stop. She clearly felt at home, although Eileen Cropper for one felt that 'you were [seen as] a weirdo if you rode a bike as a woman. The lads used to put bricks in my saddle-bag. I got to be a strong little climber, so I'd give them a hard time on the hills and they would pull my ponytail to make me slow down. Now that I didn't mind; I was as good as they were.'

One correspondent, Joan Green, wrote to *Cycling* – which she would later join as a journalist – to describe the sport as 'dominated by men and regulated by them, a man's world which women cyclists enter and they are forced to abide by the rules the men lay down.' She was responding to a letter which took the sexism of men like Foster and Harris several steps further, purporting to ask about etiquette towards women cyclists: the writer wanted to know whether he should push a woman uphill, repair her punctures, lend her his cape, 'offer to oil the legs of that charming blonde…' or sacrifice his chances in a race to 'help a crying maiden whose pedal has fallen off'. Green answers, 'any girl who has cycled for a while becomes accustomed to fending for herself when necessary.' Full stop.

Cycling magazine was typical of the time: there was constant emphasis on the looks of women who raced – they were continually described as 'attractive' or 'pretty as a picture' – and reference to their domestic skills. They were referred to by their first names – 'Beryl versus Millie' – while men would get the surname treatment. A typical headline might be 'Jean third to Russian blondes'. There was a cartoon strip every week featuring 'Ruby Lustre', which was plain offensive: a typical offering showed Ruby turning up at Land's End and asking the way to John O'Groats. Another cartoon showed two cyclists sitting under a tree holding beers, one saying to the other, 'Give me a beautiful girl, a tandem and the open country, and you can keep the open country and the tandem.' The space allotted to women's national championships was often derisory.

In 1958, the magazine, the voice of the sport in Britain, launched a 'Cycling Girl' competition, where the brief stated, 'The prizes are certainly attractive but so we are sure will be the many riders who enter. Pride in appearance is a healthy attribute, and cycling is a health-giving pastime, the attraction of this combination is demonstrated by our cycling girls who now have the opportunity of emphasising the fact.' This was a straight-up beauty contest, with each month's winner awarded 10 guineas in cash and the chance to attend events before a Grand Final; the picture of the contestants in very short shorts made it all pretty clear. The attitudes persisted, damagingly. Bernadette Malvern gave up racing in 1971, at the age of 20, partly because of the derisive attitude men showed toward women's competition. If women were made to feel racing was not worthwhile, they were all the less likely to do it, and then to persist at it.

In spite of these shockers, the British cycling milieu was far from the most backward in its attitude to women. By the time Burton began racing, the debate had begun to move on from whether women should race, to focus on whether women should race alongside men; Burton would campaign hard to achieve that end. When Burton had a major success, as at the 1960 World's, she was given due exposure on the cover of *Cycling* and *Sporting Cyclist*. Contrast this with Holland, where as late as the mid-1960s one of the most promising juniors, Willy Kwantes, had to dress up as a boy in order to race for the first time. Such attitudes delayed the progress of equality on the international stage, where it would take until 1984 for women cyclists to race in the Olympics, and even then only in a limited number of events. The UCI retained one men-only discipline in the world championships, the Madison track relay, until as late as 2016, for no particular reason other than inertia.

After the immense adulation Burton had received in East Germany, returning home to her and Charlie's council flat was an anti-climax, as it had been the previous year; in her autobiography she bemoaned the meagre newspaper reports, and concluded the chapter about the two gold medals with these words: 'I was a double world champion in an international sport and it might as well have been the ladies darts final down the local as far as Britain was concerned.' The contrast between her homeland and what she termed 'a cycling country' was made all the clearer later on in the winter, when she travelled to Belgium for a revenge pursuit match against Marie-Thérèse Naessens put on as part of the

Ghent six-day. The crowds were massive and passionate in their support.

Even so, Burton was gradually making a name for herself nationally. In honour of her achievements, the Cycle Industry Association awarded her and Charlie a car, a three-wheeled Reliant Robin which lasted them many years. There was another civic reception in Morley, and in early December the Best All Rounder concert at the Albert Hall. She finished runner-up to Anita Lonsborough, the Olympic swimmer, in the *Daily Express*-sponsored Sportswoman of the Year, and Brian Johnston – of *Test Match Special* notoriety – felt she was worth including in the BBC's *Meet a Sportsman* [*sic*] that November.

This is a brief recording, with Johnston's plummy accent and ignorance of cycling an amusing contrast with Burton's broad Yorkshire and her forbearance of his lack of knowledge. She laughs throughout, becoming borderline flirtatious as her initial shyness ebbs; she is clearly enjoying the attention. Asked to describe herself, Burton says, 'I'm the world championship massed start, world championship pursuit, BCF pursuit champion, national championship for the massed start, and 25, 50 and 100 miles RTTC champion.'

'A lot of letters but I'm sure it's very good,' replies 'Johnners'. He asks if Burton works, and is told, 'Up to a couple of months ago I did, part time on a farm… Market garden, not very heavy work… I haven't had time since the world championship, dashing everywhere, haven't gone back yet.' Her hobbies? 'I do a bit of knitting when I go away. I seem to have so much spare time when I'm away.' She subsides into laughter. When he asks her to describe her training, Johnston is surprised she goes out on her own so much. 'Isn't it lonely?' 'Naw, you get a chance to turn things over in your mind… what you're going to do the next day.' Again that laugh.

Burton was also interviewed for *BBC Sports Personality* alongside John Surtees – he with his motorbike, she with her track bike. She comes across as modest and wide-eyed, with an engaging smile and that impeccable mop of curly hair; asked how she combines family life, work and sport, she says, 'Well, it keeps you fit, all that dashing around,' with the same acerbity as Tom Simpson could show. She was also asked if she would be interested in turning professional, and replied – with a highly determined set of her jaw - that 'Oh yes,' she had had 'one or two' offers. She followed that up with a blatant pitch: '£20 a week and £1 a mile for record attempts'. That was the same deal that Sheridan had negotiated a few years earlier.

Later in the winter, the opportunity to turn professional did come, when a representative of the Raleigh cycle company arrived at the Burton home to talk possible terms with her and Charlie. In *Personal Best*, she tells of the amusement she and Charlie took at the lengthy list of dos and don'ts in the proposed contract. There was an inexplicable clause which stated she would be paid less for a record which had already been broken shortly before any attempt she made. Two elements made her turn the deal down. It was a three-year contract, after which she would probably be unable to revert to amateur status according to the rules of the time. That would effectively end her racing career. Clearly, the money cannot have been on a par with that offered to Sheridan. Buxton felt that 'she could earn more working as a machine accountant' – which she was still doing in between stints with Nim Carline – 'and of course I was still my own boss, racing when and where I wanted to'.

It was, she said, a decision she never regretted, but it left her with no opportunity to target anything in cycling other than races she had already won. The limited nature of women's cycling, with its three world championships and very little else, meant that once the record breaking option had been shut off – and she would turn down further offers from Raleigh – there was nowhere else to go.

One of those who recognised the situation that Burton now faced was Reg Harris. In an interview in early 1960, he acknowledged that the Yorkshirewoman had achieved pretty much everything that was on offer. Harris hoped that Burton would 'be sufficiently farsighted to avoid a future comprising constant repetition of past achievements'. His suggestion was that she could instead become an ambassador for British cycling: take the world Hour Record, then embark on road record breaking, with the backing of the British cycle industry, and make as many public appearances as possible – for example, 'panel games alongside well known celebrities of the sparkling screen', a cycling column in a daily newspaper, receptions and opening trade shows.

For this she would need an agent – obviously – and the subtext was presumably that R Harris Esq. might be the man. (In actual fact, Harris's commercial enterprises tended to fail.) This was patronising and hypocritical given Harris's views on women racing. He missed the obvious point: with the Olympics closed off and world championships restricted, there simply wasn't enough to achieve in women's cycling to satisfy an ambitious woman who wanted both to compete and to make a living from her sport.

Which takes us back to Sheridan and that house by the Thames, where the legacy of the UCI's reluctance to introduce women's world championships can still be felt. More than 60 years since her retirement, Sheridan remains disappointed with one thing. She says, 'I never felt like a champion because I never had a rainbow jersey.' Whatever obstacles would stand in her way, and whatever limits the men in blazers had imposed on her sport, Burton at least would not have to go to her grave with that regret.

Chapter 7

Friends and Rivals

59min 25sec: first beating of the 'hour' for 25 miles by a woman, Easterley RC '25', Southend Road, 26 May 1963.

There were few women who could match Beryl Burton at her peak. The doughtiest of the handful lives in a small house in a quiet street 12 miles outside Antwerp. Yvonne Reynders was born five months after Burton. She is a raconteur, who likes to tell long tales in her deeply accented Flemish. She waves her hands, gets up to illustrate a point or two, digresses widely, laughs loud and long, interjects the odd *Godverdomme* – Goddamit. It is the interview as a piece of performance art.

As well as sharing a birth year, Burton and Reynders had other things in common. Both had a tough upbringing. Reynders was the only breadwinner in her home, the child of an invalid mother and an alcoholic father. She was put to manual work early on, delivering coal through the streets of Antwerp on a tricycle with a vast basket on the front; later, she moved on to selling soup. Like Burton and Sheridan she began her athletic career as a swimmer, but Reynders progressed to athletics – specialising in discus, shot and javelin, and even winning a Belgian national title – before she switched to cycling.

Reynders has a practical mindset. She painted her own bike frame and put the machine together, and later helped to mix cement and carry bricks when building her own house. She now lives surrounded by sculptures of her own design, with a gardenful of sheds she put up herself to house her tools and her collection of 32 turtles, the oldest of which, she tells me, is nudging a century. As Burton did, she wants things to be just so; on the wall of her workshop is a perfectly arranged 'shadow board' where every spanner and wrench has its specific hanging place, denoted by an accurate profile drawing. Her career is detailed in immaculately kept photo albums, race by race.

There is a key difference with Burton, however, in that Reynders received some appreciable financial rewards from her racing. The Antwerp racer dominated during what the writer Marcel de Leener described as 'a golden age' of women's racing in the early 1960s, when she 'became the big star of women's cycling with plenty of contracts and firms fighting over the privilege of paying her'. Her photo albums show women's races in Belgium contested in front of massive crowds, on a par with men's professional events. In the photos, there are always sponsors' names and logos on her jerseys, be it the electronics company RadioBell or a bike maker such as Liberta or Reno.

Reynders rightly describes herself as 'a self-made woman'. Like Burton, she had fought hard; she had bought her first bike off a pile of scrap steel about to be melted down, and painted it using the vacuum cleaner at home, in blower mode, covering herself in paint as she did so. She explicitly states that her main motivation for racing was the money: up to 900 Belgian francs for a win – at a time when a good bike cost 1200 – and on one occasion 19,000 francs from a race in France, 'up and down with prime after prime'. She supplemented her income with paid demonstrations of her ability to ride on rollers. It was the stuff of the circus: she would have to keep her bike steady and keep pedalling as she took her tracksuit top off, removed and replaced the handlebars or pumped up a wheel.

In the 1960s, *Cycling* magazine considered Reynders to be 'the most accomplished all round bike rider in the game', noting that although Elsy Jacobs could 'match her nerves but not her spirit' and Burton was able to outpace her in a pursuit on the track, she outstripped the Luxembourger and the Yorkshirewoman when it came to bike handling, race sense and confidence. Those qualities helped her to seven gold medals in world championships between 1959 and 1966 including four road race titles.

The rivalry with Burton lasted from 1959 until Reynders' retirement in 1967, with the 1958 world road race champion Jacobs occasionally making it a three-way battle (although Reynders' feeling is that the Luxembourger's best years were behind her by the 1960s). Of Burton, Reynders remembers a rival whom she had to respect, but also a language barrier – she speaks no English, Burton had no Flemish. 'She was the strongest I faced. It was either me or her. One then the other. But I never really got to know her well.' Burton in turn described Reynders as a good friend off the bike and her most bitter opponent on it.

After beating Reynders to the road race and pursuit in 1960, Burton hoped to retain her world titles on British soil the following year. The men's races – a reduced programme in an Olympic year – were held in Zurich; the women's events were awarded to the Isle of Man.* In the pursuit, the die seemed cast when Reynders qualified in 4min 1.1sec, 6.5 seconds faster than Burton, but both broke the four-minute

---

** The UCI's own official listings still have all the races in Zurich but the reports are explicit that the women's races were in the Isle of Man. There is no explanation why the championships were split, but most probably it was because the Swiss did not want to run women's races.*

barrier in their respective rounds at the semi-final stage, with Burton marginally faster.

There were stormy skies for the final on the outdoor Onchan velodrome, high above Douglas Bay, with riders huddled under tarpaulins and wrapped in blankets as the wind lashed the bumpy, exposed track. It was 'an epic battle', according to *Cycling*'s editor George Pearson. Burton started fastest, and the pair swapped the lead on each of the seven laps. With half a lap remaining Burton took a three-bike-length lead, but Reynders fought back to win 'by a yard' – the official margin being just a tenth of a second. 'Afterwards, our manager Oscar Daemers told me it was the only time he had seen a pursuit won by a rider "throwing" their bike across the line, like a sprinter,' Reynders recalled.

The road race was ten laps of the four-mile Willaston circuit, based on the southern end of the TT course, and including Governors Bridge, the Grandstand and Cronk-ny-Mona. It became a three-way battle between Burton, Reynders and Jacobs, again won by the Antwerp rider. Daemers hailed his leader as the only member of his team who truly paid attention to detail, the only one who made sure to take a spare bike of her own with her to the world championships. That proved critical when her gear cable broke at Douglas; she simply changed onto the back-up machine at the pits. Although Burton and Jacobs promptly attacked, Reynders' supreme effort to close the 15-second gap showed she was the strongest, and in the final three-up sprint up to the Douglas grandstand she opened a massive 10-length gap over Burton, with Jacobs 20 lengths behind. There was a pattern here: Burton attempting to escape, Reynders riding with her head. She tells me she knew exactly what she was doing, and how to keep Burton in check. 'Races are won with the head as well as the legs,' she declares.

A year later, in Milan, Burton took a spectacular revenge on the Vigorelli velodrome, defeating Reynders in what the partisan writer at *Cycling* described as 'the greatest ride in the history of women's pursuit racing', winning in a record 3min 59.4sec. The final, according to their reporter, 'was a slaughter. Beryl led all the way and delivered the knockout in the fourth lap when she gained 10 lengths. After that it was a massacre.' Here, *Cycling*'s man wrote, 'was a better Beryl Burton than ever before, a girl [*sic*] who seized every moment all the week to train on the track, who was still sending for "sparring partners" a few minutes before racing began.'

'Beryl has speeded up her start and her stamina is unquestioned,' read the report. 'On a hot, sultry evening her magnificent ride could be gilded in only one way – by a record... the first ride ever done inside four minutes.' (The previous year's championship at Onchan included rides under the four-minute mark, but the racing was not over the full 3000 metres as the track was measured in yards; the race worked out at 2830 metres for the seven laps.) Burton clocked 4min 1.7sec and 4min 2sec in the intermediate rounds, and was asked to start in the back straight for the seven and a half lap final, so she would finish in the home straight. Why? she asked team manager Tommy Godwin – to be told that the official delegation of guests 'expect you to win, and they want to see you finish'.

Eileen Sheridan, who had been taken to Milan to act as chaperone for the women in the team, believes that '[the organisers] weren't bothered about the women. It was a men's track event; two sprinters did a standstill for half an hour with the crowd throwing things because they were so bored. And because of that the women didn't race until midnight. It was a rotten thing to happen, but Beryl was marvellous in spite of the long wait.'

Meanwhile, Charlie had travelled over the Alps on the back of a clubmate's moped, arriving late in Milan after a blow-out on the Simplon Pass. His had been an epic journey; the two men camped on the way, setting fire to their tent on night one and spending another night in a graveyard. Such sacrifices were the norm for Charlie; the BCF allowed him to travel with them to the World's largely because he acted as an unpaid mechanic to the team. He remembers sleeping outside the team's hotel somewhere in France one year – he had tried sleeping in the woods but had been woken up by some pigs. The manager Tom Pinnington came across him and moved him to a couch in the hotel's corridor.

Beryl's nerves had been frayed, understandably, as she tried to figure out where Charlie had got to. In her memoirs, Sheridan described an ice bag being applied to the back of Beryl's neck in the gym under the stands of the Vigorelli; she slugged a couple of aspirin, while Charlie 'smoked like a chimney'. 'After a while this girl of steel sat up and said laughingly, "What's the matter with you two? Nervous?"' The final was an emotional experience: 'I yelled till I was hoarse, much to the amusement of the crowd… We all stood with eyes gleaming like soap bubbles and I saw Beryl on the rostrum (with a bouquet of deep red gladioli) raise a hand quickly to remove a tear…' Both Burtons were overwhelmed; Sheridan recalled that Charlie had to be instructed to kiss his wife for the photographers.

The celebrations did not end there: 'There was a little man had a café round the corner from the hotel,' recalled Sheridan. 'He said to us, "If you have any champions bring them here." The evening ended up with a whole lot of cars driving into Milan, a big hotel, a big room, wine glasses all down the table. It was lovely for Beryl – it was lovely to see her get the attention she deserved.' There were other accolades: from the world sprint champion Antonio Maspes and the legendary bike maker Faliero Masi. However, the rest of the World's was an anticlimax: a frustrating road race on the circuit at Salò, where Reynders engineered a win for her team mate Marie-Rose Gaillard and Burton ran in eighth. She stayed in Italy for another attempt at the Hour Record on the Vigorelli, but it was, she acknowledged, a 'half-hearted' bid in which she abandoned after about 30 minutes, and the Blue Riband eluded her again.

The rivalry with Reynders continued a year later on Belgian soil, again in the pursuit, this time on the velodrome in Rocourt, the track used for the 1959 championship. The field consisted of only seven riders, meaning that the race went straight from the qualifying rounds to the semi-final stage. The planning for women's races being what it was, the three rounds were spread over five days, testing the riders' patience to the full. Reynders qualified fastest, by just 0.9 seconds; in the semi-final, where a strong breeze sent clouds of dust spiralling into the air, Burton beat the Russian Riabchenko in a time 0.25 seconds faster than Reynders, in spite of a slipping saddle.

The final was held late in the evening, under floodlights, in warm conditions, with a partisan home crowd roaring as Reynders raced into the lead on the first lap. It was blow and counter-blow: Reynders had gained three lengths by the second lap, Burton pulled her back in the fourth, gaining 20 yards, and then produced the strong finish that most expected of her to increase that to 30 yards at the bell. That prompted a 'sudden stillness' among the home crowd, *Cycling* reported, before they 'accepted the inevitable and found their voices to applaud the finest unpaced rider women's cycling has ever produced'. It was, Burton felt, the 'pinnacle' of her pursuit career; she had gone faster in Milan, but the track at

Rocourt was slower. She had now won five rainbow jerseys in as many years.

The road race at Renaix, a hundred miles away in Flanders, was a disaster: Burton crashed within 10 miles of the start when a service vehicle overtook the peloton, forcing them over to the right where Burton was moving up. She was taken to hospital suffering severe bruising to her back. This was one of a series that hampered Burton during the mid-1960s; the resulting issues with her back were still affecting her 12 months later at the world championships at the Parc des Princes track in Paris. Here, Burton lost her pursuit title to Reynders, after two other crashes ruined that championship.

The first came as she was preparing for the road race at Sallanches in the Alps, when a close pass from a car put her on the deck. The back injury from that one would have been bad enough, but the *coup de grace* was a second pile-up at the Parc, when a line of riders came down *en masse*. Burton suffered what sounds like a broken wrist, and had to ride with one hand plastered; even after receiving a painkilling injection she was still unable to hold the bars properly. Not surprisingly, she was well off her best, and a silver medal to Reynders was a startling achievement in the circumstances.

Not for the first time and not for the last, Burton's medal was the Great Britain team's high point. *Cycling* magazine had a new editor, Alan Gayfer, who flayed the British Cycling Federation in his editorial. The team won no medals apart from Burton's silver, they had not troubled to travel with rollers for the riders to use (not for the first time or the last time), and to Gayfer's disgust they were reduced to asking *him* to try and find another team with a spare set for them to borrow. Burton's hand and back issues were eventually resolved by an Italian physiotherapist – but as Gayfer wrote, 'Heaven and earth itself should have been turned upside down to get her the treatment she needed before she rode the championship. Is it any wonder she looked so glum?'

Afterwards, Burton said she was contemplating retirement. The family were moving into a new house at Woodlesford, six miles south east of Leeds on the river Aire, and she was concerned that the need to get it in order would limit her time to race. Most importantly, perhaps, the cost of racing was getting to the Burtons. It had, she said, cost her and Charlie £100 of their own money to go to Paris for that silver medal at the Parc des Princes, while 'some weekends I travel all over [the UK] to track meetings, time trials and road races and perhaps get a couple of medals and a small prize having spent about £5. With a rate of expenditure like that one cannot carry on racing any longer.' In her memoirs, she recognised the appeal of lie-ins at home in her own bed on a Sunday morning. Given she and Charlie would get up as early as 330am for a 530am time trial start, that does not seem unreasonable.

The notion of retirement came to nothing, and Burton was present at the 1965 World's in San Sebastian. Once again the British team forgot to pack rollers, but the euphoria at Tom Simpson's gold in the men's professional road race meant that any issues were overlooked. Burton fell ill before her road race, and took on the 30 miles while not fully healthy. This left her drained for the pursuit, where she failed to qualify. Reynders, meanwhile, managed a silver medal in the road race, but retirement was now on the Belgian champion's mind: she felt it was no longer possible to earn a living racing on a bike owing to new restrictions on sponsor names on jerseys.

In 1966 Reynders returned after a brief spell away from racing to win a seventh world road title on the Nürburgring circuit. It was a classic race of the type that frustrated Burton so much: she came in fifth after spending the absurdly short 28 miles trying to dislodge the other riders from her wheel. 'It was like beating your head against a brick wall,' she said afterwards. She forged an initial four-rider break with Jacobs, but Reynders was on effervescent form and bridged to the quartet. 'Every time I turned round to speak to Reynders and Jacobs about leading they made it plain they wanted nothing to do with me. It was no use, either I worked and we stayed away or the others would have come up to us.' 'Leeches,' she termed them in her memoirs; in fact, as Reynders would say, her rivals were merely using their heads.

If fault was to be found, it was with organisers and officials who felt women should not be racing more than 30 miles in a world title; such brief races did nothing to demonstrate what women could do and in Burton's case it limited her chances of dislodging the sprinters before the finish. At the 1966 World's, the *Cycling* editor Gayfer felt that the women were treated as second-class citizens in terms of the racing schedule, which was reflected in the crowd at the road race; the victory photo in Reynders' album shows three women crossing the finish line with barely a spectator in sight.

The Burtons' relations with the Great Britain national team were also far from ideal. That year, 1966, Burton had to contend with a BCF rule which stated that riders who wanted to be considered for the world track championships in late August should not race in events of more than 25 miles after 31 July. That might have been a well-intentioned attempt to ensure that the pursuiters did not blunt their speed by racing long distances, but it was a blow for Burton, who excelled in 50- and 100-mile time trials.

Another BCF idea was to prevent track riders from taking on the road race, which was ludicrous given the small pool of riders available, and considering that the road race was a mere 28 miles. Charlie wrote an angry letter to *Cycling*; he rightly claimed this was 'killing initiative with petty rules'. A week later a supportive letter writer claimed that the BCF treated Burton as if she were 'an embarrassment and an encumbrance'. Burton never felt that the BCF gave her or other women much assistance or encouragement; a women's training weekend at Loughborough in 1963 had 50 participants, but it was run by the WCRA, rather than the governing body.

Two days after the road race, on the track in Frankfurt, Burton qualified fastest for the pursuit, in spite of a planning error by the Great Britain team management, who were unaware that there were two pursuit rounds that evening. Burton was due to race at 7pm but the team had the start down as 9pm; she was about to tuck into steak and salad at the team hotel at 10 past six – her knife and fork literally poised over the plate, she recalled years later – when the mistake was discovered. Beryl was 'furious' at the mad rush needed to get her to the track in time to ride; Charlie put the steak in a plastic bag for her to get down later in the evening.

Yet again the final pitted Burton against Reynders in front of a crowd that included many British fans. 'Smooth as silk, Beryl continued on her imperturbable way,' reported *Cycling*, 'picking up a tenth here and a tenth there while Reynders gradually broke down under the pressure of a girl [she was 29] much more used to time-trialling rhythm.' This was another close encounters, with Burton putting distance into Reynders 'inches at a time' and eventually winning by 0.32 seconds. It was their penultimate battle at world level; in her memoirs, Burton described the pair as resembling 'two old pugilists who would fight until one dropped of exhaustion'.

Afterwards Burton complained about the cold, and about the scheduling, but Frankfurt left her with a truly enviable pursuiting record: seven world championship medals in seven years, with five golds and two silvers. She drew parallels with the time trials she rode for most of the rest of the season: 'I get as much fun out of pursuiting as I do out of riding a "25". I certainly don't find them any worse. I start just as hard when I do a "100" and I have to keep that up for four hours and a bit. This only lasts five minutes.'

Later in her career time trialling would stymie Burton's pursuit speed, but for the moment it helped: the self-knowledge born of her years of racing against the watch must have helped her know exactly how deep to go. She complained of her slow starting speed (and would go to the track at Newcastle-under-Lyme for coaching from Roy Swinnerton in an attempt to quicken up) but she had stamina that usually showed in the final quarter of a pursuit. Countless long time trials must have left her physically well adapted to 'backing up': riding a semi-final flat out, then a few hours later finding the strength for a final, as was the case in Germany.

Her success and, a few years later, that of the professional pursuiter Hugh Porter, led to calls for an indoor track somewhere – *anywhere* – in the UK, which continued throughout the 1970s. Ironically, at roughly this time outdoor wooden velodromes were built at Meadowbank in Edinburgh and at Leicester (1968 and 1969). The use of a perishable surface reflected a regrettably short-term outlook given the considerable investment required; it is no surprise that neither is open today. Burton was only ever able to race indoors when she travelled abroad; she had made a second trip to Berlin in 1964, and travelled to Ghent in autumn 1966 for a 'revenge' omnium against Reynders, where she took a narrow victory.

Burton had been awarded an MBE in October 1964; she wore a white woollen suit for the ceremony, where she was impressed by the queen's flawless complexion and a little surprised by her small stature. There were other accolades: in December 1965 there was a six-week invitation trip to South Africa – a massive journey at the time, and one where she made another unsuccessful Hour Record attempt, at Bloemfontein, where she struggled with the practicalities of organising a bid on an outdoor track.

She made it onto the shortlist for the Sports Writers' Association's Sportswoman of the Year award several times, while at the end of 1966 the BCF awarded her a gold medal for her world championship rides since 1959. A great deal of fuss had to be whipped up before this event was made public – in the end the ceremony took place on live television, shot by BBC *Look North* – but *Cycling* magazine felt that there should have been a massive official celebration dinner. Its editorial argued: '...this woman has brought more prestige, more consistency [to a great sport] both by her behaviour and her riding than most other members of that sport. Yet when the gold badges are handed out where is the publicity, where is the shouting and the parading?'

Every now and then, between the constant run of victories in time trials, road races and pursuits in the UK and the annual world championship medals, little bits of the real Beryl Burton would poke through, like mountaintops through mist. There were pressures and pleasures that were rarely spoken of as she moved from one race to the next, sipping tea next to a time trial result board or whipping up the pace at a track meet or road race, anywhere in England that was within reach of Yorkshire.

The travelling life that she imposed on herself and Charlie – and on Denise, depending on the distance and the available childcare – was merciless, beginning with those 330am starts. In various mid-1960s interviews, she acknowledged the pressures: 'Our domestic life is nowhere near ordered or relaxed enough. We don't get enough sleep. We do an immense amount of travelling and never have time to eat properly.' She confessed that racing too much had at times made her stale, such as at Whitsun 1963 when she and Charlie notched up 600 miles in the car – at a time when there wasn't a lot of motorway to make travelling smoother – to four races in three days.

At times Burton's race schedule was hectic to the point of absurdity; the mental pressures of scheduling, travelling and competing were probably as severe as the physical effort involved. She must have seemed like a superwoman to her opponents, given her predilection for riding to and from events where possible. Sometimes, during the 1960s, she would ride a 25-mile time trial in the morning and a road race in the afternoon, or a track meeting one day, a '25' the next. On one weekend in summer 1966, she won the BCF road race championship by four minutes, rode – and won – a '50' the next day, then pedalled 95 miles home to Yorkshire with Nim Carline.

In December 1966, Burton was asked by *Cycling* magazine what she wanted for Christmas: 'The first thing that came into my head was someone to come and dig the garden over and put a fish pond in, crazy paving and little trees and shrubs. I guess you could say I want a landscape gardener… everyone would get pleasure from it. We have such keen gardeners around us and we have been living in the house for two years – the weeds have been drowning [it] that long. Second I thought was a nice teak radiogram, and third a nice long oil painting of the Yorkshire Dales to put over my fireplace. '

Denise Burton-Cole recalls that when the family moved from their council flat in Morley to their new home in

Woodlesford in 1964, when she was eight, it was the first time that they had had a garden. 'The house was in a quarter acre plot on a corner and it backed onto farm land, which was probably why Mum and Dad liked it as well. The garden was left for a *long* time, a year or two or maybe three, then the neighbours who surrounded us on two sides began asking questions like "When are you going to do your garden, Beryl?" or "What are you going to do with your garden?". She got to be thinking they had to do something with it, so Nim came down with his small tractor and a plough and he ploughed it and they got the rotovator out and broke it all up, then of course she did her magic with it.'

Beryl's hobbies involved making things that had a practical use, that you could hold in your hand: she was a good gardener, and a passionate knitter. 'She did like the gardening, she did baking, she enjoyed it,' said Denise. 'She did [baking] every Thursday because it was a rest day and that baking lasted all week. She'd make about four different things: flapjack, fruit cake, this coconut thing with chocolate underneath – like coconut ice, just as sweet, a coconut mix with egg and glace cherries – that would go in as a traybake. She did gardening, baking and knitting.'

Burton would also go to the opera in Leeds a couple of times over the winter; she had been introduced to it by Eileen Gray on one of the British team's trips to East Germany. 'A couple of times we'd go to the cinema, and there were club dinners most weekends,' recalled Denise. 'They used to write to her – she'd say yes to most of them. She'd present the prizes, give a speech. I used to love them; I started going as soon as I was a little girl, by the time I was five or six.'

It was a life centred on cycling, with holidays spent riding between youth hostels; Burton wrote affectionately of Christmases spent hiking in the Lake District. Her Morley protégée Ann Battersby (née Pallister) recalled how the club would spend the week between Christmas and New Year at a different Lakeland youth hostel each year, with their bikes conveyed there in Nim Carline's van.

'When you think of the enormity of what my mum did, she wouldn't have had time for anything [other than cycling] anyway,' is how Denise sees it. 'She used to go to bed quite early, often by around 9.30, and she'd be up by, I don't know, 6 or 7. She didn't have a lie-in, you were never allowed to have a lie-in. Nobody was: you had to get up. If you weren't up by 8 o'clock on a Saturday you were being shouted at.'

Burton did face challenges in these years, as she attempted to take on Reynders, Jacobs and the women that the Soviet Union developed year after year, but they stemmed from physical issues. As previously noted, she suffered several major crashes in the early to mid-1960s, which clearly affected her form; the effects were exacerbated by a lack of proper medical back-up, and by her unwillingness to take breaks from competition.

The bulk of the problems arose from a crash at Manchester's Fallowfield track in June 1962, which cost Burton both that year's RTTC '50' title, and the BCF national pursuit title. She fell on her spine and hip, taking most of the skin off her back; she spent several weeks in bed as a result of the injury, and continued to experience pains in her middle and lower back. When she won the world pursuit championship in Italy in record time later in the year, she complained that she was unable to sleep, could not turn over in her bed, and couldn't straighten her back. The crash affected her for the entire winter, and she made a slow start to the following season. In the two years that followed she was adamant that she was still not 'right'.

In 1963, as she broke her records and won her fourth world pursuit title in Rocourt, she was racing and training through the pain, with one leg feeling as if it was working at half power. In British time trialling she was largely unchallenged by other women, but physically she was still not functioning perfectly; in July her back had not improved, and her leg had worsened, with pain striking from lower down her back through her groin and reaching down the inside of her leg. She was advised to take three or four months off, but she could not do so, she said, because the World's were looming.

In the world road race at Renaix that August, she was forced off the road into a ditch three feet deep – one of those that seem to run alongside most of the roads in Belgium – hit a telegraph pole, and woke up in hospital unable to move her head or neck. Her back pain was worse than before, and she had pins and needles in her arms. She finally saw a physio in September, getting relief from the pain and a proper night's sleep for the first time in over a year.

In the winter of 1964-5 she had an operation to remove a swelling in her groin, a classic cycling injury for a woman and quite possibly a lipoma, an internal fat cushion formed when an area of the body receives repeated physical damage. The four-month lay-off was probably beneficial, although she did not realise it. But in May 1965 she had 'an argument with a van' and was left with broken fingers, a knee like a football and bruising from head to toe. A bout of gastro-enteritis that hit her at the world championships in San Sebastian that year made itself felt for the next 18 months.

Along with the pain, there were psychological scars which belied the impression she sometimes gave – or that was put about by rivals and journalists – that she was a human machine who felt neither nerves nor fear. When she started a road race about a month after the Renaix crash in 1963, she was trembling all over, Charlie recalled, and had almost totally lost her confidence. She said afterwards that if she had not forced herself to ride in the bunch that day she would never have ridden a road race again.

Although Reynders and Burton crossed swords at the occasional invitation race and the world championships, that was about all. Half a century on, Reynders raises what seems like an obvious question: why did Burton not move to Belgium to try to make money in the same way as her biggest rival? The answer can be seen in the obstacles faced by British cyclists (all male) who did make this move*. In the 1960s, racing abroad was a big step, owing to the distance (greater in terms of time than now because of slower road and rail links, and not even the concept of low-cost airlines) and the language barrier. There was a pathway for cyclists to follow, but those who did up sticks tended to be those without families. The prospect of taking husband and daughter to live in Belgium would have been daunting for Beryl, especially as there were no female role models who had done this before.

Had Burton been single she might have made the move – as her fellow Yorkshire racer Barbara Mapplebeck did – but had she been single she would possibly never have set out on a career as a bike racer. She remained locked into the British cycling world in which she had started out, mixing her time trialling with the odd track meet and road race, but sticking to what she knew best. As she said, British roads provided a quieter, less stressful contrast to the crowded intensity of the velodromes of Europe. And on those roads, her record remains unmatched.

---

* I examined this in *Roule Britannia: Great Britain and the Tour de France.*

By July 1962, when she lost the '50' championship to Liverpool's Joan Kershaw, owing to the injuries she sustained in her crash on the Fallowfield track, Burton had won 13 straight national titles across 25, 50 and 100 miles. Her dominance had been absolute. As early as 1960, Kershaw complained that 'many of today's racing girls… believe that Beryl finds it easy to produce great rides week after week, and that to suffer is a condition experienced only by those who try to emulate her. They think she is unbeatable.'

In time trialling, Burton's major achievement of the early 1960s was beating the hour for 25 miles, the first time this had been done by a woman; 'breaking the hour' remains the initial target for most time triallists in the UK. A gold medal for the first woman to achieve the feat had been put up by *Cycling* magazine in July 1958, but it took Burton almost five years of whittling away at the record to get there. Rather than the relatively small fixed-wheel gears that were still the norm in the early 1960s, Burton had by now switched to derailleur gears similar to those used today, which were increasingly in vogue. She had also begun to adopt what were seen as high gears for the time, with ratios of 54x14-18.

Her time of 59min 25sec in the Easterley RC event on the Southend Road on 26 May 1963 was a spectacular 1min 9sec beating of her own record. It was seen as an immense landmark. On what Charlie described as 'next door to a perfect day', there was a rising breeze on the outward leg to the 12.5-mile turn, which Burton reached in about 32 minutes. Aware that the record might be on, she had started three yards behind the start line so as to be certain that the course was the right length.

'On this morning we saw her true greatness,' wrote the *Cycling* editor George Pearson. 'It was a day described as near perfect, so too was Beryl Burton near perfect. How else can one describe a performance of such magnitude?' Her achievement made her the fourth person to receive one of the magazine's gold medals for breaking a particularly significant time-trial barrier. Her predecessors were Leon Meredith in 1910, for being the first man to cover 100 miles in five hours out and home, Marcel Planes in 1911, for completing the greatest number of 100-mile rides during the year (322), and Ray Booty, for riding 100 miles out and home inside four hours in 1956.

At this point Burton was an all-rounder, also capable of winning road races with Merckx-esque margins: a week after she smashed through the 'hour', her 1963 victory in the WCRA road race championship came after she escaped five miles into the 45-mile race – like other British road race titles this was, paradoxically, much longer than a typical women's world championship – and gained seven and a half minutes on the field. A month or so later, she added the BCF title with a four-minute margin. The following year, in contrast, she landed the WCRA title in a 12-up sprint.

The titles mattered, but so did the times. In interviews, Burton argued for women and men to compete on equal terms in the same events rather than being segregated in their own separate races, and she had a vocal supporter in *Cycling* editor Alan Gayfer. It is said that she warmed to the idea after talking to Russian women at the world championships; they mixed with male racers, to great effect. It was on the road that Burton presented the strongest possible case: during the early 1960s she gradually began to overhaul all but the very fastest men.

On 10 May 1964 she made it onto the cover of *Cycling* for a milestone as significant as breaking the hour: finishing faster than all the men in a time trial for the first time. Her 2hr 4min 29sec in the Eastern Counties Cycling Association

50-miler was a women's competition record. Technically it was a separate event to the men's race which was run earlier, but in the view of the magazine she became 'the first woman ever to beat men on their own terms, on the same course on the same day, in what under the circumstances virtually amounted to the same event, the women starting 15 minutes after the men'. The consensus was that the wind which slowed the riders down on the return leg added about six minutes to their times, meaning that in good conditions Burton would have beaten two hours. At the finish she was 'completely undistressed, as if she had ridden a club run'. On that weekend only two or three riders across the whole country rode a faster time for 50 miles.

Burton was an outlier: in Britain in the 1960s no women could come near her. Bernadette Malvern began racing against Burton as the 1960s drew to an end, and recalled, 'riders would say there was no point starting if she was going to be there. To that extent, she was killing it off.' That was partly because Burton was probably the strongest woman cyclist in the world, but also because the pool of potential rivals was not large and the standard was not great. In *Cycling*, the writer Joan Green estimated that there were about 230 women's races each year – which was more than respectable – but they were being contested by only about 300 women, of whom only 25 managed to ride over 21mph at shorter distances. Competing against men was the obvious next step.

Green felt that Burton was unique, that the opposition was not single-minded enough, but she put that down to the way women were conditioned against being competitive. 'I don't know of one racing girl who has the true killer instinct. It isn't feminine of course. It is discouraged because it's not "nice". Of course it isn't nice, but it wins races. If you enter an event at the same time as Beryl Burton, believing before you start that she will win, then she certainly will and you deserve to lose.' This is not a new issue, and it is one that is far from being resolved.

In 1964 Burton told Gayfer, 'What I would like to do before I hang up my racing wheels is to train as much and as hard as I like for two or three months just to see how fast I could go. I have never yet got the best out of myself and it would be nice just to be able to for once.' Just once. She would have known that the interview would be read by all her domestic rivals, so there may have been some mind games going on here – imagine getting a kicking from Burton every week, then reading that she didn't think she was actually racing to her full potential. Those words still speak volumes for her perfectionism, not to mention her ambition, which was intact even after five world titles in as many years.

Chapter 8

Sweet Triumph

11hr 59 min 15sec: the time it took to ride 277.25 miles, Otley CC 12-hour, 17 September 1967.

For 70 years, there has been endless discussion in Italy about a bottle Fausto Coppi passed to Gino Bartali during the 1949 Tour de France. Half a century after Tom Simpson allegedly asked his mechanic to 'put me back on my bike' as he died on Mont Ventoux, scraps of his jerseys and vests are carried around by some of his successors, as are pebbles from the mountainside. In one Belgian museum, you can inspect a whole display case of relics from places associated with the great bike races: a bit of dust, a cobble, a flask of holy water. The Burton story includes one key object that should have a place in this reliquary – cycling's most celebrated sweet. But it was eaten at the moment it was about to become legendary.

The liquorice allsort is justly famous: Beryl Burton offered it to Mike McNamara when she overhauled him in the Otley CC 12-hour on 17 September 1967, en route to setting a new competition record of 277.25 miles. The liquorice allsort represents the high point of Burton's career. The moment when she passed McNamara was critical, the point where it became virtually certain that she would both win the '12' and beat the record. A little later she became the only woman in cycling history to hold a record of this kind outright, bettering the best male time for the distance under identical conditions. It was a feat that appears to have been unmatched in any endurance sport.

Watch a 12-hour time trial in the final miles on the finish circuit – to hand a bottle to a mate who is riding, perhaps – and you are left with no illusions about how tough it is for the bulk of the competitors. When any cyclist is under pressure, the imperfections inherent in their riding style – nodding the head, bending a knee in a certain direction – tend to be exacerbated. A 12-hour finish circuit is a parade of knees pointing every which way, heads wobbling like a toy dog in a car window, shoulders rolling hither and thither. It is painful to behold, and must be horrible to experience. The '12' was – and is – an integral part of British time trialling, as it was – and remains – one of the three events that have to be completed if a rider is to qualify for the men's Best All Rounder competition; the women's contest was over 25, 50 and 100 miles, which seems much more reasonable. There was debate over whether the '12' was simply too hard to be in the BAR, too much of a specialist skill; one writer in *Cycling* described it as 'a pole-squatting event totally unrelated to bike racing'.

Burton had prepared minutely for the Otley '12'. Like Mole going through Ratty's picnic in *The Wind in the Willows*, she told how, the night before, her race food had been lined up on the breakfast bar in their house: 'fruit salad, peaches, rice pudding, fruit and honey cake, egg and milk, peppermint and blackcurrant, coffee, glucose, malt bread, bananas, four bits of steak and some cheese.' Her clubmate and employer Nim Carline was a cyclist of simpler tastes, he of the lamb cutlet straight from the frying pan midway through a long-distance event. He came through the Burtons' door and commented, 'What on earth do you want all that for in a 12?' His protegée replied that she intended to go out for a day's ride and was going to enjoy herself. She had put in 140 miles on the Thursday, to Hornsea and back, and had visited a physio who had straightened her up after a crash a few weeks earlier.

Burton had been beating men on the road throughout the 1960s, in an informal way and in spite of the fact that the sexes were segregated. To avoid doubling up on marshals and so on, women's time trials were frequently run as add-ons to men's races, with the women starting either before or after. These would be registered as a separate race, but were the same event in all but name. Burton might be as fast as, or faster than, the men riding the men's event, and she might have started within a few minutes of them, but she would not be entitled to any of the men's prize money. Sometimes she would compete in subtly different conditions – women's events usually started before the men, and as most time trials were in the early morning, the air would be colder and thicker, so often she may have been at a disadvantage.

The riders around her would usually be women, usually going slower than the average male time triallist, so that they were less valuable as 'hares' to be chased down. Cine footage of the time shows Burton simply whizzing past slower women; if she had a faster rider to chase, that would pull her out for at least a few minutes, maybe more. If she was in a time trial where the women's event started after the men, and the distance permitted it – at 100 miles in particular - her goal would be to overtake all the women ahead of her and then try to get past slower starters in the back of the men's field. This was what she was trying to do on the morning of the Otley '12'; McNamara was the last of the line-up in the men's event. The organiser probably knew pretty much what would happen, and probably hoped it would.

McNamara was already the favourite to take that year's men's Best All Rounder. He was a genial, self-effacing man, a mainstay of the local cycling scene, a member of the local RTTC District Committee who had acted as pusher-off at the previous year's national hill-climb championship. He was 32, and worked as an instrument technician in a steelworks. He had turned up late due to the misty driving conditions, recalled 'rushing' through his pre-race preparations, had not had time to put warming oil on his legs. He was, however, a fast starter, and tended to fade later in a '12', he recalled.

The weather was gloomy and mild, with a thick drizzle which gradually cleared as the morning wore on. Burton was pushed away by the timekeeper at 7.12am*, two minutes behind McNamara. He was an obvious target for her to chase: as the report of the race noted, Burton was 'not going to let him relax'. Burton said she had no intention of 'going after' Mac', but this seems totally disingenuous. The pair had already met the previous week when the Yorkshire Century and Yorkshire Ladies Cycling Association 100-milers were held on the same course, with the women's race starting after the men's. 'Mac' had won that encounter by more than 12min. They had known each other for about 10 years; they would sometimes ride home together after finishing a '25' on one of the South Yorkshire courses.

The first phase of the '12' consisted of long stretches on local 'A' roads, before a finishing circuit where the riders' times and distances could be easily calculated by timekeepers stationed at intervals on the roadside. As they sped over the flat roads around York, Burton could occasionally spot McNamara in the distance. There was comparatively little between them on the first leg to Tadcaster, back to York,

---

* *Burton's autobiography records the start time as 7.42am. But the report in* Cycling *magazine has the event starting at 5.31am, with McNamara last of the 99 men. He therefore started at 7.10, with Burton 2min behind.*

then out and home to Thirsk. At 100 miles, McNamara was timed at 4hr 14min 44sec; Burton was 57 seconds slower. (McNamara's recollection is that he was well up on Burton at 100 miles, but this does not tally with the report from the day.)

McNamara recalled: 'My brother was looking after me, he overtook me in his car, and shouted, "Beryl's coming, coming very fast", I replied, "how far?" He yelled, "she's level with you". That was at 160 miles. I wanted to get off to go to the toilet, but I carried on down the A1. I got onto the finishing circuit, and there was this little hill; John shouted, "she's at the back of you".'

Keith Lambert (Bradford Elite CC) – a future top professional and Great Britain team manager, but then riding his first '12' at just 19 – eventually finished eighth with 255.2 miles. He was caught by Burton relatively early on – 'I doubt if I was expecting it, but I don't think many were expecting what she did that day. I knew her quite well, and she always said something; it was probably, "Come on lad, what are you doing?"' On the finish circuit, he found his legs and caught Burton in his turn, but he was still almost a whole lap behind.

Going northwards from Wetherby to Northallerton, Burton closed on McNamara. From 150 to 180 miles it was level pegging; at 200 miles, she was 18 seconds faster after covering the distance in 8hr 33min 37sec. In distance terms, that is barely a 200m lead. Burton was calm enough to stop after four and a half hours to pour a bottle of water over her head and nip behind the hedge to answer a call of nature, losing about a minute. Around this point, she was trying to fix a stomach ache: she drank ginger beer, peppermint juice, blackcurrant cordial. Eventually, Charlie passed up some brandy; Beryl was not used to it, but 'it worked wonders.' Rennies were also on offer, and helped settle her guts as well.

Burton was not a novice at the distance. She had made her first attempt in 1959, in wintry early autumn conditions in the Yorkshire Cycling Federation race, finishing with 250.37 miles to break Eileen Sheridan's record by 13 miles and beating all but two men on the day, even after a five-minute delay due to a puncture. It is said that the rider who finished third, Barry Hoban – a future seven-times Tour de France stage winner – got into his car at the finish and commented bitterly, 'Beaten by a woman!'

Back in the Otley '12', after 206 miles the riders went onto the finishing circuit of 15.87 miles, and there Burton started to close on her 'hare'. On the first lap of the circuit she pulled back 42 seconds on McNamara – who was still bursting to go to the toilet – and as she drew near to the end of the lap for the second time, at about 235 miles, she overhauled her quarry, putting in a lap that was nearly two and a half minutes faster.

Burton was in a quandary as she prepared to overtake McNamara, because she understood the significance of the moment: unless she were to crack in the next 40 miles, enabling him to catch up and then leave her two minutes behind to regain his original position on the road, there was no chance that he would beat her. 'I saw Mac in front,' she said. 'I didn't know what to say, whether to pass him or what to do. He was weaving a little, so I thought, "I'll offer him one of my favourites." I got out a packet of liquorice allsorts, tore off the top and offered Mac one, which he took. He took the best one, the sort with the coconut round the liquorice.' He remembered: 'I accepted it, I think it was in a bag on her handlebars.'

Crucially, Burton managed to remain relaxed for most of the time, with her eyes initially set on her own 1959 record of 250.37 miles. There was one glitch when her back wheel broke a spoke and began to get a wobble; as happened with her when the unexpected happened, panic began to set in. She could not stand the noise and the wobbling, she said later. Charlie was looking after her as always, but support cars were not permitted to follow right behind their riders; that meant he could not shadow his wife's every move. For a while he was nowhere to be seen, and Beryl made her feelings known when he did turn up. Even so, she covered the final circuit at almost 23mph, after 11 hours in the saddle.

For Mac' being caught appears to have been a relief: he could now stop and ease his bladder. 'She caught me at the bottom of the hill, I took a couple of minutes to go to the toilet, then when I rode up the hill, one of the spectators shouted that I was about two minutes behind Beryl.' He caught up with her again – 'I think she was beginning to feel it' he recalled – and she rode about 100 yards behind him. 'My time was up as I went down the A1, but she made it to the next time keeper.'

Burton stopped after 277.25 miles, with 45 seconds of her 12 hours still to run, meaning her distance was perhaps a quarter of a mile shy of what she might have achieved, perhaps a little more. She had not been impressed with a stiff little climb on the circuit; with no desire to struggle up it again, she came to a halt at its foot. She was surprised by how comfortable she felt, by the lack of saddle soreness; she was, after all, used to looking as though she wasn't really trying. She had even had time to pick out a 'lovely house' on the finish circuit to admire each time she went past.

McNamara finished 0.4 miles behind, having regained ground on Burton since she had caught him, but the pair were in a league of their own; the next man managed only 265.8 miles. McNamara had broken the previous men's record, and he went on to win that year's men's BAR at a record average speed; he was the best long-distance time triallist in Britain that season. This was a massive scalp to take.

Prior to that day, only four other riders had gone further than 270 miles, and in the next 20 years only another 30 or so would manage the feat – all men. The postscript was low-key; there were no elaborate celebrations. After finishing just after 7pm, two hours later Burton was in bed. Mac' was struck by how quickly she disappeared: 'she only said a couple of things to me, and was off. Normally you'd stand around the result board and chat, but she just went.' Burton's mind was elsewhere: she was up again at 1.30am to clean out all the debris that had accumulated in the car while Charlie had been frenetically feeding and watering her all day, and they were out of the house at 3am to head to London for an appearance at the Skol Six-Day Race at the Wembley Arena. She didn't get back home and into bed until 3.30am the following day, but inevitably, she was up early that morning for her usual training ride.

1967 was a golden year for Burton, the finest of her career, with a string of records on top of a clean sweep of national titles and her final rainbow jersey. At long last, she enjoyed 12 months without major interruption from illness or injury. Over the winter, she had clocked up fewer miles than usual, but she felt stronger after returning to work regularly on Nim Carline's farm. She rode the eight miles to and from work at Carline's, where she spent eight hours a day lugging heavy batches of muddy rhubarb roots. She did not actually begin training in earnest until March 1, about the time the evenings began to get longer; then she took a spell off work and knocked out 500 miles in five days by riding to Bournemouth and back. She had a new bike, 'of Continental manufacture"* *Cycling* wrote primly (respecting current rules on sponsorship), with special 28-spoke wheels, radial at the front, radial-tangential at the back.

Her season started in mid-April with a handicap road race run by the WCRA at Chobham, where she started alone, eight minutes behind the first group of competitors, and rode through the entire field well before the finish of the 23-mile course. In late April she knocked out a new women's 10-mile record at the south end of the A1, with 23min 5sec, almost two minutes faster than the next finisher, her Morley clubmate Margaret Allen. After that, she said that she had done virtually no training, although she noted that she was lighter than usual, having not gone over 10 stones all winter. That is approximately 63.5 kilogrammes for her five foot six inches (167cm); Burton was no featherweight climber, but she was well-muscled thanks to all those hours in the market garden. She was only three pounds over her previous year's world championship weight; the lingering effects of the gastro-enteritis from the world championships in San Sebastian 18 months earlier had probably played a part in that.

A few weeks later she finished faster than a full field of men in the Middleton CC 25-miler in Cheshire; they were the fastest 120 from 160 entrants. She was described as 'coming smoothly over the line in that so-deceptive style of hers to stun a large gallery into almost complete silence.' Her margin over the late Carol Boardman – the mother of the future Olympic champion Chris Boardman – was nearly nine minutes. 'Unbelievable Burton beats the boys,' ran the headline.

** It had come from the local importer and major Yorkshire cycling personality Ron Kitching. It appears to have been a Jacques Anquetil, which was later handed down to Denise.*

The record for 15 miles followed, then another for 30 miles in mid-May, not long after her 30th birthday, on a greasy, wet day when many competitors fell off at the roundabouts on the course in Nottinghamshire. 'The hazards of braking at roundabouts in the midst of motorists who were mostly either incapable or unsympathetic, put years on the lives of both marshals and riders alike,' wrote Mike Smith in *Cycling*. The fallers included Allen, and Burton actually stopped to help her get back up on her bike, but still managed to break the record. The headline: 'Beryl outrides mere males.' She also smashed her way through the two-hour barrier for 50 miles with a time of 1hr 56min, on the Boro' course on the A1 in North Yorkshire. By halfway, she had ridden through the women's field of only nine, to spend the last 25 miles on her own. Her time would have been good enough for 10th in the men's event held on the same course later that same morning, so in warmer and thus faster conditions. She hailed the result as 'a Morley club record'. Next up came a 56min '25' on the Southend road, yet another new record, described in *Cycling* as 'a performance the like of which men's or women's 25-mile time trialling had never seen'; it was the sixth consecutive time she had broken her own record. For once, she was reported to be 'breathless' after the finish, and commented that she felt she was going to pass out towards the end of the race.

There had been speculation that Burton might beat four hours for 100 miles in the women's title race in June on the Fosse Way in Nottinghamshire. In the event she put the 36 women to the sword and beat a full field of men, but not the magic barrier; nor did she quite meet her target of running through the women ahead of her and then closing a five-minute gap to finish among the men's field. That prompted a classic Burton comment: 'After two and a half hours my hands felt like dropping off the bars, but I thought, "Well it's only another hour and a half".' Her time of 4hr 4min 50sec was a mark that only a dozen men had beaten to that date.

By the time she travelled to the world championships in Holland that August, Burton had won at least 16 time trials, three road races – including both the WCRA and BCF national championships – and two track races, one of them the national pursuit title. She had also attended the funeral of Tom Simpson in the churchyard at Harworth after his death on July 13; the pair had waltzed at the RRTC Champions' night at the Albert Hall, and 'Major Tom' had kissed Burton in triumph only the previous autumn, when she overcame Reynders in Ghent. So she rode to Harworth in the pouring rain; in her vast rain cape, she stood next to Simpson's team-mate Eddy Merckx. Burton felt that she and Simpson had something in common: their desire to take the maximum from whatever life offered.

The loss of the man who had been the flag-bearer for British cycling for eight years hung heavy over the UK contingent at the world championships in Holland, but paradoxically this was to be Britain's most successful world road race championships ever, with victory in two of the three titles. Initially, on the track in Amsterdam, however, Burton fell foul of the Soviets Tamara Garkushina and Raisa Obodovskaya. They both qualified five seconds faster than Burton in the pursuit, which pretty much settled matters. She overcame her old rival Yvonne Reynders for the bronze medal, in what was to be their final encounter; the Belgian retired not long afterwards following a positive doping test which she swears to this day was a mistake.

Burton was not much slower than the Soviet duo when she posted 4min 8sec in the bronze medal ride-off, but it was not an equal contest: she was riding the pursuit without any specialised training, whereas Garkushina and Obodowskaya had been selected from a pool of about 10,000 racing women, and had prepared specifically for the distance. They spent their winters doing multi-sports – ice skating, volleyball, skiing – then put in a combination of road and track work during the summer; critically, they trained on the track every day. Eastern Bloc athletes had raised the bar in the discipline far above the point where it was sufficient to be talented, fit and healthy. Garkushina, for example, was posting a time for her opening lap that would have been fifth fastest among the track sprinters. A rider who was preparing by knocking out time trials on distances up to 100 miles was not competing on equal terms. 'I don't know where they get their muscles from, but they make me feel like a drainpipe,' was Burton's view, speaking as a woman who was well-muscled herself.

The world championship road race was a complete contrast. It started and finished in the town of Heerlen, close to the German border in the little southern Dutch enclave of Limburg and as in 1960, Burton made full use of her superior strength and stamina; she was able to dislodge the sprinters to win the second road gold medal of her career. Her single-minded destruction of the field began after five miles and ended with her coming close to lapping the backmarkers in only three laps of the eight-mile circuit. Belgian and Italian journalists compared it to one of Fausto Coppi's victories – this from men who would actually have seen the *campionissimo* race.

'For just once the watchers had seen Beryl Burton at her most magnificent, the Burton whom we have seen so often pedalling imperturbably riding away from the rest,' began the report in *Cycling*. Not long after the start, Burton went to the front of the field and strung out the 42-rider peloton – including for the first time a rider from Ireland, Roisin Troy

– to open a gap, accompanied only by the Russian Lyuba Zadorozhnaya. Burton disposed of Zadorozhnaya as they tackled the main climb of the circuit, through the village of Ubachsberg, and was on her own for the final 20 miles.

At the finish her margin was 1min 47sec on Zadorozhnaya and 5-47 on the front ranks of the peloton, where her team-mates Pat Pepper and Barbara Mapplebeck had worked hard to slow down any initial chase from the Russians and the French. So focused was Burton on her effort that she barely raised her head before the finish line, and she made no victory salute, despite having so much time in hand. Photographs taken afterwards show the British team manager Chas Messenger accompanying her to a rudimentary tent where the doping control was held; she complained of cramps towards the end but in the photos she does not have the look of a woman who has suffered greatly, as she sits waiting and sips a beer. Was she happy about the absence of Reynders? asked a Belgian journalist afterwards. 'Frankly it didn't matter. She would have been at the back shattered with the others anyway.' It was payback after seven years of frustration.

That afternoon, the men's amateur race went to Birmingham rider Graham Webb, the only Briton in the post-war years to take the title. 'Beryl was the first to congratulate me,' recalled Webb. 'On a stretch of Dutch motorway that served as a finish straight we jumped up and down together and hugged one another. The world was ours.' Burton did not watch the professional road race the following day; her mind had turned to her appointment with the Otley CC 12-hour, a couple of Sundays distant, and she wanted to train.

The road race medal was her seventh gold in eight years, and it has to be seen in the context of her defeat in the pursuit, which had left her morale broken. *Cycling* described how she 'had sat in the team hotel at Aachen, knowing that "I've failed, there's only one medal that matters".' Her morale had been rebuilt by the team masseur Eddie Soens and manager Charles Messenger. The irascible Scouse coach Soens was a legendary figure in British cycling; his final protégé was Chris Boardman. The awkward looking Messenger had been a key man in the BLRC years, the organiser of early Tours of Britain. He was in tears after Burton finished her race. Like Soens, he was an outspoken man who never fitted in well with the 'blazers' who ran the sport; a month after the Dutch triumph, Messenger was sacked. Burton was among the many who wrote to *Cycling* to express their support.

The Otley '12' came two weeks after Heerlen. 'Supreme record,' proclaimed the cover of *Cycling*, alongside the figure 277. 'Fabulous, fantastic, great, superb, none of these adjectives is adequate to describe the result of the Otley CC 12-hour…' Burton's day-long duel with McNamara, its writer felt, 'will be remembered in years to come as the greatest ever of its kind.' It was, and probably remains, the most famous time trial ever held on British soil, but the magazine added this proviso: '[The] saddest part of Beryl Burton's phenomenal ride will be that she will never get, in the general press, the credit she deserves for the rides she has done and continues to do.' Readers were encouraged to go out and vote for her as BBC Sports Personality of the Year. *Cycling* presented Burton with a medal made of antique Mexican gold, obtained with Bank of England permission, because, as editor Alan Gayfer observed, she had over 100 silver-gilt medals already. It was inscribed, 'First woman to break a men's athletic record, Otley CC 12, 17-9-67 277.2 miles'.

Among the other tributes was a page of cartoons from Johnny Helms, whose illustrations summed up British cycling in the second half of the 20th century. The best depicts a greengrocer's shop, with rhubarb priced at one shilling a bunch, alongside rhubarb 'hand picked by Beryl Burton' at two shillings. Helms loved to draw sharp-toothed dogs, and on his 'Burton page' one is shown chasing her, watched by two others, one of which says to its companion, 'He's wasting his time'.

In the backlash after Simpson's death, when it became clear that European professional men's racing should not be treated with simplistic veneration, Burton was a new heroine rooted firmly in the British tradition: she was voted cycling personality of the year, and hailed as top woman sports star by *Daily Express* readers. BBC *Sportsview* viewers placed Burton second to the boxer Henry Cooper as Sports Personality of the Year and the British sportswriters also gave her due, electing her sportswoman of the year. In her acceptance speech, she quoted a Morley Cycling Club motto: 'Smile when you lose, laugh like hell when you win.'

Burton featured on the cover of *Sporting Cyclist* for the year-end; their editor Roy Green noted that 'Beryl, most humanly, wants acclaim. That is part of her driving force. After all, she still puts as much into her racing as she did when she started in 1954. She shows the supreme champion's hallmark, by garnishing mere victories with "impossible" exploits. New aims for Beryl – are there any? Well, her men's all-rounder average [speed] this year is 24.889mph…' That would have given her fifth overall in the 1967 men's Best All Rounder competition over 50 and 100 miles and 12 hours; as Green observed, Keith Stacey had won the 1965 contest with a slower average. 'Fifth best is fantastic, Beryl, but we are sure you can go four better!'

During 1966 and 1967, Burton's consistent victories over the men had gained her more and more attention, to the point where in August 1967 *Cycling* put this headline over a race report: 'Men beat Beryl.' She took obvious relish in her successes, commenting after one '100' in which she had finished faster than the entire field, 'It makes me laugh when I see [men] flop down at the end, I've beaten them anyway.' By the end of 1967, in moral terms, if not according to the rulebooks, Burton had more than won an argument she had begun six years earlier. The campaign to open races, and particularly time trials, to women, rather than running separate women's events, had begun in August 1961 when Burton – or a ghost writer – produced a column in *Cycling* making the case for mixed racing. She suggested that for a trial period the best women should be allowed to compete 'on equal terms in all British men's events including championships'; these elite women would be barred from riding women-only races, including women's championships, and would effectively be considered women only for international races. The idea, she said, was to make women race faster and at a higher standard for international events.

She clearly had one woman in mind – initials BB – but the suggestion was radical nonetheless. It prompted a correspondence which lasted for much of the winter in the letters pages of the magazine. In December, one (male) reader wrote that 'Nothing would be more demoralizing to many a young lad in a time trial to have a fast girl riding him into the ground...' He added, however, that to resist the move would be 'restrictive, retrogressive'. A Mrs M Hood considered that men and women should race separately because of the rough tactics adopted by men and also because women 'were handicapped physically'.

A proposal was duly put to the RTTC National Council that winter suggesting that 'events other than National Championships may be open at the discretion of the promoting body to men or women or both men and women.' As Gayfer wrote, 'There can be no logical reason in time trialling at least why women should not race with men once the principle of women's racing at all is accepted.' His argument was that unlike in road racing, in time trials any physical disparity between the sexes did not matter because 'the competitors are [racing] against themselves. No problem can be raised by size. No problem can be raised by speed.' As he observed, most women might be slower than the fastest men, but so too were many veteran and junior men. The motion was voted down. Something similar was proposed at the end of 1963 by three RTTC District Councils, but that fell too.

Burton was exceptional in cycling, but there were other female endurance athletes who were pushing boundaries as well. After hiding in bushes in order to start the Boston Marathon in 1966, the year before Burton's Otley 12-hour, Roberta Gibb finished the event in 3hr 21min, ahead of 290 of the 415 men in the field, putting out seven-minute miles for much of the event. She did so in spite of wearing heavy clothing, notably a hoodie, so she would not be immediately identified as a woman.

Generalising about sports science is perilous, but the consensus is that in endurance sports the gap between men and women closes as distances get longer. The nature of that gap prompted headlines in the UK press in January 2019 when the ultra-endurance runner Jasmin Paris won the Montane Spine Race, 268 miles along the Pennine Way, finishing 15 hours ahead of the nearest competitor in a largely male field. Parallels were drawn with other ultra-endurance events: open-water swimming, where women hold the longest distance records; a victory for Lael Wilcox in the 4,400 mile Trans Am bike race in 2016; a series of victories for the American ultra-marathoner Courtney Dauwalter. Comparative studies on women in endurance sport are relatively sparse even today, but the data provides a few possible explanations. Women seem to be more resistant to muscle fatigue than men in marathon efforts, their fat consumption is more efficient, and there is speculation that their hearts deliver blood more efficiently to their smaller muscles over a long effort.

Burton's performances at 12 hours back up the science, which suggests that the greater the distance, the narrower the gap becomes between men and women. In her first '12', the bulk of the time she lost to the winner, Ken Wood, came in the first 80 miles; on the finishing circuit, she recorded better times than all the men bar Wood, whose most rapid lap was a mere 20sec faster. It was in the final third of the Otley '12', once they hit the finish circuit, that she gained most of her (admittedly small) winning margin on McNamara. Her theoretical 'third 100 miles' in the '12' would have been almost two minutes faster than Mac' would have managed, although clearly his toilet stop would have to be taken into account.

The Otley '12' was a key moment in a golden age of British time trialling which, roughly speaking, lasted from the mid-1960s into the late-1970s. It was a popular sport, counting roughly 75,000 rides per year in both 1966 and 1967. In 1971, there were 1,623 open time trials in the UK, with a total of 89,777 individual rides; in Burton and McNamara's Yorkshire alone there were almost 500 open events with a total of almost 9,000 rides.

Those years saw spectacular increases in speed, and often it was larger-than-life personalities who pushed the boundaries.

Burton was one of these, alongside men such as Alf Engers; she was referred to as the 'queen' of time trialling, to his 'king'. Like Burton, Engers was never a mainstream British sports star, but he was a cult hero, who figured almost weekly in the pages of *Cycling* thanks to his innumerable comebacks, his continual battles with officialdom and his consummate charisma. While Burton played up her persona as the homespun Yorkshire lass, Engers went down the city slicker road, sporting a thick fur coat and dark glasses and maybe shocking silver lamé for a track meet. The prizes would be less exotic: one '25' in the Midlands offered a Wolber tubular, a chain, a racing cap, an orange, bananas and a bottle of Ruddles Ale, plus a pound for fastest rider to the turn.

Throughout the 60s, as Burton broke record after record for women, the men collectively lowered their times towards 50 minutes for 25 miles and 1hr 40min for 50 miles, with every step along the way hailed as massive news in *Cycling*. Burton's Otley year, 1967, was marked by David Dungworth taking the '25' record down to 52min 28sec, riding in an extraordinarily tight crouched position. Even with advances in training, aerodynamics and materials, that would still be a rapid ride in the 21st century. The speed was partly prompted by the constant jousts between Engers and the rest, riders such as Roger Queen, Eddy Adkins, Dungworth and John Watson. Between them, they transformed time trialling from something club riders just did alongside road races and track events, usually on the same bike, to the domain of specialists: 'testers' as they were (somewhat derisorily) known.

At the start of 1969, *Cycling* introduced the Campagnolo Trophy, a season-long competition for top 25-milers on the fastest courses. It was the magazine's attempt to bring time trialling into the 20th century, to give the discipline a season-long narrative and some continental pizzazz. (This at a point when the governing body was not sure about the use of chequered flags and would not allow mention of riders' sponsors.) But as women were not permitted to ride men's events, the Trophy was not initially open to Burton, who along with Engers was the biggest name in the sport.

Road improvements contributed to faster times as well. There was continual debate about 'dragstrips' – courses on improved A roads, with agoraphobia-inducing, brutalist roundabouts – and 'suck and blow courses' such as the Southend Arterial Road, where overtaking traffic 'pulled' the riders along. These were compared to 'sporting courses' on the unimproved backroads with more twists and turns and less traffic. One major opponent of 'dragstrips' was the *Cycling* editor, Gayfer. Time trialling, he argued, was 'riddled from top to bottom with a speed mania that transcended everything else'. A picture in the magazine in autumn 1965 showed a time triallist on the Southend Road surrounded by four Ford Anglias – which were, amusingly given the size of today's vehicles, barely larger than the cyclist.

By 1967 the Boro' courses, based on the A1 not far from Burton's home in Leeds, had become the most famous – or notorious – of the dragstrips. The V153 course between Wetherby and Leeming was described by one of *Cycling's* writers as 'really super. Dead smooth surface... Straight out and back, over undulations that make a fit man give his best… An awful lot of long-distance lorries roaring along the A1. Anyone who says that these juggernauts passing a rider at about 50mph do not help his progress is kidding himself.'

In 1967, *Sporting Cyclist* magazine questioned whether time trialling was still 'unpaced'. The article made the safety implications terrifyingly obvious: 'Some top 25-milers ride near the white line, obliging cars almost to brush them as they go by, thus getting an advantage from the "tow" of the car; others openly swerve out to catch this tow from every passing vehicle.' Burton felt she had no option but to race on the 'dragstrips', but said, 'I'm so scared of getting knocked over again that when I hear a car or a truck coming from behind I consciously get out of [its] way. This probably hinders me because moving to the left gives you more of the backwash [of disturbed air] in your face.'

Cycling's most famous sweet began to make headlines a week after Burton's Otley triumph, and that lasted. The following summer, the second edition of *International Cycle Sport* devoted five pages to Burton, including a two-page open letter from the writer and fellow time triallist Mike Daniell, which included this passage. 'You have now won over 200 open time trials, the equivalent of a win a week for four years. We have never had a man who could claim this, and with it the fact of continuous improvement at all distances. You found competition record at 10 miles at 25-0 and have taken it to 22-43. You have smashed over five minutes off the '25' record, 13 minutes off the '50', 27 minutes off the '100' and added an almost incredible 40 miles to the 12-hour record in which ride last year you finally accomplished what your great promise had foretold... the greatest performance by any racing cyclist, male or female... the ultimate pinnacle. Now we admit you ungrudgingly as our peer.'

The legend has lasted well, but has perhaps grown in the telling. Nineteen years later, when she wrote her autobiography, Burton had changed her mind about precisely what kind of allsort had been pulled out of the bag: 'I can still remember that it was one of those swiss-roll shaped ones, white with a coating of black liquorice.' McNamara, who has spent the last few years living in the north of Scotland, recalled that a few years later, Burton was invited as guest of honour to the Rockingham CC club dinner; the Bassett sweet company made a presentation tin, which he gave to Burton; he was also presented with a giant allsort at another dinner. An artist in the Lake District produced an artwork with an image of Burton along with a pile of allsorts, and the sweet features on the back pocket of a commemorative jersey produced by Santini half a century after her epic ride. Like Coppi's bottle, like Simpson's alleged final words, 'Put me back on my bike', the sweet has passed into cycling legend.

Chapter 9

500 or Bust

1hr 45min 22sec: Grand Prix des Nations, Paris, 22 September 1968.

There was no world championship for time triallists in the 1960s, and there were no other races on the international stage in which Beryl Burton could demonstrate her skill in racing against the watch. A handful of major time trials were held in Europe, but they were only for men: traditionally, races such as the Grand Prix de France and Grand Prix des Nations were run in early autumn as a chance for the fans to watch the professional stars of the season speeding by. The Baracchi Grand Prix in northern Italy, a two-man team time trial, served a similar function; these late-season occasions could be portrayed by the organising newspapers as revenge matches or chances for redemption in the broader narrative of the season.

The idea that Burton might ride the 'Nations' as a guest came from the Essex-based journalist Jock Wadley, the *Daily Telegraph*'s cycling writer, who had been an informal mentor to such riders as Tom Simpson and Brian Robinson, and it was Wadley who pulled the strings to get Burton entered in 1968. It may seem strange in the 21st century that a writer might be the one to do this, but in the 1960s most of Europe's major races were still run by the journalists who headed up the cycling departments at major newspapers. The 'Nations' was no exception, being organised by *l'Equipe* and

Le Parisien, which ran the biggest men's races: the Tour de France and Paris-Roubaix.

The 'Nations' was viewed as the unofficial time trial world championship. Run on a course that covered almost 50 miles in a loop south of Paris, and finishing on the velodrome in Vincennes, it was the fiefdom of the French five-times Tour de France winner Jacques Anquetil, who had won it nine times. Anquetil was considered the greatest time triallist cycling had ever seen; he was heading gently for retirement, but his lustre had rubbed off on the event. Given Burton's constant drive for new challenges, particularly ones which pitted her against men, the attractions were obvious.

Her invitation cannot, however, be seen as even the smallest step towards equality of opportunity. As far as the organisers were concerned, they needed publicity: Anquetil was not in the field that year, and only a tiny handful of the best professional men wanted to race; they were also unable to run the usual amateur event owing to a calendar clash. Inviting Burton to ride her own private time trial ahead of the men would create some welcome headlines. For some French papers, the comparison with their favourite was obvious: 'A sort of feminine Jacques Anquetil' was how the *Dimanche Soir* newspaper saw the Yorkshire racer.

The Burtons had some help from Ron Kitching in paying their way to Paris, but still covered most of their own expenses ('all' reported Marcel de Leener in *Cycling*); Wadley arranged accommodation for them and the 1967 world amateur champion Graham Webb, who was in the first year of his brief and unsuccessful professional career. Burton attempted to look over the course on the Friday evening and Saturday morning prior to the Sunday start, but what she found bore little resemblance to the average British time trial on the A1: roadworks, town centres, cobbles and back streets all had to be negotiated. She was not the only one who felt worried: Wadley too was concerned. As he had sung her praises to the race organisers and his press colleagues, if she flopped his reputation would take a knock.

Burton started 12 minutes in front of the professional field, with the same escort as the 12 male riders – *gendarmes* on motorbikes, a support car with her name on a board on the bumper, and a press car containing Wadley, who could be seen anxiously checking his watch. Burton clearly enjoyed the experience of racing on fully closed roads, with complete freedom to choose her line at each corner, and no fears about traffic overtaking her or getting in the way at junctions. The organisers had assumed that the men would catch up with her before the finish on the Cipale velodrome; in fact, she was well ahead of them, so much so that when she arrived at the track an agitated Wadley had to persuade the officials to let her in.

Although she was allowed onto the track, it was occupied by support races to fill in time before the arrival of the professional race, and she became mixed up with a group of amateurs riding a devil-take-the-hindmost. The timekeepers were not in place, so she had no option but to ride on while they were found. She recalled that she had done two extra laps of the 500m track; the report of the race said she did one. Either way, it was hardly the most respectful way to treat a seven-times world champion, but it underlines the fact that cycling officialdom had little idea about the ability of female cyclists, and scant inclination to take them seriously. The extra lap added an estimated 40 seconds to Burton's time, but there was more; afterwards, she discovered that she had ridden the final half of the race on a softening back tyre with a half-inch nail stuck in it.

Even so, she finished the 46 miles in a time 12min 34sec slower than Felice Gimondi, the winner for the second year in a row. At this point in his career, the Italian had won the Giro d'Italia, Vuelta a España and Tour de France once each over a period of four years; on this day, he knocked out a record average speed for the 'Nations' of 29.5mph for the 46 miles. For the benefit of English 'testers', it was calculated that he would have done around 1hr 41min for 50 miles. Burton was well off Gimondi's pace, but not far off the back end of the professional field: Webb, in last place, was only 2min faster.

The 'Nations' was an event she would have liked to ride again, but sadly that opportunity did not arise. In future years she said that she would summon memories of the crowds and the glamour in darker moments, but however much she had enjoyed it her appearance at the race was a gimmick, a brief glimpse of a milieu where there was no interest in furthering her racing career or that of any other women. The writer Jean Bobet, in *Le Monde*, felt that, 'Mrs Burton's performance was all the more interesting because she did the job with a smile and a dignity that we had believed incompatible with women's cycle racing.' Which raised the obvious question: what had Bobet been expecting? A sultry frown and a flash of knicker?

Her appetite whetted, Burton said she would love a crack at the Bordeaux-Paris 'Derby', cycling's longest one-day event in which a small group of professionals was paced by pedal-assisted motorbikes over the 350 miles; that never happened. It took until 1994 for the Union Cycliste Internationale to introduce world time trial championships for men and women; the 'Nations' was to remain Burton's only appearance in an event that was in any way comparable.

Burton had travelled to Paris to conclude a season that had taken her to the final great milestone of her career, as recounted earlier: the first sub four-hour 100 miles by a woman. Her 1968 results had also included one super-fast '25' on the Southend Road, 56min 25sec, which provided a rare direct comparison with Alf Engers, the only male to go faster on that day in the (separate) men's event; 'the King' was 2min faster, but like Burton he was an outlier among his peers.

Ten years into her career, at the age of 31, Burton was, she felt, 'becoming a permanent fixture' at national level. The pattern was familiar: constant beating of women's fields by dramatic margins, regular proof that she was as good as most men, further national championships on road and track and against the watch, a flying start mile record at Herne Hill. The sheer brilliance of her record in the Otley '12' the previous year was underlined when the best time triallist of 1968, Martyn Roach, fell 140 yards short of beating her distance (he did post a new male competition record but that was rather a hollow victory).

Burton had also made her eighth appearance in the final of the world championship pursuit, landing her ninth medal at the discipline. Again, that World's in Rome showed how cycling officials struggled to accommodate women, even though it was ten years since they had begun competing at this level. Burton rode a strong, consistent series: she qualified second, a whisker behind Raisa Obodowskaya (4min 6.19sec to 4min 6.04sec), then beat Audrey McElmurey of the US (a full-time biochemist who had paid $1,400 of her own money to travel to Italy) in the quarter final and Nina Korotaeva of the USSR in the semi. The quarter-final stage, however, was a farce, with only the redoutable figure of Eileen Gray standing between the women and the incompetence of the UCI after a heavy thundery shower shortly before the women's pursuit quarter finals made the boards of the outdoor Olympic velodrome dangerously slippery. Attempts were made to dry out the track using dishcloths, sawdust and hot air blowers; all failed.

The track had been deemed unsuitable for the male sprinters, but the officials were under pressure to get racing underway to please the paying crowd of about 1,000. They wanted the women to race; Gray would not have it. Two things broke the impasse. Gray challenged the chief commissaire René Chadelle to go for a ride on the track, which he declined, only for the British official to put on suitable clothing, wheel her own bike onto the track and call his bluff. A quarter-final between Obodowskaya and Elizabetta Maffeis of Italy was started, only for the Soviet to skid and then fall off. That prompted the commissaires to call off the day's racing; to add insult to injury they put the cancellation down to the riders' 'nerves'.

'You have won,' one commissaire said to Gray the next morning. This was far from the first or last battle fought by the combative Gray, the future mayor of Kingston on Thames and future president of the BCF. She had pushed hard 15 years earlier to get women into the World's, she was still campaigning for women's cycling to be included in the Olympics, and she stepped into the breach again in later years when she felt women were being overlooked.

Part of Chadelle's concern had been due to a regulation which stated that three rounds of the pursuit could not be run in a single day. That rule was put to one side; when Burton and Obodowskaya took to the track for their final at 11.30pm, they had begun racing at 10am, and had two rides already in their legs. 'What demands the clowns of the UCI were making of us,' wrote Burton in her memoirs*. Her silver medal was richly deserved: Obodowskaya opened an early gap of three seconds, before Burton fought back with her usual rapid finish, losing by less than a second. However, this was followed by a familiar outcome in the road race, where she worked hard on the circuit at Imola, whittled the field down to 15 over the derisory 34 miles, but was unable to produce the necessary speed in the finish sprint.

Burton's defeat in the 1968 world pursuit championship prompted suggestions that she might be in decline. That was mere speculation. On the other hand, the following year did see the first major public setback of her career. The Mersey Roads 24-hour time trial was a turning point. It was her biggest challenge to date, the one women's record that she had never held: like the Grand Prix des Nations, the '24' took her into unfamiliar territory and pitted her directly against men. It went horribly wrong.

Racing for 12 hours non-stop was considered too extreme by many die-hard time triallists – let alone laymen – but the '24' took that to another level. There were only a handful of such events each year: the organisational logistics were overwhelming and the number of riders prepared to take on the challenge was small. The '24' was the province of specialist hard men such as Burton's boss Nim Carline, whose influence hung heavily over her attempt to push past a huge landmark: 500 miles in a day. The fact that Carline had himself gone

---

** Burton's memoirs state that the rain debacle happened during her final with Obodowskaya, but she appears to have misremembered: the report in* Cycling *is adamant that the delay came at the quarter-final stage, with the rest of the racing rescheduled for the following day; hence her harsh words about three rounds being run in one long session.*

within four miles in 1966 was an obvious incentive for his protegée to do better.

Burton prepared for the '24' in the Carline style, putting in outrageously high mileages beforehand – 640 one week, 500 the next – and taking on additional challenges such as riding home from Essex to Leeds with a clubmate after winning the national women's '50' championship (she posted a super-fast 1hr 56min 15sec for her 31st national title). It was summer, and the workload on Carline's farm had quietened down, but even so, to prepare fully for the race at the end of July – '24's are held in high summer to take advantage of every minute of daylight – she had to miss out on the national road race and pursuit titles and decline selection for the world championships.

'The "24" was the only event I ever took time off work to train for, and only because I knew I had to do it,' she recalled. 'Working for Nim, I knew he had time off work. For the last six weeks before the "24" he'd do 100 miles each day, nothing less. I thought if he had to do it, I'd have to. The difference [with Carline] was that when I'd done my 100 miles I wasn't finished. I remember one day I rode to Hull and back, about 130 miles. I always made sure I was back in time to cook Charlie's dinner and I stood ironing for about three hours after that.'

With Burton's notoriety at its height after the '12' and '100' records, a huge crowd turned up, fully expecting to watch her break the 500-mile barrier on a course that stretched along the north Wales coast and back, then down through the Cheshire plain into the quiet villages of north Shropshire. Over 100 cars were parked in a field near the finish; countless other cycling fans turned up on their bikes. When Burton started on the evening of July 26, she was expected to face two male rivals: Carline and the Doncaster rider Roy Cromack, who had ridden the previous year's Mexico Olympics. Cromack was a grammar school teacher and – like Burton – a supremely talented all-rounder, capable of winning a pursuit on the track or completing the toughest international stage races. His ride that day would earn him a citation in *Cycling* magazine's Golden Book, which noted that he 'won medals at disciplines ranging from the 4,000m pursuit on the track to all the RTTC standard distance national championships.'

Burton was one of four women in the field, alongside 74 men, and the only one to be asked to ride on precisely the same course as the men, because – obviously – she was expected to cover at least as much distance as they would. In fact, she was the fastest in the entire field from the start in the village of Tarvin, just east of Chester: 2min 10sec ahead of Carline at 30 miles. In steady rain, she passed through 100 miles in 4hour 11min – fast enough to win any women's event by a street, and to make the top 10 in many men's races – with Carline 9min behind and Cromack, with his crew cut and green and white striped jersey, at 13min.

'Beryl was astounding everyone with her fantastic pace; this was the men's championship and it was as if she were an intruder come to upset the apple cart,' wrote Mike Smith in *Cycling*. Thus far, it looked as if a repeat of the Otley triumph was in the making. In the darkness of the brief July night, wearing a 'natty woollen hat', Burton overhauled Cromack, as she had intended to, with the remark 'What's keeping you, Roy?' (but no liquorice allsort). She caught Carline on the coast near Queensferry, the 150-mile point, which she went through in 6hr 22min, 20min ahead of her clubmate and 23min faster than Cromack. Carline and Cromack fought it out behind her for 50 miles until finally the Morley rider cracked, and abandoned to support Burton.

'Still she pounded away,' wrote Smith, 'creating havoc behind her, making timekeepers check and recheck their watches.' According to Cromack's calculations, Burton's maximum lead was 27 minutes at about the 12-hour point, which she passed at 268 miles – not far short of her Otley '12' total, and a distance that would have won many men's '12's. She looked to be heading for a total well over 500 miles, but in fact her knees were beginning to give out. 'Her lead had already started to fluctuate before 270 miles,' wrote Cromack later. Smith estimated that Burton still had a lead of 23 minutes at 345 miles, but ten miles later her race was over. Repeatedly, Charlie had urged his wife to slow down; later on, she stopped briefly while he attempted to massage the pain out of her knees.

Burton later revealed that she had been having treatment on the joints for the previous five weeks (they would remain troublesome until well into 1970). The pain had, she wrote, 'given cause for concern', although it had not stopped her from training, or from winning other races. Charlie recalled: 'A bit further on [from her first halt], she pulled in and said, "I can't go any further, my legs won't move." We had a car with no back in it, she lay down in that and couldn't move. The veins and muscles in the back of her knees were like wire.' Meanwhile, Cromack went flying past, reportedly flinging Burton's earlier remark back at her.

Back to Smith: 'The word quickly got around, and one could feel a sense of anticlimax; after all when she retired she was still the fastest rider on the road, almost an hour inside "evens" [20mph]'. Charlie's view was that his wife had over-trained, trying to emulate Carline. There was also the way she had raced, 'eyeballs out', with no pacing whatsoever. It was, Beryl had said, '500 or bust'; she said later that she knew she was taking a gamble on her knees, but felt she had no option.

Similarly, she saw no point in trying for anything other than a record, so there was no use in throttling back.

Cromack, on the other hand, went on to do 507 miles, but it was far from straightforward. He rode more and more slowly in the final minutes until he was 'completely sold out' and fell off his bike in a dead faint with ten seconds remaining. His record stood for a further 28 years. 'I suspect Beryl is somewhat embarrassed by references to the event,' he said many years later. 'She made a right pig's ear of it, charging off from the start in enormous gears at a lunatic pace. It says a lot for her that she lasted 350 miles, and maybe it is significant that she has never been back to finish the job off. Her [career] record is beyond comparison and is unlikely to be surpassed. There is no need to gild the lily.'

Burton's knees dictated the rest of her season. Her sole focus on the '24' meant there was no chance of redemption in the world championships. Two weeks after the '24', the RTTC '100' championship went the same way when she started flat out, stormed into an early lead, then quit in distress. Burton had started against medical advice, and paid the price. Thirty miles in, she had overtaken all the starters apart from her clubmate Maureen Wroe; 12 miles later she had to stop, 'weeping unashamedly' at the side of the road as the field flew past. Charlie was close to tears as well. The victory went to Wroe, a 'modest, attractive girl' according to *Cycling* (she was a more than decent cyclist, as well).

It was only the fourth time in 36 consecutive women's national time trial championships since 1958 that any rider other than Burton had won, and it brought an end to an unbeaten run across the title board – 25, 50 and 100 miles — that went back to 1965. For the first time since her illness as an 11-year-old, her body had failed to meet the demands she made of it. Her first thought was that this might be the end of her racing career, and she was not the only one to wonder.

Burton did not travel to the World's in Brno. In her absence, another British woman achieved a road race medal; Bernadette Swinnerton* – now Bernadette Malvern – landed silver on a mountainous course (which would have suited Burton) winning the bunch sprint behind the solo winner, McElmurey of the USA. Meanwhile, Burton was attending St James Hospital in Leeds – where she had been treated for chorea at the age of 11 – for daily treatment on her knees. The joints recovered rapidly, suggesting that if she had only had the patience and self-belief to back off her training for the '24', her collapse might have been avoided. It took only four weeks for her to be fit enough to break two hours again for 50 miles, and in late September she managed to break the competition record at the distance, with a time of 1hr 55min 4sec in the Teesside RC 50 at Catterick, which was good enough for seventh in the men's event. But it was a far cry from what she had aimed for.

The '24' was a gamble that had not paid off, and despite her recovery she remained concerned about how her knees would hold up to subsequent challenges. Midway through 1970, in an interview with the local journalist Colin Willcock, she said she would not try again. 'It's the only event I have ever changed my training schedules for. I had to train my own way for it so I could ride it my own way, and changing all my

---

** Born into a cycle-shop owning family in Stoke, Swinnerton was part of one of the finest cycling dynasties Britain has produced. Her father Roy was a national track champion; siblings Frances, Margaret, Catherine, Paul, Mark and Bernard were also more than proficient, winning a variety of national titles and racing internationally.*

training times and everything caused too big an upset with everything.'

There was, however, one major victory that autumn, when a joint meeting of the RTTC and the BCF – working in tandem for once - agreed that from the start of 1970 women would be permitted to compete against men in all types of race in England and Wales. It was eight years since Burton had started campaigning. 'Racing Goes Unisex', proclaimed *Cycling*. Time trialling was already run on an equal basis in Scotland, and that October Burton travelled north of the border to compete in a 25-mile time trial between Dundee and Perth that had been specially organised for her by the Heatherbell Ladies Cycling Club; she broke the Scottish women's record, beat 28 men – including Charlie – and finished second to Jock Ritchie of the Central Scotland Wheelers, who was 19 seconds faster. Merely having Burton in the event was a massive draw, with hundreds turning out to watch her race in heavy rain and mist.

Burton hailed the change for the opportunities it would bring, 'not just from my point of view but for the younger girls as well – it will teach them how to handle their bikes better and more quickly. I would rather be off the back and chasing hard in a men's event than riding women's road races. They're either like time trials or we are only doing about 17 miles per hour and that's not racing.' A few years later, she reflected that the introduction of mixed racing had 'improved all my performances. Whether a competitor is male or female doesn't bother me. Whoever's on scratch [i.e. starting last and thus nominally the fastest rider in the field] is the one I pick out. That's the one I've got to beat.'

In February 1970, Ann Horswell of Plymouth RC, the reigning BCF road race champion – Burton had not started the previous year because of her training for the '24' – became the first woman to ride a 'unisex' road race, the Mid Devon Road Club handicap. Burton herself would take advantage of the change to ride two-up team time trials with Nim Carline and other male clubmates, while the entire family – Charlie, Denise and Beryl – would occasionally be seen competing together in handicap races, albeit in different groups.

The main target for Burton in 1970 was the world championships, held in Leicestershire, the first time that both men's and women's World's had been put on in the UK. But she had reached a career impasse since the disaster of the Mersey RCC '24' the previous July: there was nowhere new for her to go. 'The only thing that holds my interest these days is trying to improve on what I have already done,' she said in an interview that May. Burton was in a cleft stick: she could still win any time trial, as she had shown for the last ten years, but there was nothing else to achieve. There was no point in turning professional because she would not earn a great deal more and races were few and far between. That explained her urge for unusual challenges such as the 'Nations', the '12' and the '24'.

Her retirement was not exactly a subject of public speculation, but the question was an obvious one: when would she hang up her wheels? In May 1970, her answer was, 'Not yet, not until I'm stalled – you know, not getting the results. Then I'll retire, but not while I'm still enjoying it.' Unfortunately, the races which gave her the most pleasure and satisfaction, her regular time trial wins throughout the season, were gradually beginning to stymie her performances at the world championships. To compete to the full in British 'testing', Burton had had no option but to adopt the same big gear, slow pedalling strategy as her male rivals; like Alf

Engers, she had made a successful transition from the fixed-gear era of the 1950s. The golden age of time trialling was the era of peak chainring, when gears became ever larger, with a 'soup plate' at the front and five close-range gears at the back.

Engers felt the use of the big gear depended on concentration and sophisticated technique: 'By the late '60s you had "testers", who used enormous gears. It was a real art; you didn't push the big gear, you rolled it along. You didn't point your toe like a dog trying to dig a hole in the road, you didn't try from your guts, you kept calm, got into a rhythm and rolled the gear over with your heel down.' Burton hinted at something similar, pointing to the way she pulled herself forward on to the peak of the saddle and thrust with her legs rather than spinning the pedals; that meant plenty of pulling with the arms and shoulders, moving forward in the saddle to get her body weight over the pedals.

However, her perfection of the technique meant that road racing and pursuiting became more difficult. Riding a pursuit on a fixed-gear track bike relied on spinning a low gear and possessing the explosive power to make a rapid standing start. Road racing entailed sudden changes of pace where the ability to change cadence every second was paramount. Week-in, week-out, Burton rode time trials which called for precisely the opposite quality: steady, rhythmic and relatively slow pedalling using sheer strength and unstinting concentration. That mattered less in her 20s, but as Burton grew older her natural speed and explosive power declined, even as she perfected the big gear style. There were ways of combatting this for an older rider, but weekly time trialling was not one of them.

During the early 1970s, this difficulty became increasingly visible as Burton took on younger competitors. There were other issues: her knees were still a problem and she also began to express publicly what amounted to a fear of failure. So she sought safety in what she knew best: time trialling. The first sign of this gradual change was that she became increasingly frustrated with riding the world championship road race. It had begun to bug her in the early 1960s, but her irritation became more marked: '…they don't let me ride away any more these days, everybody watches me and if I can't drop them I can't win,' she said. 'All I get is a pat on the back from the others and, "Well done, you made the race."' The writer Geoff Nicholson put this firmly down to time trialling. He described Burton as, 'clearly the strongest competitor' at one world road championship but added, 'devotion to time trialling has developed only her ability to set and keep an unyielding pace… she hadn't the sudden change of speed which would enable her to break away from the hangers-on.'

The issue was underlined in May 1970 in an international stage race run by the Women's Cycle Racing Association, where she was heavily marked by a four-woman Dutch team. *Cycling* magazine described how they 'deployed their forces in a successful attempt to outmanoeuvre Burton from the start, clinging to her back wheel leech-like … Time and again … she tried to break away but each time she opened the slightest gap there was either a Dutch girl or [Bernadette] Swinnerton inches from her back wheel.' The upshot was an angry disagreement among the British women after the finish, with Burton threatening not to ride the World's.

In the event, she was selected for both the road race and the pursuit, but refused to ride the former. This was partly due to frustration at her own inability to escape the pack and partly to avoid playing second fiddle to Swinnerton. Burton explained that she knew that the Mallory Park circuit would give her 'no chance'. She added: 'I felt reasonably certain that I could not win no matter how I tried, especially with some members of our own team riding against me.' In the event, Swinnerton crashed late on in the race at Mallory Park, but she too hated the circuit. 'It was disgusting, so flat and short.' Burton was castigated in the letters page of *Cycling*, accused of being 'afraid to meet the possible superiority of foreign competition ... One can hardly admire or respect anyone who behaves in this unsporting manner...' Her form beforehand was more than decent: she broke her own 25-mile record, yet again, the week before the track racing started at Leicester.

The 1970 World's in Leicestershire were a qualified success. There were good crowds but the event was run on a shoestring. There was poor coverage in the national media and heated debate for weeks afterwards over where to direct the blame. The British stars were Wolverhampton's Hugh Porter, who won gold in the men's pursuit, and Stoke's Les West, who claimed an unexpected fourth in the professional road race behind Jean-Pierre Monséré of Belgium. Burton landed a bronze medal in the pursuit behind her perennial Soviet rivals Tamara Garkushina and Raisa Obodowskaya. 'They are not unbeatable,' said Burton, who felt that she was 'riding worse than I've ever done'. She qualified last of the eight who went through to the quarter final, but improved as she often did to rap out 4min 10sec in the bronze medal ride-off to beat Katie Hage of the Netherlands.

The 'Ford Girls' – hostesses who looked after the VIPs – received as much coverage as the racing women, and were listed as the host nation's number one achievement. (*Cycling*: 'All the official visitors loved the Ford Girls – it was great, they thought, being able to load their problems on pretty girls who could speak their language.') Burton made the news for allegedly sleeping through Prince Philip's official visit for the second round of the pursuit, on 8 August; she was also more than miffed that just as she was racing Geneviève Gambillon in the first round, the VIPs all got up as one and left in order to have lunch with HRH.

Among the more appreciative members of the crowd who came to see Burton race at Leicester was a five-year-old called Ernie Feargrieve. He was taken there by his father, who had driven Burton and team mates to the 1959 world championships (see chapter 5). 'We were sitting on the grass bank between turns three and four, below the beer tent. Beryl, Charlie and Denise came and sat with us; Beryl was cooking steak on a camping stove, because that was what she wanted to eat before she raced in the final.'

The 1970 World's indicated that apart from Burton and Swinnerton, the standard of British women's racing had declined. There was still no coordinated road racing calendar for women, and the Federation's financial input was minimal: a total of £100 had been invested in coaching for women in the three years leading up to Leicester. Eileen Gray compared UK women's racing unfavourably with that in the Netherlands, the country that had been unwilling to host a women's World's in 1959. A mere five years after they had first recognised women's racing, the Dutch already had a system of two races per weekend, run to standards which matched men's events and with prizes down to 15th, while their riders enjoyed extensive coaching – for novices and experienced riders alike – from their Federation. They also had sponsored women's teams, while Katie Hage – the Marianne Vos of her day – would receive a £25 fee for starting a race.

Other countries had also advanced, including the USSR, which had been targeting the sprint and pursuit on the track for some years. The pool of riders in France had increased to almost 250, in comparison to only 40 or 50 women road racing in the UK. However, the various nations had moved at different rates: in Italy, there were still only a dozen or so women racing, while in the US McElmurey was paying her own way. Questions were raised over the viability of holding women's world track championships when the number of entrants was so small. There was a simple reason why the growth was sporadic: women cyclists were not permitted to race in the Olympic Games, and thus many governing bodies, unlike the enlightened Dutch, did not view them as a priority.

The 1970 World's left the BCF short of money, and the governing body was willing to pay for only two women to attend the 1971 World's in Mendrisio, Switzerland. Riders were 'invited' to pay their own way, and did so; one, Margaret Gordon-Smith, invested her life savings on the trip, but now believes it was a disaster for her, as she was simply not ready to compete at this level. Mendrisio was a disaster for the British across the piece, with stand-up rows between the men's road team and their manager, and one rider, the late Phil Edwards, sent home in disgrace. That set the tone for a decade in which British cyclists struggled internationally; the nation seemed to be in a backwater, and there was existential angst every year after the world championships.

Cycling in Britain became increasingly divided as time trialling and road racing went their separate ways. The RTTC was still debating chequered flags, whether organisers should request self-addressed envelopes from race entrants, and whether women should be referred to by their initials or their first names in result sheets. British cycle racing was a parochial world, in which Reg Harris could come back to sprinting successfully at national level in his 50s and where Alf Engers' deeds and alleged misdeeds were the focus of intense debate. The Great Britain national team did not run to providing its riders with cotton racing hats or – still – rollers to warm up on, let alone luxuries such as proper accommodation. Burton's and Porter's bronze medals in their respective pursuits at Mendrisio were minor relief amidst a logistical nightmare.

The team endured a 23-hour journey to Italy, their hotel was a heaving pit of 'local night life', manager Tommy Godwin missed a change of schedule, one of the male sprinters never made it to his race, and Burton and Bernadette Swinnerton almost missed the pursuit qualifier in a near repeat of events at Frankfurt in 1966. They were rushed to the track with a police escort, had to change immediately and with the rest of the team looking on ('the men loved it,' said Swinnerton wryly), then went straight onto the track without a warm-up.

Worse was to come on the key day of the pursuit. Burton was scheduled to ride a semi-final, with high hopes of reaching the final as she had qualified second fastest to Garkushina in a very rapid 3min 59.79sec. In the quarter-final Katie Hage had punctured while in the lead against Polanska of Czechoslovakia; the Dutchwoman was given an estimated time for the round which was faster than the time Burton had managed in beating Tartagni of Italy. Burton arrived at the track the next day for her semi-final assuming that she would be riding against a slower qualifier – Hage or Lyuba Zadorozhnaya – and thus could reasonably expect to make it through to the final.

She was utterly dismayed when she suddenly became aware – five minutes before the start gun – that Garkushina was on the other side of the track. She had been kept in the dark by team management. 'I was devastated. Had I been told first thing in the day it would have been a blow but I would at least have had the opportunity to make a mental readjustment... [Our] officials should know their riders and consider how they react to given situations.'

She was duly beaten, by eight seconds, but then pulled herself together for the bronze medal ride, which proved incredibly tight. Her final margin of victory was a mere 0.16sec from Zadorozhnaya, a remarkable achievement for a 34-year-old who had to treat pursuiting as an optional extra. Burton now held a unique record: no cyclist of either sex had won as many medals in world championships as she now had – seven gold medals, four silvers and three bronze. She had overtaken the legendary Dutch sprinter Arie Van Vliet, whose tally was four gold, six silver and three bronze.

As *Cycling* noted, this record had been achieved, 'very quietly and almost un-noticed.' Eileen Gray concurred: 'The girls still do not receive full recognition and support which brings me back to the lack of recognition for Beryl compared to the excitement if, say, Eddy Merckx had just won his fourteenth medal, or even in the case of our own Reg Harris when he won his fifth.'

Burton's greatest achievements – the Otley '12', the gold in Heerlen — had made her a household name in British cycling, but the narrative of ubiquitous victory was rarely put into proper perspective. She was so prolific that her successes lacked any element of drama for the press; the statistics — record after record, championships by the dozen – were simply taken for granted. Rivals appeared and went on their way once they realised there was no getting past her. By the early 1970s, Burton had yet to endure a sustained challenge from an adversary who would hold out for more than a couple of years. However, that was about to change: a serious opponent was about to emerge, from disturbingly close to home.

Chapter 10

A Funny Feeling

1hr 35min 55sec: national women's road race, 36 miles, Harrogate, 1976.

Denise Burton became aware of a change in her mother a few weeks before the national championship road race at Harrogate in early August 1976. Beryl was always relatively subdued around the house, but she tended to become quieter than usual in the run-up to a major race. She would seem to be constantly running through the race in her mind, intently working out what she would do in every situation that might arise: 'rehearsing the whole thing over and over', as Denise put it. But before this race, Beryl was even more withdrawn.

That year, the championship was the climax to Harrogate's International Festival of Cycling. The national road race was often a low-key occasion, but the tie-in had dramatically raised its profile, helping to attract sponsorship from *She* magazine. Now long gone, the festival was a huge occasion, largely inspired by the fact that Yorkshire's 'Mr Cycling', Ron Kitching, had based his company in the spa town. 'Harrogate Week' drew thousands of cyclists for a massive trade exhibition – the catalogue of exhibitors ran to 50 pages – and a wealth of races that included professional criteriums, invitation time trials, grass-track racing and mass touring rides.

Beryl Burton had begun her Harrogate week by knocking out a new competition record for 50 miles in the Nunbrook Wheelers race on the A1: her time of 1hr 51min 30sec would have given her fourth place among the group of British-based professional cyclists who rode the race. Also competing in that '50' was Denise, who finished a colossal 12 minutes behind her mother.

At 20, having spent virtually her whole life in the saddle, Burton junior was coming into her prime. At the previous year's world championships, she had taken a bronze medal in the pursuit – her mother's old speciality. Beryl had been as happy as her daughter at the result; to mark the occasion she had bought Denise a bronze candle in a bag trimmed with bronze beads. (It had also earned Denise an appearance on the Superstars television programme). On the road, the pair had crossed swords many times, with the outcome following a clear pattern: Burton *fille* tended to be faster than her mother in a sprint, while Burton *mère* would knock spots off her daughter in a time trial. Beryl had observed as early as 1970 that Denise had a good sprint, 'unlike her mum. She can hammer me over the first two miles of a Sunday run.'

It was a 25-mile trip from the Burton family home in Woodlesford to the national championship race headquarters in Harrogate's Rudding Park. On their way out of the house to travel to the race, and completely out of the blue, Beryl turned to Denise and told her bluntly, 'You aren't coming in the car.' Denise, totally nonplussed, asked her mother, 'Well, how am I supposed to get there?' There was no answer, but it was obvious: on her bike. Beryl was unwilling even to let Charlie load their daughter's race wheels into the car boot, so Denise did the only thing she could: put the wheels onto the sprint carriers which fitted onto the front of her bike and set off. What had just happened might surprise parents of today, but – as Denise said years later – for her mother, 'Everyone was a rival. I was a rival.' Still, at least her parents took her race bag.

Halfway to Harrogate, Denise met Charlie, who had dropped off her mother at the race headquarters and turned around immediately to search for their daughter. They loaded her bike into the car and her long-suffering father – whose conflicted feelings can only be imagined – drove her to the start. Over 40 years on, Denise recalls she felt relatively unfazed and chose to look on the extra 12-mile ride as a warm-up. 'I was fine: I got changed, Dad put the wheels in and everything. I had a cup of tea, I tootled up and down and that were it, we were off.'

The eight laps of the four and a half mile circuit included one steep climb and one long uphill drag; within sight of the start, the race had begun to split as Beryl Burton set about her usual task of trying to dislodge the rest of the field. It was a tactic that had worked time and time again over the previous 20 years, including as recently as 1972 and 1973: on both occasions she had won by several minutes. After a single lap, the field had been split into three, with both the Burtons in a seven-strong leading group – including Catherine Swinnerton, sister of 1969 World's silver medallist Bernadette – that had been whittled down to three by the finish. It was Beryl who did most of the whittling, betraying her stress when she turned round to the rest of the front runners after one surge to taunt them, 'Doesn't anyone know how to attack?' It was reported that on the sixth lap, Swinnerton and another leader, Terrie Riley, 'tangled and crashed'; eyewitnesses said it was as a result of the erratic way Beryl Burton was riding, so keen was she to get the other riders off her wheel.

At least one image from the race shows Denise chasing down an attack from her mother; afterwards, she explained that she had ridden tactically, knowing that she could use her sprint in the finish. 'I did go to the front, but I didn't go as hard as I might have done. If some girls can sit in, why can't I?' At the finish the bronze medal was always destined for Carol Barton of Long Eaton Paragon; the sprint for gold between mother and daughter was 'fearsome', according to the editor of *Cycling*, Ken Evans. Beryl chose the right of the road, Denise the centre, Barton the left. 'A bitterly fought finish,' felt Evans. 'The increasing rivalry between the two meant there were no holds barred. In the last 20 yards Denise found the extra to push her bike ahead and the title was hers.' The finish picture shows Denise with her elbows wide out and an expression of total immersion in the moment as she took the gold medal. She did so by a generous bike length; in her memoirs, Beryl merely conceded that her daughter had won 'by the proverbial whisker'.

For a cyclist approaching 40, it was still one hell of a finish, second place or not, but Beryl Burton did not see it that way. Primly, Evans wrote, 'There were no motherly words of congratulation on the podium.' In other words, Burton did not acknowledge her daughter in her moment of victory. Beryl wrote later that she felt that Denise had not done enough work to keep the break away, and that, as usual, she had 'made the race.' She had had to endure the scenario that had frustrated her time after time over nearly 20 years – attempting to break away, but being kept in check by a sprinter who then pipped her at the finish – but this time her own daughter emerged as the beneficiary.

Her old friend Eileen Cropper also rode that race, but abandoned after a few laps. As a result, she was already in the changing rooms, washed and brushed up and ready to go home, when Beryl appeared. Cropper saw Burton sitting on the floor of the changing room, hitting the surface with her fists – in that same state of frustration as when she dropped her ball as a child – and heard her scream, 'Charlie does everything for her!' (referring, of course, to Denise). 'She was seething, really mad,' Cropper told me. Afterwards, Cropper found Denise and congratulated her: 'I told her I was really pleased for her.' In an obvious state of emotion, Denise apparently said, 'I wish you were my mum.'

'It was a bit strange,' Denise told the writer Robert Dineen. 'I don't know why she did it. Just silly. She just wanted to win and got herself completely mixed up.' Beryl admitted that her feelings about losing yet another race in a sprint became intertwined with the issues arising between her and her daughter at the time. 'This is a real life narrative about basically ordinary people with jangled nerves and emotions, our bitter conflict played out in almost gladiatorial fashion,' she wrote in her memoirs. 'I was surrounded at the finish but Charlie was not with me and it was the final straw... [I felt] choked and miserable.' She added that she recognised that in refusing to congratulate Denise afterwards she had done her sport 'a disservice'.

Beryl Burton claimed that the episode came at a time when her relationship with Denise was tense, and that this was because Denise had not been pulling her weight around the house. Denise Burton-Cole does not remember it that way. She was allotted a long list of tasks, and 'my mum used to delegate all the jobs. There was no way she would do them all herself.' 'My view would be that they both had different ways of training,' said one contemporary, Maggie Thompson. 'Beryl was old school. She would go out and ride her bike. Denise would do it in a more scientific way. You rest when you need to, and when you rest, you do nothing. If you were running around trying to run a home, I can imagine that would be irritating.'

Denise Burton-Cole says that the flare-up at the national championship did stem from something deeper. 'It was a long build-up to that day, definitely. It's not that day in isolation, definitely not. It was a couple of weeks at least, things being a little bit icy, and then that day it just exploded. It must have been quite distressing for her, not having that control the same that she had [had], and the fact it was me – not in time trialling so much but in pursuiting and road racing – that was beating her, and other people by then. She was getting older herself, she was past her best by then. I think she did find it difficult.' Other riders of the time agree that Burton's dispute with her daughter was part of a bigger picture, as she became aware that a strong group of much younger riders were threatening her hegemony; Denise was one of that group, who also included the Swinnerton sisters, Riley and Barton.

According to one witness, Beryl Burton was 'discovered wandering through Rudding Park caravan site in a distressed state' by the then national secretary of the RTTC, Phil Heaton, who took her to his caravan to provide tea and sympathy. In the further aftermath of the national championship, she moved briefly out of the family home. One source I spoke to who had been close to her for many years met her not long after the 'national' episode. 'She wanted to come and stay with me. She was going to move into my house. She said, "I've had enough, he [Charlie]'s taken Denise's side and doesn't give two hoots for me – you've got a spare room."' Burton herself recorded that she went to her mothers to 'sort herself out.'

Beryl Burton's relationship with her daughter was unusual, probably unique. Denise's upbringing had been entirely unlike that of her peers, but there was more: even as they were trying to work through the normal issues that create conflict between any young adult and his or her parents, Denise was fighting for the same medals and the same international selection slots as her intensely competitive mother, who was as dominant a force in the household as she tended to be in a race environment. There are no other comparable instances of a mother and child competing head to head at the highest level in an endurance sport.

Even without Denise to threaten her supremacy, Beryl Burton would have been tense. As she approached 40, she had to cope with the beginnings of the inevitable decline that is universal even in the most gifted champions. The looming loss of her physical ability had forced her to confront the re-awakening of some of her old mental demons. These challenges must have been thrown into stark relief by the development of precisely the opposite qualities in her daughter, who was gaining strength and speed by the year, and showing the exuberant confidence of youth. To make matters worse, the relationship had to be played out in the public eye, even if the public was made up of the relatively undemanding folk within British club cycling.

Forty years later, Denise is keen to emphasise the positive elements of her childhood within the tightly knit Burton family, a trio set slightly apart from those around them by their complete focus on her mother's chosen sport. 'We spent hours and hours together, weekends away, touring, holidays, events, we were always together as a unit. That was *us*. We were the Burtons. We had good times, many many years of good times.' It's a spirit encapsulated by footage of mother and daughter from the finish of the national '25' championship in 1970: Beryl in her winner's racing cap, a 14-year-old Denise with her hair in bunches, the pair shoving each other side to side with their shoulders in shared hilarity.

Those happy memories are coloured by the other side to their relationship, which developed as Denise gained maturity and grew as a cyclist. Her conclusion is stark: 'There was love there, but [Beryl] didn't like it when I was winning, or living in the same house.' As their sporting rivalry intensified, their personal relationship became complex and troubled. To this day it still colours many of Denise's memories of her cycling career, which was cut short first by anorexia and then by a horrendous accident. Denise seems happy in her own skin now, but that has been possible, one suspects, primarily because she has acknowledged what took place between her and that idolised, dominant parent.

After Denise's birth in 1956 she was not allowed to get in the way of her mother's racing career, although she did become a ubiquitous presence in every photo shoot for every magazine article. A photograph of Beryl from 1957 in *Cycling and Mopeds* magazine showed her shopping at a butchers, in a checked jacket and cut-off trousers, probably home made, with Denise, age 16 months, in a push chair clutching a book.

In a 1958 article in *Cycling*, Burton describes Denise as a keen cyclist at two and a half, adding – with an early hint of resentment – that 'her main pleasure seems to be in running around finding all the puddles and dirt possible to increase my daily wash'. 'They call her "boot-button eyes", for that's what her lustrous brown orbs look like,' wrote an interviewer in *Sporting Cyclist* when she was four years old. Beryl said later that Denise was put on a bike at 12 weeks; she travelled with her parents to most weekend races apart from 100-mile time trials, where it would have been tricky to have her running around while Charlie was handing up bottles of tea and wet sponges to her mother. She would be left with her grandparents for those.

If the race was within 60 or 70 miles of home, the trio would ride there, with Denise travelling in the sidecar or on the bike trailer to the weekend's accommodation, occasionally sleeping in a drawer in the bedroom. She was not indulged with fancy kit to ride and race on at a young age: Beryl made the point in a 1970 interview that she and Charlie made their daughter progress gradually through steel components and heavy wheels and tyres to lighter, faster parts as she grew older and went further in the sport.

The relationship was not exactly close, recalled Denise: 'We weren't the family that talked a lot. Both my dad and her had quite a Victorian upbringing, quite strict parents. I talk with my children – chat, chat, chat – but not my mum and dad. He was more chatty, but Mum didn't talk much unless she needed to.' She was not allowed to sit on her mother's lap as a young child because she might hurt Beryl's legs; after being told that several times, she went and sat on her father's knee instead.

Charlie and Beryl did not go to functions at Denise's school – parents evenings, sports days and the like – because it would have cut across cycling. 'They weren't that kind of parents,' said Denise. The one time that she recalls her mother visiting a school sports day was in her final year at junior school, when Beryl was injured and was unable to ride her bike.

Denise raced for the first time in May 1968, aged 12; she made the pages of *Cycling* for riding a five-mile club time trial (which she covered in 16min 58sec, on an 18-inch bike with 24-inch wheels). Less than 12 months later, she competed in her first open time trial over 10 miles, winning the schoolgirl prize with a time of 31min 50sec, finishing 6min 20sec behind her mother in 19th place. She rode a machine way too big for her, with massive handlebars compared to her tiny arms, and the saddle dropped down as far as it could go; it had clearly been handed down from Mum or Dad.

Her rise was meteoric. In 1971, aged just 15, she became the youngest ever rider to win a medal in an RTTC national championship, after finishing almost 10 minutes behind her mother in the '25' championship, where Beryl took her 37th national title. She and Beryl took the team prize for the Morley, together with Ann Pallister, who was two years older than Denise. They were the first mother and daughter to win a RTTC national team prize. Although Denise's own cycling career was not to be anywhere near as prolific or lengthy as her mother's, she rapidly proved that she was world class. At 15 she finished fifth in the national road race title, blocking in the bunch as Beryl rode to victory by 7min 20sec. A year later Denise was selected to ride in a race in Holland for Great Britain, performing more than creditably for a 16-year-old.

Her mother, meanwhile, was continuing as of old, still beating the men – as in the Glade CC '50' in Essex, described by John Coulson as 'a magnificent licking to the entire field', with the second rider 90 seconds back. On occasion she would race two-up and three-up team time trials alongside men, as in the Doncaster RCC race in early 1973, in which she and Morley team-mates Roy Caspell and Billy Hudson finished second but beat some noted time triallists in other teams, including, again, Mike McNamara.

In the summer of 1971, Burton hit some of her best time trialling form, winning her 40th national championship in the '50' at Newark, nearly 10 minutes ahead of Maureen Pearson (*née* Wroe) and winning 'mixed' time trials with rapid men in the field. In July she lowered her '25' record to 54min 44sec in a rare head-to-head with Alf Engers, who finished two minutes faster having unshipped his chain, punctured and then switched to a bike which was the wrong size; Burton, on the other hand, was 21 seconds clear of the third-placed rider. On her day, she was capable of beating most of the best 25-milers of the day, men such as Roger Queen and Mick Ballard (in the Colchester Rovers '25' that September), but the scalp that always eluded her was that of Engers, the finest short-distance specialist of them all.

That year, 1971, Beryl landed another national record at 10 miles, pushing her time down towards 22 minutes, and the next day she triumphed in the national road race championship, escaping after just three of the 34 miles to win by 6min 10sec. At that race there was a hint of what was to come four years later: 'I had time to rub down and watch the sprint for second place,' Beryl wrote. 'Denise was sixth and I was a little angry with her and some of the other girls for hanging back for the sprint in a slow race. The mental attitude to road racing was all wrong…' According to the report in *Cycling*, she said, 'You've only yourselves to blame for it coming to a sprint': although her comment was also directed at the other riders, she had her eyes squarely on her daughter.

That irritation with 'sit-in sprinters' was not limited to Beryl Burton. It had been a broader part of British cycling culture in the 1950s and 1960s. Bernadette Malvern recalls, 'when I was growing up in cycling in the 1960s, it was [seen as] bad to be a "sit-in sprinter". You always had to do your "whack". I always said that if I hadn't done my work at the finish of a world championship I wouldn't want to sprint. I think that's why she didn't like it when Denise got that medal.' That cultural element was yet another side to the complex mix of emotions working on Beryl Burton on that August 1976 day in Harrogate.

Burton had never liked 'sit-in sprinters' and would do her best to intimidate them. Malvern recalled breaking away with her in the 1971 national road race championship. 'I hung on and it shocked her.' It took a while for the younger woman to recover from the effort she had made up the hill when Burton had attacked. Burton pulled to one side to let her rival 'come through', but she then realised Burton was actually going faster. It was a classic technique to break a rider who was close to rupture. 'She said, "if you can't come through, get back where you belong". I sat up, my eyes filled with tears, and I let the others catch me. It really upset me – we'd put her up at our house, fed her who knows how many steaks over the years.'

In August 1972, Beryl and Denise achieved another landmark, becoming the first – and probably only – mother and daughter to ride a world championship road race together. It was a hilly course near Gap in the French Alps, with a proper climb; as a result, Beryl managed to split the field, paring it down to a group of six, out of which she finished a profoundly unhappy fifth. She complained at the way the other breakaway members had ridden, saying of the winner Geneviève Gambillon, 'The only time she went to the front was when I pushed her into the lead,' and adding that, 'The rest were all soft-pedalling.' She described the race as 'another failure of mine to take a medal against class riders who were afraid of me. How I would have loved it if the distance had been 100 kilometres instead of 60.' Denise Burton-Cole, in contrast, remembers that she felt 'secure' travelling to France and racing with her mother: 'My mum was there, my dad was there. I was very nervous, I was only 16, but they were there.' She finished 23rd.

The pursuit on the Marseille velodrome was even more disappointing for Burton, because she had been in such outstanding form. Suffering from stomach troubles, she was unable to back up a solid qualifying round in which she finished third; she eventually lost the bronze ride-off to Lyuba Zadorozhnaya. Burton was beginning to feel that pursuiting was no longer worth the mental strain. She put her defeat down to 'nerves, a mental block.' Early in her career, she felt, she had thrived on the stress, which stimulated her to greater effort. Since 1968, she felt, it had been the other way round and the 'nerves' had not driven her to success as they had used to do.

Burton's final world championship medal came in August 1973 in Barcelona, when she beat Carol Barton in the bronze ride-off; both were well adrift of the perennial medallists Tamara Garkushina and Katie Hage. In the road race, both Burtons finished in the front group, with Beryl 8th and Denise 20th. Back home the season had been another success: a solo victory in the WCRA road race title, a super-fast 10-mile record – 21min 25sec – the 50-mile record pushed below 1hr 55min, and a personal fastest in the British Best All Rounder thanks to another sub-four-hour '100'.

Burton had taken 15 world championship medals since 1959, out of a total of 22 medals by British women. It was an amazing record, but there was still no willingness within the British Cycling Federation to follow through by funding the women properly, or to structure women's racing to enable them to develop in a meaningful way. In 1970, Burton had said she felt that the under-16s got more help than the women. With relatively few places available at each year's World's, there was little incentive for women to race internationally. Most young women cyclists idolized her but Burton's exceptional talent had a counter-productive side. No attempt was made to figure out why her occasional rivals fell by the wayside, and there was no pathway for those looking to follow her.

In 1974, both Beryl and Denise travelled to Montreal for the world championships. Denise was on good form, having won the French Havro–Cauchois stage race (a year after her mother had taken it), but she crashed twice in training before the World's road race, and a third crash on lap one ended her chances. Montreal was Beryl's final world championship; she was eliminated in the quarter-final in the pursuit and ended up fifth in the road race – on one of the hardest circuits she had raced on – after opting not to attack on the final climb of Mont Royal. 'It was a decision brought about by my lack of aggression,' she reflected. 'The adrenalin just did not flow. I had to be left with the satisfaction of knowing that despite my seniority in years no other woman in the world could shake me off, and given enough miles I could beat them all.' The Beryl Burton of Heerlen 1967 would not have settled for that.

Suddenly, Burton felt that she could no longer deal with the anxiety that accompanied each world championship; she recalled that she 'just froze'. She had always been afraid of failure, as her nervousness had revealed; the difference was that now that she was getting older, her fears were more likely to be realised. In 1975 she preferred not to contest the British national pursuit title, on the grounds that if she won it there would be pressure to ride the World's. Instead, it was Denise who travelled to Italy, and landed a bronze medal at her first attempt.

In early 1976, to counteract the lack of support from the BCF, Denise and a group of other younger women joined together to race as a unit, so that they would be prepared for future international events. At roughly the same time, 14 potential riders for a Great Britain's women's national squad were invited to the Lilleshall training centre in Staffordshire for the first get-together of its kind. Beryl Burton was not included. (Denise was apparently invited but was unable to attend). There could hardly have been a clearer statement from the governing body that it was not interested in working with the country's most prolific medallist; this was hardly respectful, and must have been hurtful for a rider who had competed so hard for so long.

Piqued perhaps by this rejection on the part of the governing body, Burton stated that she wanted to return to the world championships that year. She was adamant that she had got over her anxiety, but it kept emerging. For example, in the WCRA stage race that May at the newly opened Eastway cycling circuit in London, the tension that was beginning to emerge between Beryl and her daughter became evident when Denise broke away and Beryl chased her down. At the finish, Beryl crashed heavily 15 metres from the line with Catherine Swinnerton; she was reported as being 'strongly critical' of Swinnerton's riding. (Funnily enough, Swinnerton's mum did not agree.) There were frequently issues between the Burtons and the other riders: 'There's a lot of them and us in women's racing and to a lot of racing girls the Burtons are "them",' was the view of *Cycling*.

Road racing and pursuiting were proving more difficult, but Beryl Burton was still managing to time trial extremely rapidly, pushing her record for 25 miles down to 53min 21sec, a time that would be viewed as remarkably fast even today. That drought summer, 1976, she broke the hour for a '25' for the 100th time since 1963; only eight other British women had gone through that barrier since she had first managed it. She was still doing it her own way: she rode 40 miles of the way to the start of that year's national '25', before Charlie picked her up in their van to drive the rest of the journey; afterwards they rode off together to look for a river where they could do some wild swimming to escape the heat.

On a graph showing the progress of Beryl and Denise Burton's respective racing careers, with international success plotted against the passage of time, the national road race championship in Harrogate would come at pretty much the point where the two riders' lines intersect, with Denise progressing and her mother in gentle decline, notwithstanding her enduring ability to time trial the living daylights out of any stretch of road in Britain.

Shortly after that extraordinary day in Harrogate, Denise went on to win the national pursuit title, while her mother did not ride. Astonishingly, however – given the scenes at the national championships – they were paired in a Great Britain team at the Havro-Cauchois stage race in France not long afterwards. Here, Beryl came close to overall victory, winning the points title but losing the overall lead after a dangerous rival was allowed to go clear and the team misunderstood the instructions of their manager to chase the move down.

Beryl was not named in the Great Britain team to race the world title at Ostuni in Italy in 1976; Denise was selected, but there were no medals. Her mother's former rival Katie Hage won the road race eight years after her first gold, and more incredibly still Yvonne Reynders made a comeback at 39, taking the bronze. Reynders looked back at that race with astonishment: 'I couldn't believe it. There was another Burton there!' Nearly 30 years after women had first been allowed to ride at world championship level, officials were still doing them few favours. In Italy that year, there was no race to decide 5th-8th place among the women sprinters, and the organisers did not trouble to specify the exact start location for the women's road race: it was left up to the teams to figure it out for themselves.

At the end of 1976, whatever the facts on the ground, in Burton's mind her international career was far from over. Having seen her old rival Reynders take a bronze medal at the age of 39, Burton declared she would be looking to gain selection for the World's in Venezuela in 1977, and was aiming to beat Denise in the national pursuit championships. 'If life begins at 40, I just can't wait,' she told Dennis Donovan. 'Age doesn't bother me. Ever since I've started I've found that I learn something every year… If you are going well, you've got to ride both [pursuit and road].' Donovan concluded: 'That look comes back into her eyes, as if to say she will be going well and she will be riding both.'

Before the 1977 World's, Burton had hard words for the Great Britain team – she felt they had not 'ridden as a team' since the 1960s – and more generally for her rivals within the UK. 'I can't really say I've been impressed with anyone. Unless someone's snapping at your heels, you can't be impressed. Since I've been riding mixed events I tend to think of what men I can beat instead of how much I beat the females by.' She expressed little respect for those who preferred women-only races: 'I can only think they want their little bit of glory. I would rather finish well up in men's events than win a women's event.' She also kept a studious eye on the pursuit, taking a swipe at her daughter: 'I thought the winning ride [at the national championship] would be a 4-3, yet a 4-10 was described as fantastic. When I heard that, I knew they wouldn't do well at the World's.'

The cycling relationship between Denise and Beryl Burton was curious: on the one hand Denise would probably never have taken up cycling had she not been born into a cycling household, on the other hand she never enjoyed a great deal of support from her mother. They never trained together. Sometimes both left the house independently within minutes of each other to train on their bikes; Denise recalled passing her mother as they went in opposite directions going up and down the A64. They did wave.

As Denise recalled, Beryl was far from reticent when it came to making her views known, so she must have doled out some nuggets, but Denise has no clear memories of it. 'I won't say she never passed on any useful information because she might have done when I was younger, said the odd thing, but certainly as I got older and was more of a competitor who was more likely going to challenge her, I didn't get any helpful advice at all.' Denise never went elsewhere for advice, but she observed others and learned to adapt her training for particular events. When pursuit time came round in the summer, she would put a stopwatch on her handlebars and head for Methley Straight near Rothwell, to replicate as best she could the conditions on a tarmac velodrome.

Denise noticed that her mother did not praise her very often – Beryl would say 'well done', but little more – but she would make a point of congratulating other people in public and expressing her eagerness to see young women rising up the ladder. 'I wouldn't let it bother me. It maybe did bother me deep down, but outwardly I didn't let it. Because if you let something bother you that means it will affect what you do.' To Eileen Gray, there was something slightly out of kilter in the way that Burton dealt with her daughter. 'You couldn't call it rivalry, but there was no motherly help,' she recalled. Gray recalled how on one occasion at the Leicester velodrome Denise punctured, but her mother would not let her have a spare wheel on the grounds that she herself might need it: 'She had tunnel vision, and that was it.'

During the winter after the Harrogate episode, 1977, the Burton family unit finally broke up. Charlie acquired a new job, and was offered a flat to go with it. Denise's parents informed her that they were moving and she needed to find somewhere else to live. 'I said, "Where am I going to live then?" And [my mother] just says, "Well you'll have to find somewhere". Denise was left with a fortnight in which to uproot herself and move. With hindsight, she can say, 'The new job that my dad had got came with this flat, so I can understand that bit, but the fact they didn't tell me so I could prepare for it, that was the shock.' Being effectively thrown out of the house was disturbing and disruptive for her: 'I was in a pattern of being taken to races. It was a case of "this is your life", so to be told it's not, without warning, was a shock. And I had no money.'

For Charlie, caught between the two women who were the focus of his life, the years of tension between Denise and her mother must have been agonising. 'He worshipped her, and he loved me; to be in the middle must have been horrible,' says Denise. 'We didn't argue – mum said stuff and that was it. That was the law. I never answered back – well, I might have said, "Well I'm not" or something.' The problem was a familiar one: Beryl, with a strong element of the control freak in her make-up, ran the household in her own way. For example, Beryl had tried to teach Denise how to knit: 'it was a jumper or something, and she took one look at it and pulled it all out and knitted it herself again because it was a waste of wool, the way I'd done it.' All of a sudden, as Denise grew up, Beryl found herself faced with someone who was equally determined, and who would not back down. 'I would question things, I was probably just as strong-minded,' concedes Denise. 'With two strong-minded people [in the house] it was never going to work.'

Denise moved in with her aunt and kept racing through 1977; by now she was engaged. The rift between her and her mother never really healed, at least as far as Denise is concerned. Not surprisingly, it remains on her mind, even after 40 years have elapsed. It is the kind of life-defining issue that can probably never leave a child, or a parent. The following year, 1978, she developed anorexia, which may well have been linked to the stress of living through the tensions with her mother while at the same time trying to compete on her bike at the highest level. It took her several years to recover, wiping out what should have been the best years of her career; her first marriage also ended, in 1980. In the early 1980s, Beryl bought a tandem for the pair of them to ride while Denise built up her strength; eventually they raced on it, setting a British record for 10 miles. In 1985, aged 29, she returned to racing and briefly relaunched her international career.

'It did bother me and it still bothers me,' she says now. 'Sometimes I think, "Maybe if that hadn't happened, this wouldn't have happened and maybe I shouldn't have got ill." My mum and dad were very close and he'd give her a hug and stuff like that, and he'd hug me, but my mum just didn't do it. But I would imagine that [as] I've got older, I would have been [hugging] her. I'd like to think I'd have forced it upon her. You can't blame any one thing, but I do wish some things hadn't happened. It's a funny feeling, beating your mum.'

Chapter 11

'BB' and Beryl

53min 21sec: competition record for 25 miles, T254, Catterick North Yorkshire, spring 1976.

In the aftermath of the contentious finish to the national championship in 1976, the complexities of Beryl Burton's relationship with Denise did not fade away. Beryl's autobiography described how by 1977 the atmosphere at home 'had been smouldering for some time', but does not mention that Denise had effectively been thrown out on her ear. When mother and daughter met in the semi-final at the national pursuit championship at the Leicester velodrome in August 1977, all those present would have been aware of the events of the previous year.

It must have been hugely stressful for both women. The track centre in a velodrome is an exposed area meaning that any emotions on view can be read by the public and the press. One obvious dilemma at the race was whether Charlie would look after his wife or his daughter; in the end he took charge of Beryl, while Denise was in the hands of Tom Hargreave of the Women's Cycle Racing Association, who had been present when her mother won her first and second world titles at the discipline. Beryl complained of nerves and a lack of power, and praised her daughter's race: Denise, she said, was the stronger on the day.

'Watching from the Press box,' wrote Dennis Donovan in *Cycling Weekly* in 1992, 'I could see Beryl wearily get off her bike, her shoulders slumped in defeat, with her back to her daughter. Denise walked over to face her mother, and suddenly the two women were in each other's arms, crying and hugging, and the rift had been healed... a terrible ordeal for both had ended. They were friends again.' Donovan implies that Denise made the first move, and this is also the impression given in Beryl Burton's autobiography; Denise Burton-Cole claims it was the opposite. Donovan's account cannot entirely be trusted, as he states incorrectly that the incident occurred after the final of the race. The writer must have wanted a neat ending to the story: this should have been the final not the semi; mother and daughter should have been perfectly reconciled.

In Burton-Cole's recollection, the 'reconciliation' was the work of the BCF's women's coach Val Rushworth, and it was not as straightforward as it looked. Partly, she suggests, it occurred because Beryl realised she was beaten. 'I can tell you what it was. It was stupid because it upset me so much I didn't win [in the final] – I got silver and that is why. I was so upset about it all. [...] Val brought my mother over to me and said, "Your mum's got something to say," and my mother says, "I'm sorry," and then someone throws a blanket or a towel over both our heads and my mother's sobbing, well that got me all sobbing, and that was me. I'd finished. That was my gold medal out of the window, because no matter how hard you are, or how hardened to the thing, you can't help but get upset, can you? So that I... Ooh, I was furious actually.'

The winner of the race that day, Maggie Thompson, still feels a distinct sense of pride that her victory contributed a little to bringing the two women back together. However, Burton-Cole does not feel that she and her mother ever truly moved on, partly because theirs was not a relationship where they ever engaged with the underlying issues. 'It's not that we weren't friends or anything like that. It went on as before.

She wasn't a person, for me, that you could get close to. She wasn't the mum who I could go to and say, "Oh Mum this", or "Oh Mum that" and have a cuddle or anything. You couldn't say, "I've got this problem" or "Can you help me with this?" – she wasn't that kind of a mum. She was just totally for what she wanted.'

Beryl and Denise Burton's falling out over the 1976 national road race championship made waves in the small world of 1970s British cycling, and not merely because it was a tasty item for lovers of gossip. Beryl Burton was one of the most celebrated figures in British cycling; this was a rare glimpse into her character, showing how driven and fragile she was. There was a disconnect between the public persona she had forged for herself over 20 years, and what was actually going on under the carapace. 'You have to understand that there were two Beryl Burtons,' a long-standing observer of British time trialling said. 'There was the BB you met around the result board, which was how she wanted everyone to see her, and then the Beryl Burton we never really met.' Burton's behaviour at the national championship in 1976 was just the tip of the iceberg; the real Beryl Burton was more insecure, more complex and harder to read than most contemporary accounts suggested.

The common view of Burton was a simplistic one: approachable, likeable, in control, plain-speaking, modest. Her victories were always viewed as relatively straightforward but, as we have seen, a close examination of her career reveals several episodes when her emotions got the better of her. Denise Burton-Cole recalls, 'She used to get quite nervous about things. The build-up… the tension before an event was immense, and the bigger the event the more immense the tension was beforehand, and then when it was finished – especially if she'd won, but even if she hadn't – she'd be much more relaxed, which is quite a usual thing, but the tension [beforehand] was ultra. You could cut the atmosphere with a knife.'

Eileen Cropper, too, feels Burton was complex: 'I can't understand how her mind worked, because she could be so nice. I remember her having a screaming fit [at Charlie] outside the van, because the bike wasn't right; it was really offensive. Charlie shrugged it off and let her get on with it. When she was on the bike she was the star and that was it.' The *Cycling* writer Mick Gambling observed, 'Charlie has to watch his step [before a major race] and just try getting into the house smoking a cigarette or wearing shoeplates.'

The theme of 'BB and Beryl' was first put forward by the writer Bernard Thompson, who saw more of UK time trialling between the 1960s and the 1980s than any other journalist. He probably got closer to Burton than most, but it took him the best part of a dozen years, during which he turned up religiously at major time trials to take at least one photo of every participant before typing out a report that would be sent in to *Cycling* magazine. In 1974, he produced one of the few full-length interviews with Burton, which he titled, *'How many Burtons are there?'* His premise was that there were essentially two Beryl Burtons – a hard, unrelenting competitor and a woman who remained 'as starry-eyed as they come when the talk is of her family, her club or her holidays awheel'.

Denise Burton-Cole and others agree with Thompson that there was a difference between Burton the celebrity, on show at races and events, and the Beryl that her family knew at home. However, far from seeing her mother's racing persona as the 'hard, unrelenting' side, Burton-Cole appears to consider the reverse to be true. She told me: 'There was my mum at home and my mum with other people – as I get older and can look back and see it as an adult, there's no doubt about it. I hear people say, "She was this, she was that, she was the other," and I'm thinking, "Hmmm, OK." At home she was not a nasty person, but very different.'

After races, most people found Beryl friendly, chatty, patient, down to earth and good-humoured. **After** races. 'When she got on her bike, she zoned out, she got into her own shell, and then when she had finished she would be back to normal,' recalled Alan Sturgess, who together with his wife Ann gave Burton lifts to races in the 1960s. 'She didn't mess about,' said Ann Battersby, who – as Ann Pallister – travelled frequently with the Burtons to races. 'When she was getting ready to race she would sit in the car, we had to leave her for a bit.' Burton was invariably described as being tetchy and withdrawn before a race start, but probably what left the biggest impression was the shared time afterwards at the prize presentation or around the results board. 'When she finished the race she was a different person, very sociable,' said Battersby. 'She didn't strut about, you would never have known she was a world champion.'

Beryl Burton admitted to Bernard Thompson in 1974 that away from racing, she turned in on herself. 'By nature I am a very quiet person, often at home I do not talk to anyone for hours, not even Charlie or Denise. It has nothing to do with moods or with falling out with people. It's just my way and they all understand this at home. I spend hours thinking, mostly planning the future.' (There are echoes here of another Yorkshirewoman, Lizzie Deignan, who is similarly 'a thinker, a planner'.)

'In our house she was quiet, she was quite serious,' recalled Denise Burton-Cole. 'Not a lot was said unless it needed to be said. We didn't have a discussion or play a game. Some people would say it was quite Victorian how she brought me up.' One contemporary from the 1950s, Shirley Robinson, described Beryl Burton as, 'very insular. She rode a race and she went home, whereas we rode, and then stopped and chatted. You never got a chance to be close to her. I don't know who her friends were. Nim Carline was a friend, but I don't know who among the girls.'

Beryl Burton liked to project herself as a typical Yorkshirewoman, and here the journalists were happily complicit. 'A simple lady, a kind thoughtful soul; maybe a typical Yorkshire person,' was the view of the writer Mike Breckon. Writers worked the White Rose clichés to the full: a terrier, a Tyke, a down-to-earth, self-deprecating person. Burton also liked to play up the image of the tight-fisted Tyke. (She is not alone: when I helped Lizzie Deignan with her autobiography, she noted that her family liked to save money, and commented with tongue-in-cheek that this was a characteristic typical of Yorkshire folk.) Immediately after crossing the line in a national championship time trial, Burton told Bernard Thompson that she had spotted some cheap potatoes and was going back to buy some. Another writer described seeing her make a U-turn at the start of a race to pick up a penny from the road.

A delightful story about Burton's frugal attitude comes from Peter Whitfield's *12 Champions*. 'I had a day off,' she told him. 'It was a lovely sunny day and I was going to do all sorts of jobs, then I thought, "Blow it, I'm going out on the bike." I had picked up a lovely rabbit, just got its head knocked in; I thought, "Lovely, that's tonight's tea," and stuffed it in my saddle-bag. I dropped down Bishopdale then towards Middleham, up a small rise, a car comes the other way, a woman jumps out, mutters something about "too late", started running the way I was going. I could see why: a pheasant in the road, looked as though they may have killed it. I gave a quick look back, car on my tail, thought, "Blast," car went by; I did a quick sprint but she just beat me to it. I said, "Are you taking it?" She said yes, so I said, "I suppose I shouldn't be greedy, I've already got a rabbit".'

This was not the only roadkill story she told: there was another, about using the rabbit for rabbit sandwiches, in a speech to British sportswriters in 1967. Burton relished telling the tales, but this is not solely about saving money; it also stems from a lust for every little victory over whatever life throws up, a need to put one over on the world at every opportunity. It was the same spirit which led Burton, in a speech at an RTTC dinner, to sarcastically express, 'thanks to the men in unisex events. I know they love to look at their start sheets and see my name there.'

There were other stories that expressed her dry, unemotional side: when she had to wait for a train at a level crossing and took advantage to nip into a hairdresser's for a quick trim, or when she told another Yorkshire cyclist, Sid Barras, that her rainbow jerseys 'made great dusters'. These are straight out of the unrelentingly macho copybook originally written by Nim Carline. Following that template made it seem normal for her to ride 113 miles from Yorkshire to Rutland for an interview with Thompson, with a crosswind both ways. The same could be said of another occasion, when she was cycling home from London, went onto the A1 motorway by mistake and then – the punchline – was fined £3 by police.

Burton liked to parade her toughness, in public at any rate. At the end of 1976 she told Dennis Donovan: 'We're getting softer. We're pandering all the time. Distances come down, circuits get easier, that's why [the riders] get a shock when they go abroad.' 'The predominant impression I got was that she was tough,' was Whitfield's verdict when the documentary maker Ray Pascoe asked him to sum up Burton: 'there was no time-wasting in her life whatsoever.'

As we have seen in her relationship with Denise, Beryl Burton liked to get her own way, and was not used to being gainsaid. Her brother Jeffrey recalled that she would 'play hell' with him over his smoking. On club runs, once she had found her feet, she was an assertive presence. 'I get fed up with the sound of my own voice sometimes,' she said. 'When some of the young lads come out on club runs with no mudguards, I refuse to let them come anywhere near me. They get told to go to the back and stay there. I get really annoyed about that. I can get wet enough when I've got mudguards and a cape on, let alone them spraying water over everybody.'

Thompson felt that Burton was virtually impossible to read as she raced, unlike most other cyclists, who had no inhibitions about betraying their effort. 'One of my unmet challenges in time trial action photography is that of Beryl Burton,' he wrote. 'I must have taken hundreds of photographs of "The Queen" but am rarely satisfied with the results. "BB" has a solid style that displays very little of the effort she is putting into her riding; her face appears to be impassive more often than not, thus most of my pictures of Beryl are to me unsatisfying portraits of the woman who has done more for British cycling than anyone.'

As we saw in chapter 3, Burton's apparent lack of effort as she rode went back to her very earliest days as a cyclist, when she did not want Charlie and her other clubmates to know how hard she was working; later, she must have realised that this impassivity was a potent psychological weapon. It was also related to the habit among British 'testers' of using a big gear – with as little wasted effort and as much concentration as possible – and it became a key part of her race persona until the very end of her career.

Similarly hardcore was Burton's unwavering conviction that she worked harder than everyone else, be that at Carline's farm, on her bike, or in the home. 'I'm not crying men down,' she said, 'but most come home from work, have their meal put in front of them and that's them finished for the evening except for their training. You know [as a woman] that you come home, start the meal, then it's washing up, then there's other things. Even if you go training you've then got your washing and mending, your windows to clean and your baking to do. To me, those are the things you have to do, it's not a matter of not having the time. I've been brought up that you find time. Nothing is neglected because of racing and training.' It was not just men but also her younger female rivals about whom she said this. Again, this was about proving herself, making space for little victories over the world, and – as her career declined – hinting at a reason why those medals weren't coming her way as readily as they used to.

As with Eddy Merckx – and later with the Frenchwoman Jeannie Longo – Burton's dominance meant that those who followed her fortunes ran out of ways to describe her success. The tone of the reporting suggests that Burton's victories were unsurprising, inevitable: a national championship might be described as 'duly' won; one report remarked of her 1966 national road race win, 'Burton again, of course', adding, 'so much in command was the Morley lass that the others might as well not have started'. This attitude was not limited to the men who tended to produce the reports. Even Eileen

Sheridan wrote that Burton was totting up championship wins 'with monotonous regularity'.

The writers were sorely tested when it came to dreaming up new variants on 'Burton wins again': 'The unstoppable Beryl Burton is the only person who has not lost count of the number of titles she has won' (1969); 'Beryl is such an obvious favourite for whatever she rides that we often wonder whether she gets bored with her continual successes, secretly longing for the days when she passes her peak and comes down to the level of the girls she now dominates… what else can we do but offer our consolation to [her rivals]?' (1970). Or, as Bernard Thompson put it poetically (also in 1970): 'Just as surely and predictably as the cock crew on a neighbouring farm on a warm summer morn near Bicester, so Beryl Burton collected her 13th RTTC gold medal at the distance in the 27th national championship "25".'

This total dominance was eventually seen as stifling the sport. Burton's '100' title win in 1970 was described in *Cycling* as 'leaving unrippled the ditchwater inevitability which permeates women's championship racing'. The writer of that article, Les Woodland, added that the description should be taken not as a criticism of Burton, but as a compliment. There are obvious parallels with the way that journalists dealt with the dominance of Eddy Merckx: 'Who will be the man to beat Merckx?' or 'The Merckx story continues.'

The default view was that Burton was somehow inhuman, 'a machine'. After one 1965 national championship, a report stated, 'It's hard to imagine The Burton ever being beaten.' With this dehumanisation came a portrayal of her as both aggressive and devoid of emotion. Coverage of her second world pursuit title was headlined 'Remorseless'; a report on a victory in the Isle of Man in 1960 described a 'ruthless,

In full flight,1985 RTTC ‘10’ championship

18 The crowds throng, but Burton will fall short: Mersey RCC 24-hour, 1969.

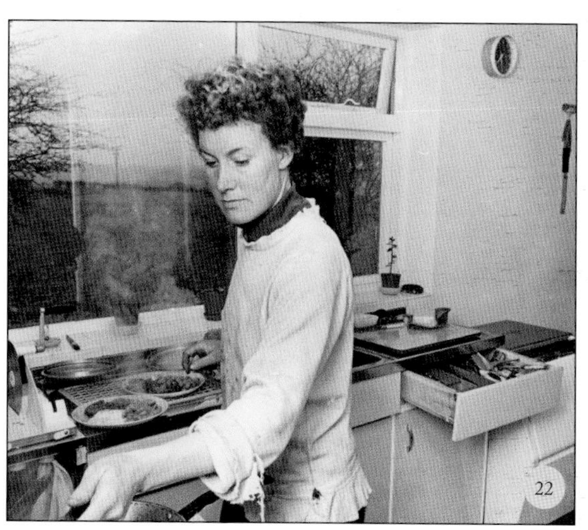

Domestic bliss, tribulation on the road: left, with a young Denise; top right, mother punctures, daughter waits, two-up time trial, Bedford, mid-70s; right middle; with Denise, centre, and Carol Barton, right, on the podium after the national championship finish in 1976; bottom right, the sparsely furnished Burton kitchen.

The 80s and beyond: Top left, Burton (right) meets the great campaigner Eileen Gray (left) at the RTTC National '10' title in 1985; bottom left, selecting images from *Cycling* magazine's archive for her autobiography; top right, remembered in the Morley town-centre mural, which seems to replicate the spirit of this photograph from the late 1960s, below.

Morley
Bloom
25

26

'BB' as most remember her, smiling with the Sunday morning time trial safely behind her.

unemotional efficiency', and another victory was supposedly taken 'with contemptuous ease'.

If Burton was not entirely the Yorkshire Tyke of cliché, or the unemotional winning machine the writers described, what was she really like? One writer, perhaps eliding racing style and personality, described her as 'blunt and unimaginative'. That seems a little unfair. Burton had her own hinterland, and she was clearly open to new impressions. She told Bernard Thompson of a trip to Morocco: 'We slept in the open, visited the market places, saw the locals carrying entrails of animals home for their dinner, cutting up live animals for sale. It's gruesome, cruel and often sickening, but it is how they live and I like to know how other people live.' That is not the comment of a woman who is only interested in life inside her own bubble.

She was also aware of the issues around her trip to South Africa in 1965, at a time when the question of sport's relations with the apartheid régime was beginning to hit public consciousness. The following passage occurs in her memoirs: 'one day I saw a group of black men being rounded up and searched in the street by police. I thought it repugnant that they should be under suspicion because of their proximity to the alleged offence, but was even more appalled by their public humiliation.'

Burton had her less serious side. *Sporting Cyclist* in 1960 described her as a person who 'loves to dance. She's very fond of music and is the "Top 20" programme's most devoted listener. Rock'n'roll, light opera – Beryl finds something in all of them. I would say that Elvis, Cliff Richard and Lonnie Donegan have quite a high rating among her pin-ups.' The journalist Phil Liggett recalled her love of dancing. 'I remember dancing with her at the Sports Writers' Association dinner in the 70s and honestly, she threw me around the floor so fast, I thought she was going to kill me. It was like being hugged by a giant panda!'

She would go to watch an opera once or twice a winter, having picked up the taste for it from Eileen Gray on a trip to East Germany; she would listen to it in the kitchen as well. The co-writer of her autobiography, Colin Kirby, recalled her discussing the merits of various tenors, not a sign of someone with a merely casual interest. More improbably, she apparently liked Westerns, too. She also loved clothes, and could spend hours wandering around shop windows comparing prices and styles. Peter Whitfield recalled Burton in her mid-40s as being 'attractive in a tomboyish way', but Alf Engers saw another side to her: he recalled her as 'very feminine', a woman who 'liked girly things', who would wear a wig on a special occasion because she wasn't delighted with her short curly racing hairstyle.

The picture Denise Burton-Cole paints of her mother is of a constantly active woman, who felt that every hour of every day should be filled with occupation. 'She was always busy, always doing something. She wasn't very good at sitting down and relaxing. She would sometimes listen to music, but she would listen while she was knitting. She used to knit for everyone: the lads in the club, I had a lot of knitted stuff, Dad did, Nim did. She was very good at it – she knitted a lot of stuff for both my children – really beautiful stuff as well.'

Knitting in the way that Beryl Burton would do it must have taken up plenty of her time and imagination. For a cyclist, it has one major attraction: it is sedentary, permitting the mind to remain active while the body rests. It is also rhythmic, which makes it a soothing way to recover from exercise. As Burton-Cole says, it was far from a casual occupation for her mother: 'It was very intricate what she was doing. It must have taken her mind off everything else, [although] you would only concentrate if it was very intricate or around the sleeves – when it was only rows on the back or front of a jumper you can let your mind wander a bit.'

The complexity of the stitches, designs and different wools appealed to a side of Burton which was largely hidden from the public: her attention to detail was close to that of a control freak. 'She was a perfectionist in almost everything she did,' said Burton-Cole. '[Before a race] things had to be just right, in their order.' As her mother told Bernard Thompson, 'I look after my clothes, it's a thing with me. I always make sure we all turn out for every race in clean clothes, tracksuits, the lot. Shoes! There are dozens of pairs in our house and I used to clean them all until a short while ago [this is in 1974] when Denise began to chime in a little.'

That attention to detail went to extremes, as Burton-Cole recalls: 'The thing is with my mum, she did the ironing. She ironed everything, knickers, everything – we used to say, "But nobody sees them." It was funny. Even my dad used to say, 'You don't have to iron my socks.'" This was in part a generational thing; many women in the 50s and 60s felt that they were judged on the standard of their 'housekeeping'. However, given how much standing all that ironing would have involved, you would have expected a serious racing cyclist to have skimped on it.

Obsessive ironing apart, the Burtons' domestic life was pared down to the point that almost everything revolved around cycling. The household had no telephone or television, not – as some imagine – from a desire to save money, but because it would have been a distraction. Beryl famously said that if you put her in front of the television she would never get away from it. 'She consciously didn't have one because it would have been a total time waster as she saw it,' says Burton-Cole. 'She knew that she would have had an obsession, so to solve that problem we didn't have one… She'd go and visit my auntie, her sister, she'd go visit her mum and dad – she used to call at their houses on a training run, so I'm assuming part of this training run was watching a TV programme… As for the telephone, that was because she didn't want people phoning her up when she was doing something.'

Burton had other fetishes. We have seen that she didn't like Denise sitting on her knee because it would affect her legs, but in addition she was unwilling to have a bath – or go swimming – from April to September, because she felt it would weaken her legs. Instead, she would just have a wet wash with flannel and soap. By 1985 she wasn't even walking a great deal as 'it interferes with my legs too much'. (Bradley Wiggins did the same before winning the 2012 Tour de France).

Beryl Burton's perfectionism and desire to keep things just so meant that the Burton house was an extremely neat one, according to Denise (apart from the garden in the home at Woodlesford, which went unweeded for years, as we saw earlier). Beryl herself said that if Charlie left a piece of cycling equipment lying around, it would go straight into the garage. 'Our house, honestly, people used to think she'd tidied up for them to go there, [but] it was *always like that*," said Denise. "It was like a *show* house – it was so tidy, it was so minimalist' – the emphasis in her voice hints at a vivid, and perhaps unwelcome, recollection – 'without any ornaments or anything, pictures on the wall.'

A photograph of Burton in her kitchen reflects this. All the surfaces are devoid of anything other than the bare necessities – a gas lighter, and a utensil or two – and some pot plants, which are clearly kept well trimmed. The walls are bare. 'It wasn't a happy, cluttered, comfy, easygoing existence – it was very, very tidy and clean. She had to be in control,' Denise recalled. 'Her mum, my grandma, was a cleaner for some very rich people, so maybe it came from that, and she spent time in a convent. They would have been minimalist, clean and tidy. For a large part of her upbringing it would have been like that.'

What's clear is that Beryl Burton had the ability to concentrate on one activity to the exclusion of all else. Denise Burton-Cole said, 'she had to focus – but everything else was put out of the way for her to focus on what she had to do... Nobody else existed.' As Charlie said: 'When she decided to do something she did it and to hell with everyone else.' That single-mindedness was what gave her the ability to time trial so brilliantly: churning that big gear so efficiently demands powers of concentration that border on the obsessive. Burton was only ever focused on the present: she struggled to remember past victories (although she was not alone in that – many greats feel the same way). Bernard Thompson wrote that Burton could hardly recall the host countries where she had won her world titles, while the question of whether there was 'one event in particular she could recall' evoked a 'blank look and a long pause'. Thompson suggested the legendary Otley CC 12-hour – "I suppose it would be something like that," responds Burton *without enthusiasm* [author's italics]'.

Burton appears to have had no detailed memories of actual races. 'Once a championship is won or a competition record broken, it is almost immediately forgotten, and I am looking forward to the next event,' she said, adding that, 'When I started, I could never see as far ahead as a world championship, for instance. At first I was possessed only of the urge to win the club's "10". I wasn't even aware that there was any other kind of race to ride. Someone suggested I ride an open event; that was a new one on me.... These were all stepping stones, each had to be stepped upon before going on to the next.' This might explain why Sid Barras's story about the rainbow jerseys being turned into dusters seems like only half a joke, or why another contemporary described Burton getting her world championship medals out of the biscuit tin where she also kept her buttons.

It was the peripheral incidents that stuck in her mind: the episode from the 1962 world championship in Italy when she was dragged away from her dinner to ride her pursuit qualifier was one she spoke of in a 1986 television interview; she remembered putting the steak in a plastic bag so she could eat it later. She also recalled the training accident at the Parc des Princes in 1964, after which her hand was strapped to the bars because of the painkilling injection, which meant she couldn't grip.

Thompson also noted that when Burton rode to visit him, and he asked her how long the ride had taken, 'She had not the faintest notion, she could not even remember accurately what time she had left home and certainly did not know what time it was when she arrived. It bore absolutely no importance.' But on the other hand, she cared enough about her bike to have bottle caps specially fixed on the ends of the wheel spindles to keep the rain out of them.

Denise Burton-Cole's recollections of her mother could suggest a lack of empathy with other people. But Beryl Burton was clearly capable of a thoughtful gesture: when her old rival Shirley Killingbeck returned to cycling after 12 and a half years off, Burton sent her a national championship entry form, to prompt her to race again. Ann Battersby, (née

Pallister), recalled how she was taken under the Burtons' wing – she was a year older than Denise – invited out on a club run, escorted around the Yorkshire countryside, and then dropped off at home again. 'They were fantastic. They took us everywhere. The calendar was thin, so you'd be racing all over the country, so they just put me in the car. They really looked after me.'

Another example was when Maggie Thompson beat both Beryl and Denise in the national pursuit championship in 1977: 'Never having been in the No. 1 position before I was totally elated, but hadn't a clue what to do,' she wrote to me. 'Beryl whispered to me to wave to the crowd to acknowledge their cheers. That was such a kind gesture from her in my moment of awkwardness.' The point is probably this: these were situations that Burton the cyclist would have encountered herself, and where she was in control.

Generally Burton is remembered as uncompromisingly forthright: 'She was very blunt, very, very blunt, said what she thought,' recalled a cycling friend, Barbara Penrice. 'It was how she spoke about people. She wasn't nasty or spiteful… I don't think she had much sympathy for people in general.' Eileen Cropper matched that with her direct way of speaking: 'She called a spade a spade. She was very much her own person, did what she wanted to do.' Alf Engers remembered her at an RTTC Champions' Night, observing Jacques Anquetil's fashionably clad wife Janine and commenting, 'I've seen Jacques and he's with a right flashy piece.'

The journalist Dennis Donovan recalled that Burton was more than direct after he had let himself go to seed: 'When I was overtaken by middle-aged sloth, [she said], "Dennis, you are disgusting!" She wasn't being unkind, just truthful, and [she] didn't like being around people who had let their bodies go to waste, or waist in my case.' However, Donovan also recalled that Burton was one of the few stars who took the trouble to travel to his official retirement party as *Cycling Weekly* commemorated his long career in cycling journalism.

Other anecdotes show a woman slightly out of kilter with the world around her, yet utterly determined to do things her own way. Barbara Penrice recalled riding out into the Dales for a Christmas lunch with the club on a foul day, to a pub which was 'icy cold'. 'She said, "Come with me up to this bathroom, I'm going to change into something else."' The rest of her clubmates were sitting by the fire in the bar, drying out as best they could, but Burton – the planner, the thinker – had brought a change of clothes in her saddle-bag. 'Get that cloth and rub me down,' she instructed her clubmate, who was dumbfounded as Burton simply stripped her things off in front of her.

'She was slightly contemptuous of other people who didn't have this great drive to succeed, that ambition, that self-belief,' observed Peter Whitfield. 'One of her favourite sayings about people was "They don't know they are alive"… [It was] one of her favourite put-downs when she was trying to indicate that people weren't living properly, and they had no determination.' Another refrain of Burton's had two words: 'no point'. She would, she said, never go to a world championship if she did not think she could win, 'there would be no point for me.' She did not feel calm when racing; in fact, she thrived on the nervous tension that racing inspired. 'If it was [a tranquil experience] there would be no point. I wouldn't even go.' On another occasion, she said, '"I enjoy absolutely everything I do, riding a bike, housework, racing, working in Nim's rhubarb sheds. If you don't enjoy something you are doing there is no point!'

Burton had had a life opportunity unfairly snatched from her at the age of 11. She had been given more than a glimpse of life as a bedriddden invalid. That would amply explain why she might feel a compulsion to prove to herself that she was 'alive'. If she urgently wanted to profit from every instant life offered her, that would lie behind the intensity of her dancing, the need for every hour of every day to be filled with something worthwhile. If she did things by halves, there would be 'no point'.

Hence the lasting impression that what she truly enjoyed was simply riding her bike, as opposed to the races in which she felt impelled to compete. Burton's final words to Dennis Donovan were an invitation to come and stay with her and Charlie – similar to the kindness she showed Maggie Gordon-Thompson – and an admonishment to begin riding his bike again. That is a reminder that one thing that should never be overlooked is her sheer, irrepressible love of riding her bike, for the things that had drawn her to it in the first place: freedom, independence, discovery of the world.

She would speak warmly of the moment when the last race of the season was over and that heavy winter bike on which she rode to visit Bernard Thompson would be pulled out of store. 'At that very moment I cease to think of training or racing at all, from then on I ride the bike as distinct from training on it. I always prefer to be alone; I feel much more relaxed. I go out on a cycle to relieve mental tension. It's the most relaxing pastime possible. I often get wound up with people and circumstances but once on a bike I unload it all and feel much better.'

Chapter 12

The Best All Rounder

26.665mph: Beryl Burton's fastest average speed for any of her 25 British Best All Rounder titles, set in 1976.

The Road Time Trials Council's national prize presentation ceremony on 7 January 1984 was intricately choreographed. The prizes for the previous year, 1983, were handed out following a formula that dated back at least to the 1960s, the glory years when Tour de France winners such as Jacques Anquetil or Louison Bobet might turn up at the Albert Hall to present the prizes in front of a cheering crowd of club cyclists from all around the country. The main change since the Champions' Night of the 1960s was that the orchestra had been replaced by a 'Disc Jockey' in 1984, and that the ceremony had moved from London to Derby.

The instructions can be found in the late Bernard Thompson's archive, currently held by Cycling Time Trials, the successor organisation to the RTTC. The neatly typed sheets of paper painstakingly list the citations for the champions, state precisely where they will walk, where the various spotlights are to be pointed, and where the compère will stand. The copies carry a handwritten note at the top: *Bernard Thompson's – hands off!*

The schedule for the evening was laid out in detail. At 8.50pm 'approximately', after the completion of the Interval Dance, the Disc Jockey was to ask the company to return to their seats. At 9pm 'precisely', the presentation ceremony began; the guest of honour was Dr Mary Peters, the Olympic pentathlon gold medallist in 1972. The trophies were placed 'on the left side of the stage in the order which they are to be presented,' with two assistants delegated to ensure that Peters was given them in the correct order. The prizewinners were to assemble 'at Point A', with two marshals to ensure they came on the stage in the right order. The Champions and Best All Rounders were at Point D. Certain prize winners were to have their names announced after they arrived on stage; others before. Some returned to Point C, others to Point B. Some returned to Point A via points B and C, others went to Point D via points B, C and A to be given further trophies.

However, the rigid protocol had been turned on its head in one critical way. The men's Best All Rounder winner – in essence Britain's leading male time triallist – was always announced last, as the climax to the evening. On this occasion, Ian Cammish, who had won the men's BAR, was brought on stage to receive his trophy before the winner of the women's contest. The climax of the evening was the celebration of Beryl Burton's 25th successive victory in the women's season-long competition. It was a unique achievement, one that will probably never be repeated, and it had cost her dearly.

After Cammish – men's '50' and '100' champion and Best All Rounder for the fourth year in a row – had left the stage to sit with the other champions, Will Townsend, the RTTC's former chair, took to the stage (from Point A), to read a lengthy citation. Townsend began by praising Charlie Burton and inviting him to join his wife (referred to as Mrs C Burton in the table plan) on the stage.

'This Magnificent Morley Marvel,' Townsend read, had 'forced herself upon the national scene in 1957, when she was second in the 100-miles championship and went on to a fifth place in the Women's BAR... how little any of us realised that we had seen the sporting birth of the greatest British woman cyclist of all time.'

Townsend went on to list Burton's world championships and her greatest records, and concluded by hailing her 70 national time trial championships, 49 time trial competition records and 25 Best All Rounder titles. Given the long-standing friction between the RTTC and the British Cycling Federation, it was understandable – if rather petty – that he did not trouble to enumerate her national pursuit and road race titles as well. He concluded, 'Accompanied by her husband Charlie, I call upon you to receive and acclaim on the occasion of her silver jubilee of Women's Best All Rounder triumphs, cycling's Golden Girl.'

As Burton's name was read out, the stage lighting was lowered, and the spotlight shone on her as she made her way to the stage; a projector was switched on to display her picture on the screen at the rear of the dais. In her speech, she paid tribute to the runner-up Sue Fenwick and to the sacrifices that Charlie had made, and added that she had spent much of the season convinced that the victory would be beyond her. Her final word was a classic quip: 'I don't know about next season. It's not me, it's the engraver – he's retired.' After Beryl had been presented with a special golden necklace, she and Charlie were carried shoulder high around the hall. The standing ovation from the crowd of 850 lasted five minutes.

Late that night, the Burtons and the rest of the Morley Cycling Club met in the Midland, the ornate, neo-classical early Victorian hotel near the station. In the small hours, Burton ended up sitting on the floor, munching cake and sipping apple juice. Thus was marked the final act of a quarter century of being hailed as the country's best female time triallist. It was a feat unparalleled in cycling at the time, and quite possibly in endurance sport. Derby's Assembly Rooms had not witnessed the absolute end of Beryl Burton's career that January evening, but this was the final climactic moment.

For the previous seven years, however, Burton's performances had been in gradual decline as age and injuries took their toll. In racing terms, she still ruled the time trialling world, but as far as international competition was concerned, the Great Britain management had lost patience with her; a new generation of younger women with quicker legs and sharper reflexes had come along, including Denise. The Lancastrian Mandy Jones was the best of the newcomers: in 1980 she landed a bronze medal in the road race on a climber's course at Sallanches, and came close to a medal in the pursuit. Even as they attempted to push her aside, however, Jones and other women racers all held Burton up as a role model.

Leading up to the national pursuit championship in 1977, where she fell to Denise in the semi-final, Beryl Burton had been having doubts about whether she was still suited to the discipline. She had reduced her usual volume of training miles – at the suggestion of national coach Val Rushworth – and at the age of 40, she was increasingly aware of how difficult it was to adapt from time trialling to the intense four-minute effort. She did beat both Maggie Gordon-Thompson and Denise at the WCRA championship in Birmingham, but there was no place for her in the Great Britain team that travelled to the world championships in Venezuela.

There was another trip in the offing, however: late in 1977, Burton was invited to ride a stage race in the US city of Tucson the following spring. She always had a penchant for slightly outlandish challenges that involved travelling outside the UK (such as her Grand Prix des Nations ride in 1968 and her trip to South Africa in 1965), and according to Charlie she also had her sights set on a place at the World's in 1978; some early season racing in good weather would further that goal. In preparation, she continued training well after the time trialling season ended. That November, having ridden over 50 miles from Harrogate across the Dales to Ingleton, she was 'scorching towards Skipton' – as she put it – down the A65 on her way home, when a car turned across her path. As she observed, she had just gone past a roadside snack bar, and had briefly contemplated stopping; had she done so, the next few years might have been very different.

Burton remained unconscious for several minutes, the time it took for an ambulance to arrive and to transport her the dozen miles or so to the Airedale Hospital near Keighley. The list of injuries was horrific: two compound fractures of her right leg, her left leg badly bruised and swollen, a cracked right shoulder blade, and head injuries which required almost 60 stitches, including one ear which had been almost torn off and had to be re-attached.

This was the first of four major crashes that wrecked those final years. Burton, however, made Monty Python's Black Knight look soft; the tough persona she had forged for herself permitted nothing less. Within five days of her 1977 crash she was sitting up. As she lay in her hospital bed, she told journalist Colin Willcock in predictable style that 'it could have been worse', and complained that she wouldn't get her Christmas cake made in time. Still more predictably, when she saw Eileen Gray for the first time after the accident, one of her first questions was about the RTTC's newly instituted 10-mile time trial championship. At the RTTC awards dinner the following January, the trophies were brought to her by the organisation's three most senior officials as she sat at her table with her leg in plaster. She was discharged from hospital after three weeks, but it was March before she resumed training, having set a target of returning to racing on 22 April.

She and Charlie bought a rowing machine and a stationary bike, and she did her household tasks on crutches. The muscles in her calf began to reform, but did so at such speed that her lower leg developed an infection under the plaster. To avoid the vagaries of the English spring weather, Burton trained in Majorca and Arizona – the invitation to the Tucson stage race still stood even though she was unable to race – but although she returned to fitness, the effects of the crash would be felt throughout her 1978 season. Her victory in the '25' championship – ahead of Denise, who was recovering from a broken toe – prompted the headline 'Beryl Burton just won't be beaten!' (The field that year was large, at 118, following an upsurge in the numbers of women racing; *Cycling* magazine put this down in part to the fact that Burton had become less active in international competition.)

After winning the '25', Burton told Ken Evans that 'until recently, my right leg just didn't seem as though it belonged to me when it was pressing on the pedals'. Her shoe plates had had to be changed because her broken leg had been re-set at a slightly different angle compared to its previous alignment. Even so, she was also victorious in the inaugural '10' championship on the Fosse Way, with Denise and Carole Gandy tying for the silver medal. 'The specialist has told me to keep exercising the leg, but not to overdo it. But how do you know when you are overdoing it?' she joked to Bernard Thompson.

At the RTTC prize presentation in January 1979, she made a point of walking up to the microphone with an exaggerated limp; a few months later, in June 1979, she landed her 21st 25-mile title, joking that she had wanted to climb off because of the pain. In second place was Shirley Killingbeck, who under her maiden name, Jo Bowers, had finished second to Burton in 1963. The margin between the pair had changed little over the years: 2min 6sec in 1963, 2min 40sec 16 years later. Killingbeck still viewed her old rival as impossible to overcome: 'The only chance I've got of beating her is if she's not fit, and if I did beat her I would rather she be fit and me fitter.' In fact, Burton was far from satisfied: 'I've done so little consistent training, my body feels as if it's the end of March,' she said.

'Beryl appears determined to convince herself and those who follow the time trial scene that she is not faltering,' wrote Mick Gambling in *Cycling*. That year also saw Burton take her 21st women's Best All Rounder win – in its 32-year history the contest had had only nine different winners. As the 1980s dawned, she was still time trialling as fast as the fastest men on her better days. She remained dominant in national women's time trial championships in 1980, landing a clean sweep of the '10', '25', '50' and '100' titles, and the Best All Rounder for the 22nd time. However, she was increasingly becoming limited to time trialling; road racing and pursuiting now looked to be the province of younger women such as Mandy Jones. Still, as far as time trialling went, the younger generation might push Burton hard over 10 miles, but for the moment they lacked the stamina and the skill to beat her over longer distances.

As other avenues closed, Burton was still looking for new challenges beyond time trialling, no matter how outlandish they might seem. In autumn 1980, she travelled to Australia to ride the Melbourne to Warrnambool handicap, a 167-mile race founded in 1895. She finished 1hr 34min behind the winner, amateur John Hine, in spite of injuries from a crash 10 days earlier, most notably a hugely swollen left hand which resulted in a permanent purple scar. X-rays showed no fractures, but those present believed that she had chipped a bone in her shoulder and fractured a bone in her hand. It was far from ideal for a cyclist who already felt that physically she was 'something of a wreck': her knees and back were feeling the pace, so too her breathing.

Burton started with a half-hour handicap – in the middle-marker group, with only the fastest men behind her — and rode strongly in her group of about 30 for 45 miles. Later, when heavy rain and strong winds hit the race, the strain of the injuries told, after which she rode the final 100-plus miles largely alone. 'Dozens of highly fancied opponents, including some of her critics, abandoned,' wrote the president of the Australian Cycling Council, Bill Long. 'Two officials asked her if she wanted to quit, but received the same answer, "get lost".' When the winner, Hine, crossed the finish line, she was still 22 miles distant, and by the time she did finish most of the crowds and officials had left for home; she was outside the official one-hour time cut, but still registered as the first woman to finish. It took her an age to get warm again afterwards.

Later that year, Burton described the race in a BBC interview: 'To my shock, about two days before, someone said, "Don't forget, you carry all your own drinks on the bike, all your own spares, and if you have any mechanical trouble there is no outside assistance whatsoever." I sort of froze on the spot. I thought, "Oh dear, it'll be all cold drinks." They kept emphasising, "Don't forget to take plenty of food and eat it within the first 40 miles, because if not you will take a real hammering later on." I was getting quite worried about this food business, and I packed the pockets of my racing jersey with all sorts of different things to eat. And when I finished I had most of the stuff still in my back pockets – I'd just existed on the drinks.'

This was because she was unable to grip the bars with her swollen hand, which made it difficult to eat with the other hand while riding. This sounds like hell, but as she tells the story, Burton has the tone of a woman who relished the whole challenge, painful and extreme though it may have been. At the age of 43, she still wanted adventure and novelty, and still yearned to test herself. If there was any consolation for her lowly placing in the race, it was the chance to visit the Sydney opera house.

For 1981, Burton announced that she would be making a comeback to international competition in her 45th year; she had her sights set on gaining a place in a sponsored club to enable her to finance trips to the Leicester track to train for the pursuit. After three years, her leg finally felt as if it had returned to normal, and at the end of the 1980 season she had been feeling 'tremendous'. She had good cause to be motivated: after almost a quarter of a century, Britain's cycling women were beginning to get what they needed in order to compete on the international stage: a salaried national coach in Rushworth and a season-long national women's road race series to showcase their talents. This had nine events – more than it does in the 21st century – lasting from the end of April to mid August.

There was another boost: Jones's bronze medal in the world road race championships at Sallanches in the French Alps, the first British world road race medal – for either sex – since Bernadette Swinnerton in 1969. The Lancastrian Jones had essentially gone about her training in the Burton way; her equivalent of Nim Carline, in terms of training at least, was the hard-riding professional Ian Greenhalgh, and she had worked independently of the BCF, as Burton had done before her.

Burton had cause for optimism. In the newly instituted 10-mile time trial championship, she had been pitted directly against the GB team's road racing and pursuiting women and had managed to beat all of them, including Jones. 'Those girls have been going faster than I ever did [in the pursuit], but I've never ridden on the new surface at Leicester,' she noted. (In a move that made the track faster in the short term, but not sustainable in the long-term, the outdoor Leicester velodrome had been resurfaced with timber in 1978.) A further incentive was that the world road race and track championships would be held in the UK in 1982.

Burton estimated that it would cost about £500 to fund her racing for the 1981 season, mainly to cover the cost of travelling to the track in Leicester to race – hence her need to join a sponsored club. Eventually, however, she opted to remain with the Morley, after a local private donor made some money available for her to pursue her ambitions. Her plans came to nothing: outside time trialling, the 1981 season was a disaster, affected by a heavy crash early on while she was riding a two-up team time trial with her Morley clubmate Malcolm Cowgill; she touched his wheel and fell, cutting her head deeply, breaking two ribs and developing an infection within the bruising to her hip. Even so, she continued to race, building to the national '25' and '10' championships, where she narrowly overcame Jones.

Illness was increasingly affecting her form; this was hardly surprising given that she was in her mid-40s and was constantly having to fight back to fitness from one major crash after another. By early 1982 she was experiencing difficulty in breathing during races; she had begun using an asthma inhaler before racing, and was competing against medical advice. That summer she experienced defeats in both the 10- and 50-mile titles; Jones, building up to the World's at Goodwood in Sussex, was the winner on both occasions. Although Burton triumphed in the '25', she now seemed vulnerable for the first time since the 1950s. To her annoyance, she was not selected for the world track championships in Leicester. 'She expected to be picked because she was still winning; she was more or less an ambassador, and she should have been picked. She was upset she wasn't picked, definitely,' said Denise Burton-Cole.

Instead of racing, Burton turned up at the East Midlands track to be interviewed by BBC television. At 45, her jaw was still as determined, the curls were still there, but her face had been tanned by constant exposure to wind and rain and there was a slightly hardened look about her, like a statue. In the interview, she confesses that she is 'not a very good spectator, I can't really get excited'. 'You're still competing,' the interviewer says; 'you're doing well I hear.' The reply is laconic – 'not too bad' – and he chides her for her modesty: after all, she has just won a '50' by seven minutes. (She had also just beaten Jones in a '25', shortly before the latter took the rainbow jersey of world road race champion.)

By 1982, the IOC had finally agreed to admit women cyclists to the Olympics, beginning with the 1984 Games in Los Angeles, and the interviewer can't resist the question: what about competing at 47 in the Olympic Games? At this, Burton opens up and starts to smile: 'It's in the back of my mind. I think the thing is to forget how old people are. To me if they are producing the speed or the rides or the times or whatever, age shouldn't be taken into account...'

Whatever she may have wanted, Burton came nowhere near a place in the Games. Her road racing ability had always been dependent on the sheer power she needed to get rid of the opposition; she had never found this straightforward at international level, and the new generation of British women were all faster and sharper. The pursuit was also closed to her, as she had lost her ability to switch over from time trialling, so here again the younger women had superseded her. In terms of racing objectives, she was left with the Best All Rounder and national time trial championships.

The BBAR had been founded by *Cycling* magazine in April 1930, with a perpetual shield and a prize of 25 guineas. It had been taken over by the RTTC after the Second World War, the women's competition had been instituted in 1948, first won by Susie Rimmington. The standings were calculated by working out the average speed for each of the three qualifying distances (50, 100 and 12 hours for men; 24, 50 and 100 miles for women) and taking an average of the three figures. It has always been a homespun competition. For many years the speeds were worked out on a three foot long slide rule in the house of the RTTC competition secretary Tom Barlow; at one time the certificates, some 500 across four competitions (men's, women's and juniors) were written out by hand by Burton's time trialling rival Christine Minto.

The format was a perpetual topic for debate, although when the RTTC got around to examining it at the end of 1976 they found no reason to change it. The BAR's simplicity and ubiquity were at the core of its appeal; you could travel to a fast course if you wanted fast times or you could ride locally if you merely wanted to qualify. When told that the BAR was 'unfair', the long-standing master of the slide rule Barlow answered, 'It's been said so many times. Of course it's unfair. Life is unfair. You find a better compromise.' Attempts were made over the years to get the country's best time triallists to compete over the fastest or the hardest courses, but such moves proved of relatively limited appeal. The original format, on the other hand, made the competition accessible to every time triallist prepared to ride the distances involved. The focus was firmly on each individual's time – the founding principle of the sport.

Feature pieces in *Cycling* questioning the validity of the competition were a staple of the winter months, usually accompanied by a picture of a rider being borne down upon by a threatening motor vehicle. One article in 1976 stated that time triallists were 'asking for start times to coincide with the greatest traffic flow … moving out at risk to life and limb to benefit from passing traffic … [getting] following cars [to slow down] overtaking vehicles to "store up" a handy slower moving queue of them…' It could be a dangerous business: the time triallist Ken Workman described an occasion when he was pulling out of the slip road onto the A1 on the 'legendary' V134 Boro' course when, as he nipped in behind a lorry, Burton closed at 'a great rate of knots'; they nearly collided. 'Had Beryl not possessed good bike handling skills she (and probably me also) would have hit the deck in front of another rapidly approaching juggernaut.'

There were safer roads, but no simpler alternatives to the BAR. Some of the solutions proposed were outlandishly complex: handicapping, par systems. Burton preferred the status quo because 'most of the alternatives were either unwieldy, impractical, or just incapable of catching cyclists' imaginations'. She added, 'The beauty of the present system is that no matter when a rider reaches peak form, no matter what other commitments a rider may have, it is possible at some time during the season to fit in the qualifying events.' She accepted that the 'miles per hour' system had its drawbacks, but added, 'what system of points can replace the simplicity and excitement of working out that "old Fred has only to improve 30 seconds at 50 miles to put him in front of Frank"?' That kind of calculation would be at the front of her thinking throughout 1982 and 1983.

Burton's battles to take her 24th and 25th Best All Rounder titles were fought as much against her failing health and the fickle British weather as against human opponents. The calculations were not merely about the figures posted by 'Fred and Frank', but whether she could get through a given time trial on a given day, and whether the conditions would be fast or slow. These last two titles bore little resemblance to the previous 23. For much of her career, the Best All Rounder had been important, but it had never been her principal objective in any given season. Compared to world championships, it had been an optional extra. As a competition it entailed what – for her – were relatively relaxed outings to time trials where she felt under less pressure than at a world or national championship.

In the final years, however, the fact that she *had* to win the BAR in order to achieve a meaningful outcome to the season lent a different tenor to the qualifying rides. Burton was now far from assured of victory thanks to the arrival of a new generation of competitors such as the Essex racer Sue Fenwick, not to mention the resurgence of old rivals such as Killingbeck. A BAR campaign was not a simple matter of travelling to whatever time trial course she fancied and riding as fast as she could. Burton had to keep an eye on the times her immediate opponents were posting, and calculate what the implications might be.

She and Charlie would have to make an informed guess as to which race would be the fastest in the country on any given Sunday before she entered anything. Many years of racing had told them which courses were the most rapid, but with a two-week closing date there was no way of knowing how the weather would affect a given race. If Burton entered a time trial and her closest rival entered the same race – as would often be the case, since the fastest courses were widely known – she would have to turn up, no matter how she felt physically. There would always be a chance that that particular race might end up being a 'float day' – when the weather conditions or the traffic or both meant that fast times would be posted – and she could not risk missing out.

The mathematics meant that towards the end of the campaign Burton knew pretty much to the minute what time she would require to push her average ahead of a given rival. However, facing a timekeeper knowing that – for example – a 4hr 15min '100' was needed on a given day was a kind of pressure she had not really had to deal with in her prime, when she just went faster and faster year after year and the records tumbled happily one by one.

The pressure was not strictly age-related; competing in the BAR was common for more mature cyclists. The distances involved meant that the competition was better suited to an older athlete, and in his history of the RTTC Bernard Thompson lists several BAR careers which lasted for over 40 years. The longevity of some of the competitors reflected the perennial attraction of time trialling compared to road racing or track: the ultimate rival for any time triallist is him or herself, the target to beat is his or her own fastest times.

Although Sue Fenwick, the runner-up to Burton in the 1983 BAR, was only 19, there were other women of Burton's age or older posting qualifying times and seeking out those fast days. Joan Kershaw, Shirley Killingbeck, Margaret Allen and June Pitchford all enjoyed a longevity that rivalled Burton's.

Mary Dawson, a maths teacher from Teesside, had won the BAR in 1954 and 1955 and finished third to Burton's fifth in 1957; over 20 years later she was still capable of finishing in the top 10, coming ninth in 1980. Daisy Franks was another, finishing second under her maiden name of Stockwell in 1951 and ninth in 1979.

With her compulsion to make it a record quarter century of victories in a row, Burton was piling pressure on herself. During 1982 she struggled with her breathing, but she duly chased the events in order to gain an advantage over her old rival Killingbeck; her main issue was finding a fast '100', which in the end meant racing a fast '25' in Essex on a Saturday in September, then heading to Nottinghamshire early the following morning for the final 100-mile event of the season. A time of 4hr 14min 37sec ensured her the 24th title, but she was in doubt as to whether her body would hold out for another one.

The 1983 season turned into a desperate battle against failing health. In April that year, Burton was knocked over by a car close to her home, suffering broken ribs and bruising to her back and legs. This crash also left her temporarily without a bike. Her back caused trouble all through that spring, and it was Mandy Jones who dominated the 10- and 25-mile championships; Burton managed bronze medals. By the summer, back pain was still affecting Burton's riding, and there were other issues: she was finishing rides feeling dehydrated, and was struggling when the weather was hot. Given that she was now 46, and that temperature regulation is recognised as an issue among perimenopausal and menopausal athletes, it seems at least possible that her hormone system was affecting her performance as well as the injuries.

During that summer Burton posted rapid 25-mile and 50-mile times – 56min 32sec and 1hour 58min 42sec respectively – and won the 50-mile title ahead of Jones. However, although her form had improved, she faced two issues: firstly her need for a fast 100-mile time, and secondly the fact that the doctors had advised her not to race, having diagnosed spinal concussion – presumably the result of the crash – and anaemia, plus other 'deficiencies' which she did not reveal. Meanwhile, Fenwick had become 100-mile champion – Burton had skipped the title race – and, more threateningly, she had posted a rapid 4hr 9min in a '100' in Essex, the fastest time ever at the distance by any woman other than Burton. (This only goes to show how far ahead of other women Burton had been when she set her 1968 record.) The best the 24-times BAR winner had managed that season was 4hr 19min in an event in Nottinghamshire; she attempted to race in a '100' in Yorkshire, but was forced to give up after 51 miles.

'I really did drive myself over the final few events, because I couldn't afford to miss one,' she said later. 'Sue Fenwick had got in some exceptional times, and I had to go where she went. I drove myself, and as a result I felt drained.' Having no chance of a fast time in the '100', she could not afford to let Fenwick or Killingbeck gain any ground in shorter events, so she had to keep racing right up to the end of the season.

The key event was to be the Otley CC '50', not far from her home, on August 21st, a warm, breezy summer day. 'Her fight to retain the BAR became a grim battle of willpower,' wrote Peter Whitfield in *12 Champions*. '[At Otley] she faced all her big rivals with her morale at zero, unable to train properly, suffering pain in her back, legs and lungs, but she turned in a classic ride of 1hr 56mins 33sec to win decisively. She finished more drained than she could ever remember, and no one around her knew what it had cost.' Burton described the race as 'slog, slog and more slog… the pain, the elastic legs, the rasping breath… I somehow forced myself to finish.' It was, she felt, one of her greatest rides. On the V153 Boro' course, 25 miles up the A1 from Wetherby and back, she left her old rival Killingbeck over 3 minutes behind, while Fenwick was almost 4 minutes slower. She received all of £5 for her efforts, as well as the £1 which was refunded to all those who completed the race.

Even then, she could not relax, because of the risk that Fenwick or Killingbeck might find the right form on the right course on the right day. She attempted another '100' and again abandoned, then travelled south for two races in Essex on the final Saturday and Sunday of the season, with, she wrote, 'low morale' and 'foreboding', fearing she would fall at the last hurdle. Burton crossed the line in the last race in a state of exhaustion, but fortunately Fenwick's form had faded as well. It was not her narrowest victory margin in the contest – that was in 1982 – but her average of 25.118mph to Fenwick's 24.601 was in a different league compared to the period in the 1970s when she would regularly win by two miles per hour or more. Perhaps most importantly from Burton's point of view, she had already won the title six times by the time Fenwick was born.

The length of that winning run, 1959-83, is astonishing. In 1959 the Mini was launched, while 1983 saw the first episode of *Blackadder.* Burton's BARs began in the year that Tom Simpson made his professional breakthrough with fourth place in the world road race championship, the year that Brian Robinson won his second Tour de France stage. Barry Hoban turned professional, won eight Tour de France stages and retired, after one of the longest careers in cycling, comfortably within that 25-year timespan. Three men had dominated professional cycling in that quarter century: Jacques Anquetil had won four Tours de France,

Eddy Merckx's entire career had begun, flourished and ended, and Bernard Hinault had spent six years at the top of professional cycling. Elsy Jacobs had gone, Yvonne Reynders and Katie Hage had been and gone (and in Reynders' case, even enjoying a nine year hiatus), and Jeannie Longo had arrived. There had been six British prime ministers, from Harold McMillan to Margaret Thatcher; Elvis Presley, John Lennon and Sid Vicious had all risen to fame and suffered untimely deaths.

Immediately afterwards, Burton said that she would never go for the competition again, because the pressure of chasing fast times around the country had turned racing into a chore. 'For the last six weeks I felt as if I was carrying a block of concrete on my head, and there were times when I just didn't feel like going out on my bike,' she said later that autumn. The doctors warned her that it could take six months for her to regain her full strength; characteristically, her first thought was how far into the 1984 season that would take her.

Chapter 13

On Your Own

57min 47sec, winning time in 25th national '25' title, Hampshire, June 1984.

'The fall is part of the destiny of an exceptional creature, the ultimate show of pride, a masochistic stubbornness that makes them go ever lower.' Olivier Dazat

After Burton had dragged her 25th BAR kicking and screaming into her trophy cabinet in 1983, the following year was, she said, a 'washout'. Compared to previous years, that is: she still managed to win the '25' championship, for the 25th time, and took silver in the '10' championship to Barbara Collins. Both results were remarkably close: Collins's margin of victory was one second in the '10', Burton's final advantage in the '25' just four seconds, after she had been behind for most of the distance. On Burton's own terms, however, the season was a failure. Her aim had been to target a variety of events that would form a total contrast to the chore of chasing BAR qualifying times: they included road records, tandem racing with Denise, road racing and, in particular, a start in the inaugural women's Tour de France.

Burton was still battling ill-health due to crashes and advancing years, as she had been since the late 1970s. She was now heading towards 50, at which age recovery becomes harder and the body fails to respond to training stimuli as readily as it once did. A three-month training camp in Spain early in the year failed to produce the form she wanted, probably because she was still carrying the effects of her battle to take the BAR, but perhaps also owing to a heavy fall while out walking which left her with what may have been delayed concussion.

By her own admission, Burton struggled to return to road racing. 'Just having others around me seemed to disorientate me. I couldn't concentrate on what I wanted to do and where I wanted to go,' she said at the end of the year. She was shocked at how long it took her to get used to riding in a group again; even when she was off the back, Charlie told her, she was not actually chasing at the speed she could hit in a time trial. She was 'legless, mentally and physically'. In May she was still struggling; by late June and the national road race championship she felt more like her old self, but it was too late.

Given Burton's struggles to find her feet in road race bunches on home turf, it was understandable that the selectors would be conservative when it came to her principal goal, the inaugural women's Tour de France*. In April that year, the Great Britain team manager Jim Hendry named her on a shortlist of eight for the race, but she did not make the initial cut. As Hendry explained: 'Her results have not been up to it.' It was humiliating but logical: Burton's best ride was 18th in the national road race championship, which was light years away from her form of old.

The day before the start of the Tour, however, Hendry called the Burton house, which had finally been fitted with a telephone. Because of the withdrawal of two riders who had been selected ahead of her, Barbara Collins and Margaret Herety (née Swinnerton), Hendry now wanted the 25-times

---

** Le Tour de France Féminin was run alongside the men's race from 1984 to 1989; it was succeeded by the Tour Cycliste Féminin and Grande Boucle Féminine – run by a different organiser which did not have the right to use the term Tour de France – from 1992 to 2009.*

BAR and 15-times world championship medallist to travel to France.

When Charlie called Beryl at the farm where she was working, her answer was that she would not go. 'Are you all right?' Charlie asked. Burton later explained that she felt if she was good enough she would have been picked in the first place: being taken as a reserve held no interest for her. In addition, she had told her boss at the farm that she would be available for the raspberry picking. It was a clear-cut case of her gut reaction getting the better of her: she was probably in sufficiently good form to ride the race, having knocked out 1hr 57min for a '50' not long before the Tour was due to start. *Cycling* (probably prompted by a BCF source) primly wrote that Burton 'did not have sufficient time to get ready'. Her place went instead to a 19-year-old, Louise Garbett.

This was a huge psychological blow for Burton. She had thought herself into the Tour: she felt the duration of the three week race would suit her ability to recover day to day, and that the fact she had worked all her life would mean that every day would be easier than she was used to. 'It wouldn't matter how hard the racing would be... When the final team was selected, I was floored, knocked for six. Some of the girls that went I'd actually beaten in road races. They weren't road racing girls any more than I was.'

Just as when she failed the 11-plus, the mental shock seems to have had physical effects, and she became ill: 'I felt [as if] someone had dropped me from the top of a building.' It was probably a virus, but Charlie for one felt at the time that it was directly down to the stress of her rejection from the Tour. It was not just the fact that she could not ride the race; it was what that decision represented: the point at which it finally became clear that there was no way back into the international fold. Burton's season ended early – she was not going to have another go at the BAR, which went to an old rival, June Pitchford – but she kept talking determinedly about having a further attempt at road racing, with the Tour still on her mind. It is on this hopeful note that she concluded her autobiography, *Personal Best*.

In an interview in January 1985, she spoke of giving up work for the year – for once, she said, she wanted to put all her energy into racing. She envisaged a return to Spain to 'sort herself out', she speculated about a potential road racing programme that would include the Tour of Texas and the Coors Classic in the US, the women's Milk Race (a series of circuit events run alongside the round-Britain Tour) and the Tour de France. None of it happened. She did produce a few results that year, including seventh in the '10' championship and a lone medal, bronze, in the '25'. She started a few road races, but her mind was elsewhere.

In the later years of her career, Burton had begun seeking out fresh ways of testing mind and body, new venues where she might find press and public willing to laud her ability. Riding in the Grand Prix des Nations in 1968 was the first of those instances, as was her desire to ride the Bordeaux-Paris one-day classic. The challenges she set herself became more outlandish, starting with a 2,000 mile sponsored ride around Britain in 1971 in aid of the Samaritans. In spring 1978 she had been invited to the Schlitz Light international stage race in Tucson; her crash the previous autumn meant that she was unable to race, but she flew over as a guest anyway, riding the one-day race that preceded it and clocking up some valuable training miles in a warmer climate. Her ride in the 1980 Melbourne-Warrnambool marathon was another trip outside the comfort zone, so too her attempts for selection for the women's Tour de France. She also contemplated riding the End-to-End – Land's End to John O'Groats – as Eileen Sheridan had done.

In 1985 came perhaps the craziest race of her life: the Spenco 500 in Waco, Texas. The world's longest single-day cycle event, the Spenco covered 500 miles across the plains of central Texas, through towns described as 'straight out of Westerns' and passing Lyndon B Johnson's ranch along the way. It was sponsored by a maker of gel-filled pads for bike saddles, ironically for a race that would induce saddle soreness in many of its participants.

The 320-rider field was made up of both amateurs and professionals, given special sanction to compete together by the US governing body; that year's start sheet included a seven-strong British professional contingent headed by Yorkshireman Keith Lambert, who had ridden the Otley CC '12' alongside Burton in 1967. Burton was invited by the organiser, expatriate Yorkshireman Mike Breckon, who planned to get her onto the *Good Morning America* television show on the day of the race: 'It would have paid back the sponsor in full for his investment,' he recalled. The interview didn't happen.

Burton had travelled to the US with her own supply of food – 'loads of different things, cheese and so on, all the stuff she lived on to get her through the week,' recalled Lambert, who flew out to Texas with her. US customs confiscated her store, leaving her distraught, although it is unclear whether this was at the prospect of having to eat whatever she could find in the US, or at having to tap into the $50 a day that the organisers gave the guest riders to live on during their time in Texas.

The race started at 5pm and blew to bits in crosswinds when the European professionals put the hammer down after the first hour; Burton was among those left behind. After that, wet and freezing conditions through the dark of the night – after most of the field had been told to expect temperatures around 20 degrees Celsius – forced riders to borrow extra kit wherever they could, and sapped the morale and strength of most of the competitors. 'She rode the race with poor support,' said Breckon. 'I couldn't find anyone who really knew what they were doing, to look after her.' Burton managed 200 miles, climbing off her bike near the Johnson ranch; it was the last time she attempted a distance event such as this. Lambert and another Yorkshireman, Dudley Hayton, finished second and fourth.

By the mid 1980s, Beryl Burton's cycling career was not quite over, but the quarter century of Best All Rounder trophies had been the final landmark. Burton had blazed her trail in her own way, within the limitations imposed upon her by her sport's refusal to give equal racing opportunities to women. That makes it more meaningful to assess Burton's record in its own terms than to compare her directly to the champions of men's cycling. There is perhaps a single equivalent: her dominance of women's cycling within her home country in her prime resembled the way Eddy Merckx ruled men's professional road racing in Europe. The sense of utter hopelessness Burton and Merckx induced in their rivals was similar, but British time trialling was a far smaller world, with the result that Burton's dominance was far more absolute. There was a similar aura around the Frenchwoman Jeannie Longo during the late 80s and the 90s, but again the parallels are not exact: Longo's *palmarès* was forged in an era when women enjoyed greater opportunities.

Burton was spectacularly dominant. The proportion of women's races she won relative to the races she started can be conservatively estimated at over 75% during the peak of her career, from 1958 to 1982. The records are not complete, but she was riding at least one time trial per week from April to September (in 1970 she said she raced on Sundays, and twice during the week) and she lost only one or two time trials a year for nearly 25 years. She rode far fewer road and track races, but still won a high proportion of those over the period from 1958 to 1975. 'Over the years there's always been times when I've been beaten in a season, at least once,' she said. 'Jo Bowers [later Shirley Killingbeck] used to do it once a season, regularly.' That statement should still induce a wry smile: how many endurance athletes can say anything similar?

At times, Burton's strength compared to the opposition seemed simply ludicrous. In 1965's British national road race championship, for example, she escaped with Ann Horswell, then waited for her time after time to ensure that Horswell did not get swallowed up by the bunch and was guaranteed second place. When she felt it was the right moment, she rode away. In the late 1960s, she would be started off eight or 10 minutes behind her rivals in handicapped races, even though they were usually under 30 miles; in one race in April 1967, with an eight-minute handicap, she rode through the whole peloton, overtaking all the other starters in their various groups, to win by 47 seconds. Put off 10 minutes behind, she might finish around a minute behind the bunch.

'I don't think I remember anyone beating her until she was close to the end of her life,' recalled one contemporary, Mary Horsnell. 'It was just taken for granted she would win. It was very demoralising for riders like June Pitchford and Shirley Killingbeck, who won so little. It was sheer determination, I don't think it was any physical attribute.' After the 1970 '50' championship, which Burton won by seven minutes in spite of a crash the day before at a track meet – she had to ride with a strapped elbow and injuries to hands, hips and head – Ann Horswell, the bronze medallist, expressed her despair: 'Will I ever beat her? I can't see it, for Beryl looks as if she will go on for longer than me. It's really no fun racing for second place all the time and that's all the rest of us are doing. It wouldn't be so bad if we ever got any nearer to her, but we don't.'

A rival who dominates time trialling is a far more daunting prospect than one who is the strongest in road racing. In time trialling, performance is far more predictable and measurable, compared to the more random nature of road racing, where the potential for multiple tactical outcomes means hope is never dead. In UK time trialling, Burton's rivals knew exactly what times they had to do to beat her: in 1968, for example, the BAR runner-up, Horswell, knew she would have to manage 55min for 25 miles, 1hr 54min for 50, 3hr 59min for 100. This was obviously an impossible task. Worse still, any time triallist with a remotely mathematical mind could work out the rate at which they would have to improve year on year, how many minutes they would need to chip off a personal best, in order just to compete with Burton. 'Ann Horswell possesses great fighting spirit and immense patience and forethought,' wrote Roy Green in *Sporting Cyclist*, before adding, devastatingly, 'She thinks that her improvement will be too slow *ever* to catch up with Beryl's standards.' 'Ann was as serious as Beryl,' believes Bernadette Malvern. 'She had backing from [the] Holdsworth [bike company], she was out training all the time, she was very very serious about racing, but she couldn't beat Beryl.'

Internationally, the picture was different: the pool of riders was larger, and the road racing experience of riders such as Yvonne Reynders and Katie Hage made them tactically more astute, if not always as strong as Burton. In addition, the short distances of women's races favoured sprinters over 'stayers'; Burton was conclusively the latter. Within Great Britain, it was a different picture: Shirley Killingbeck reckoned that over her long career she had beaten Beryl four times – 'in a 25 twice. In the national pursuit once, and once in a road race. I always aim to beat Beryl. You have to aim that far.' Even in that, she was something of an exception. 'Most of the girls seem to be afraid of Beryl,' said Carol Barton, who finished third to the Burtons, daughter and mother, in the 1976 national championship. 'A lot of them are beaten before they even start.'

Burton's rivals found it unrewarding constantly banging their heads against a wall, and understandably discovered other more worthwhile occupations. Her fellow Yorkshirewoman Barbara Mapplebeck went to race in Holland after Burton put six minutes into her in the national road race championship, then retired at 20 to become a missionary in the Far East. Horswell took to record breaking – her Land's End to London record in 1970 earned her a spread in *Cycling* – but eventually hung up her wheels to breed dogs.

Burton was always convinced that she did not have innate cycling talent. She said that the notion that she was a natural athlete was for the birds. She would argue that she had not begun her cycling career by going spectacularly fast, but had improved gradually through her early years; she would also frequently point to the fact that her doctors had ordered her to take things easy as a teenager, owing to her illness. There was an element of truth in this, but however much she wanted it to be her personal narrative, it wasn't that simple.

On behalf of *Cycling* magazine, Dr CR Woodard looked into the reasons for Burton's success in 1964. Having examined her, he concluded, 'I can only describe her physique as exceptional. I examined her at a time when… in her own opinion she was far from fit. Her pulse rate was regular and slow (48 at rest) and she carried no excess weight. Her muscles were wonderfully supple. The most outstanding thing about her physique was her powerful thighs. They would put even the men stars to shame. She has powerful shoulders and arms and a fine if not exceptional chest expansion.'

Twenty-one years later, in 1985, Burton went through physical testing at Leeds Polytechnic's Carnegie School, largely in an attempt to prove to herself and the Great Britain selectors that she was still capable of riding for the national team. Her physiological results were, she said, on a par with a 20-year-old male; in addition, her body fat level was spectacularly low, so low that the doctors could not record a reading. She was shown a picture of a skeletal marathon runner on the wall and told she was even thinner. Her oxygen uptake and the efficiency with which her body processed oxygen were both higher than expected.

That sounds like an exceptional athlete, which was certainly how Alf Engers saw her: 'She was immensely strong, stronger than everyone else. She had the strength and resolve. Full stop. She was still [in her position on the bike], there was no rock and rolling, it was all power. Poetry in motion.' Burton's view, in contrast, was that she was simply possessed of a greater will to win than others; Charlie – who probably knew her better than she knew herself – saw it differently. 'We tend to disagree quite a bit on this,' he told Yorkshire television. 'I agree that she has put lots of effort into it and she has polished herself up, but with the initial equipment that you are issued with, I think that Beryl shopped at Harrods and I shopped at Woolworths.'

For one contemporary, Mary Horsnell, Burton showed an edge lacking in many mere mortals. 'I remember she asked me what I was doing for Christmas. I said I was with my family; she replied, "You won't get anywhere like that. You have to be selfish." Her club would be going to the Lakes for the Christmas break, and she was going with them.' What struck Horsnell was that Burton said exactly the same thing to her on a second occasion, at a race near Oxford where Horsnell had travelled to support her husband. 'I don't think she meant it in a bad way; she meant that you have to isolate yourself. She never gave the impression of being unpleasant.'

'We never took ourselves as seriously as Beryl,' said Horsnell. 'We would go for a racing weekend away, there might be three of us. The day before the race we'd go and hang around in a bike shop and have a chat, go to the pictures, the guys would go for a beer. Then we'd ride our race and meet the club for lunch. We never took it that seriously. I don't think I ever hurt myself properly. It just came up lucky if you won something; it was a totally different outlook on life. For us, it was a way of life rather than a sport. Beryl was one of the first to come along with that determination.'

Eileen Sheridan's view was that Burton's success could be put down to the hardships she endured in her childhood and her teens: 'She has had to fight all the way. She has the most amazing guts.' Ron Kitching felt that Sheridan and Burton were chalk and cheese. Sheridan, he said, had 'no nastiness, no aggression, she didn't seem to want to beat anyone'; Burton, on the other hand, 'was very different. Her upbringing was very different, and the way the sport went for her must have made her into a very ruthless person. Once she sits on that bike, nothing else matters.'

Burton liked to underline that she was competitive by nature: 'Whether it's growing plants, knitting, baking a cake, washing the windows, the competitive urge is there to do it the best.' This was something she cited almost as often as her drive for hard work. 'I just enjoy competition. Even if it's buttering bread against someone else buttering bread then I've got to do it longer and better. I can't help it.' It was a theme she expanded on for Dennis Donovan: 'If I am sharing a kitchen with another woman and have to do the washing up, I have to do it quicker and better than she does… Knitting, playing ball, shaking a rug, anything. It comes out in all forms. It's there.'

There was nothing reflective about Burton's approach to her cycling: she was typical of most great athletes in her ability to move forwards immediately to the next target. 'They used to say when I broke a competition record, "Are you pleased?" and I'd say, "Well, it's all right for now." And once I'd done a "56" [minutes for 25 miles] I'd put it out of my mind and start thinking of a "55"… some people must have thought I was big-headed but you've got to look forward. That's been my style all the years I've raced.'

To explain Burton's basic motivation to devote her life to cycling, we have to go back to the 11-plus, to her 'failure' and her illness: this had a devastating, life-long effect. She told Bernard Thompson: 'I was the best pupil at my school and I passed all my early exams, then I failed my 11-plus… I felt as though I had been cheated and I think it must have sparked off a life of proving myself.' Her analysis seems spot on: she was a hard-working, perfectionist child, with a strong competitive streak, who was deprived of the success she sought and effectively branded a failure. She was then 'punished' with severe illness and a two-year separation from her family. That would seem to be more than enough to instill in her an obsessive lifelong determination to make a mark on the world in her own way.

Burton may have looked cool and controlled when faced with a major objective, but it is clear that in fact she suffered from acute anxiety. She would over-react when things went wrong. Her conduct after Denise's victory in the 1976 national championship is one instance, but there were others. When she broke a spoke in the national '50' in 1968, she was reported to have 'got madder and madder' – despite being miles ahead of the rest of the field – 'until the affair almost broke her to the point of packing [giving up], not just the event, but her entire career! Her concentration was such that once broken even by such a triviality, her ride almost went to pieces...'

She was clearly – and not surprisingly – driven by a colossal fear of failure. It is not uncommon in the greatest champions, no matter how they appear on the surface: most have their demons. Burton described the running race on sports day at Denise's school in terms that make it clear: 'It was only for fun but I lined up shaking like a leaf. I knew I had to win, everything depended on it as far as I was concerned. Everything I do is like that. I have to win.'

Burton never truly articulated what she was seeking in cycling. She was adamant that she wanted 'recognition', but it was never clear what precisely this involved, and throughout her career she complained about a lack of acknowledgment of her success. She did receive recognition for her achievements – she was made an OBE and an MBE, she was honoured by the British sportswriters in 1960 and 1967, and she was given civic receptions in Morley – so it would be inaccurate to say she remained in complete obscurity.

Sometimes Burton's complaints were – justifiably – directed at Fleet Street's finest. Her reaction to coverage of her first world title and the Otley '12' record were pretty much the same, eight years apart. 'One press report was kind enough to call it "incredible… amazing… a record to end all records", but the national press generally – and more importantly to me the papers in my own region – gave it scant regard, as indeed they had my world title, and sadly I had to accept that the press "play" the favoured and cyclists are not among them in this country.' In May 1970, Burton told journalist Colin Willcock, 'The press has been good to me, but they could do a great deal more for the sport as a whole. Surely events like national championships are worth a write-up, even it is only a little one.'

Admittedly, cycle racing was a 'marginal' sport, but the lack of attention and respect she received was surely related to the constant underlying sexism in the sports pages of newspapers. It is impossible to imagine a male cyclist who enjoyed this level of success being treated so casually. Even specialist publications were not blameless: Burton's long-term monopoly on national championships clearly led to her achievements being taken for granted rather than acknowledged for what they were.

It was not just print, however. Take the BBC *Sportsview* Sports Review of 1967, after Burton had won her second world road race title. Although she finished runner-up to the boxer Henry Cooper in the nationwide poll, the BBC merely paid lip service to her achievements, along with those of the other world champions such as cyclist Graham Webb, motorcyclist Bill Ivy, ice dancers and water skiers. None of them was asked to speak, and the BBC did not even show footage of her victory. It is little comfort, but Burton was far from alone: as recently as 2003, when Nicole Cooke was in her prime, 'Auntie' was barely able to raise an eyebrow.

Burton became frustrated with bigger issues than her personal press coverage. Quite early in her career, she became aware of how unfairly women were treated at international level in terms of racing opportunities, and had no fear when it came to speaking out. 'One of the few regrets I have over cycling is that there are no events for women in the Olympic Games or the Empire [now Commonwealth] Games,' she said in the early 1960s, listing the various Games held during her career to date and adding, 'We women cyclists can only watch from afar. We watch with admiration tinged with envy, itching to get in there and compete, but relegated to the position of spectator. Perhaps one of these days one of the host countries may agree to run events for us and then, although I know it will be too late for me, I shall be in there pushing the pedals around with our girls.'

Although Burton longed for more international opportunities and greater fame and fortune, she focused her activity on a sphere that offered neither: time trialling. She did not do so unwillingly, or with any sense of resentment; if she had, there is no way that she would have gone on 'testing' for as long as she did. It was not just about the victories and the (minimal) prize money. There were other sides to racing solo against the watch that drew her. As she told Marjorie Lofthouse on *Woman's Hour*, it offered the opportunity to take flight mentally: '…during the event there's all sorts of things run through your mind. Your mind sort of splits. I suppose it's like driving a car. Half of your mind is on the road, watching the traffic and one thing or another, and the other half is whatever comes into your mind at the time. It might be, "Oh,

I must go see Auntie next week" and "I must write to so and so" or "We'll go out to see a show." It's like having two minds in your head at the same time.'

The time trialling experience is cycling pared down to its essentials – you don't have to worry about the dynamics and tactics of a bunch, as in a road or track race – which means it is a more natural escape route for the mind. Burton's description of mental 'separation' is not a million miles from the words of another BAR, Frank Colden, who described reaching a Nirvana-like state when in 'the zone': 'I have been aware on a few occasions in races (always successful ones) when I have experienced a feeling which could only be described as a drifting sensation… large parts of a distance race seem to come and go without any real register in my mind. Is this part of the clue to concentration as the springboard to mind control?' His comparison was with South Sea Islanders, who 'purify their minds' and are able to walk over hot coals without pain.

Burton's *Woman's Hour* interview reveals another side of racing against the watch that must have drawn her. 'Time trialling,' she tells the broadcaster, '…is done on the road, 10 miles up to 100 miles, 12 hours, 24 hours… there is a timekeeper, they say 5-4-3-2-1-go, and you are *on your own*' – Burton says this very decisively – 'and you cover the distance – that is timed, an individual effort, on your own. If you catch someone you have to pass them, you are not allowed to sit behind them and take pace or anything.'

Time trialling would have attracted someone who had been deprived of so much by circumstances outside her control. Unlike in bunched disciplines, in a time trial by and large other people can't mess up your race for you. It must have been addictive for a control freak such as Burton – so keen to ensure that everything in her life and home was just how she wanted it – to compete and succeed in a sphere where, once the timekeeper had said the magic words, the result was solely down to her.

There were many things Burton enjoyed as well as her cycling – baking, gardening, keeping her home just so, knitting – and she enjoyed them because she could do them well, and because largely they depended on her rather than anyone else. There was no room for contented mediocrity in her constant quest for personal validation. However, that quest was stymied by the lack of recognition for cycling in general and by the specific limitations placed on women cyclists: hence her need to keep winning on her own terms, for so many years and in the face of reason. For Beryl Burton, any level of achievement could never be enough.

Chapter 14

Overtaken

27min 36sec: 69th place, national '10' championship, Newmarket, May 1992.

'I strike a blow to my body and make it my slave.' Corinthians 27

At her home by the Thames in west London, Eileen Sheridan has a small collection of photos of Beryl Burton, folded into a signed first edition of Burton's autobiography, *Personal Best*. In one, from the 1950s, Burton and Sheridan stand in a rank of bright-eyed young woman in racing jerseys and shorts, lined up as if at a school speech day. However, it is another that grabs the eye; in this one, Burton is wearing a pink racing jersey, while Sheridan, on the right, is clad in a raincoat, standing almost a head shorter. Although Sheridan was more than 60 when the picture was taken in the early 1990s, she looks about 40. It is Burton who has the haggard face of an old woman. She is light years away from the bright young thing who lined up for the group picture.

It upsets Sheridan to take out the photo. 'She was worn out,' says Sheridan. 'I'll never forget [it] – I'm looking at her and laughing about something, I'm a normal weight, but her face looks so gaunt. She was killing herself... She was riding a "50" in Yorkshire, a celebration for one of the clubs – it was pouring rain, freezing cold. I was shocked when I saw her. The next thing I knew, she'd dropped dead in Harrogate.'

It is an image that sums up the final years of Burton's career, when she kept racing, racing and racing – against medical advice, against common sense. Why did she never hang up her wheels? Why did she continue to race through injury, fatigue, respiratory illness and finally cancer? She could have retired in 1969, with her best years behind her, or in 1983, when it was obvious that her body was unable to cope with the workload. What compelled her to continue racing for so long? No one could work out why.

Sheridan recalled meeting Burton at a dinner in 1989. 'Beryl came to me and said, could she chat? She came and sat on a seat next to me; she was so skinny, so light.' (Here, one cannot help thinking back to those physiological tests in Leeds in 1985, where Burton's muscular figure with its low body fat was discussed; the hint of an eating disorder is not hard to pick up.) 'She said she wasn't feeling well, and didn't know what to do,' continued Sheridan. 'I said, "Why not retire? Twenty-five years winning the BAR, no one can beat that. Why not do that, travel about and do different things and go to different places?" She said she was going to ride a two-up [time trial] with Denise and then give up.'

However, the principles that had guided Burton since she teamed up with Nim Carline in the early 1960s did not allow for admissions of weakness. 'If [I'm] ill or have an injury or anything I just compete the same, do the best under the circumstances and I feel better – even if I've been beaten, I've done my best under the circumstances,' said Burton in 1986. 'I couldn't not go and compete and feel I'm not well or whatever; it doesn't satisfy [me] at all.' (Her former boss, Carline, went down a similar road. He had made a comeback in 1973 to win his sixth '24' title, and kept targeting the event until 1979, but in the end he developed heart problems and his hips gave out; typically, he refused to pay for hip replacements on the grounds that he had paid his taxes and the NHS could do its bit.)

Burton had expounded her philosophy to the writer Bernard Thompson in 1974: 'To ease off once would just be the beginning of the end; it's like packing in a race, once you have done it, it is easier to do it the next time and so on.' This was not mere posturing. The first occasions on which she ever gave up in a time trial were in 1969, when she abandoned in the Mersey Roads '24' and then in that year's national '100'. In her final BAR season, she stopped in several races but these were exceptions. She had hardly ever spared her body during the racing season, no matter what her state of fatigue or injury.

Throughout Burton's entire cycling career she always took considerable satisfaction from the fact that as a teenager she had been told by doctors not to exert herself; in that sense she had flown in the face of medical advice for 30 years. She was far from the first, or last, athlete to continue racing while ignoring the obvious warning signs from mind and body. The capacity to put risk and pain to one side is part of the competitive mindset: the greater the ability to do this, the better the competitor. 'Racing madness' is not restricted to men by any means.

Burton had frequently been asked when she would hang up her wheels, and had usually said that she would continue to race only if she was still enjoying it. But whether she gained much pleasure from her racing during the 1982 and 1983 seasons must be a moot point. 'I plugged away as best I could, forcing my reluctant, wheezing body to answer the call weekend after weekend, riding out of instinct and determination,' she wrote of the 1982 campaign.

One writer, Peter Whitfield, believed by the end of Burton's career that her life had become 'unbalanced... She seems to have extinguished everything in her life except cycling. The intellect, the emotions, any thoughts about religion, politics, literature, social issues – none of these held any place in her life. Her self-absorption was total, and her interest in the world outside cycling was minimal.' Whitfield describes her as 'the loneliest person in cycling, pursuing her own private battle without reference to another soul'. He writes that 'her commitment was so extreme, so single-minded that one has to ask whether it was rational.' The same could be said of many athletes: sport at the highest level is far from a rational way of life.

Perhaps the picture was more nuanced than Whitfield allows. Burton clearly had other things in her life: gardening, knitting, cooking, opera, travel and, later on, her grandchildren. Denise Burton-Cole believes that Burton continued racing mainly as a social activity, but also because by the end of her life racing was simply what she did. 'She just could not stop racing. It was something that she needed to do. I think by then she had accepted the fact that she wasn't going to win, she was going to come last perhaps, but she enjoyed the company of everybody because it was still the same crowd out at events. And they loved to see her.'

Burton-Cole continues: 'I'm thinking that she did it because it gave her a purpose to think about what [she and Charlie] were going to do that weekend, and two, she did like the [time] around the results board, cups of tea, stuff like that. She could have just gone out and done that, she didn't have to race, but it gave her a purpose. I think she had no purpose really, she didn't have any particular hobbies by then, she didn't have a TV, she still did some knitting but she didn't have to do much baking because it was just my dad and her. She used to clean up and housekeep for a couple at Flaxby – again it was a purpose.'

Time trialling has always been an accessible sport, once you have worked out where the races actually are. Burton was not frequenting the dog-eat-dog world of professional road cycling. The time trial was an environment where you could happily turn up, be sociable and face no adverse comment if you weren't winning. Every weekend, Burton would have bumped into people she knew; they had all been going to essentially the same races for over 30 years, albeit with various interruptions along the way. It would have been a close-knit group, with an immense amount in common, but large enough and sufficiently varied from weekend to weekend to ensure that it remained interesting.

Burton's own justification of her reluctance to stop racing backs up the theory that she needed purposeful activity in her life. Asked about retirement by Liz Jackson for *Cycling* in 1985, she said, 'I've answered that question for the last 15 years. I just don't know.' It was not, however, that it had not crossed her mind. As she told Jackson, 'I think about it every time I have a crash, [but] I'm not a person that can sit about.' The problem as she saw it was that without racing she would not know what to do. She would not go running ('I'm like a sack of potatoes'), and listed knitting as her only hobby. 'I have to use up my physical energy somehow. I don't feel as if I'm doing anything unless I'm working physically.'

Another explanation is that Burton enjoyed cycling for its own sake. Interviewing her in 1980 on *Woman's Hour*, Marjorie Lofthouse gave her an open prompt: 'There must be something about cycling that enables one to carry on well past the age of normal top sportsmanship…'. Burton chimed in rapidly: 'I think it's because you don't have to compete to enjoy it. You can just cycle for pleasure. Really, I wouldn't be upset if I gave up the competitive side of it, because I really do enjoy cycling just for the pleasure of cycling, going out and riding about and looking at the countryside. You can't do this in other sports. You can't do it in running or swimming so much, but you can do it with cycling.' She added: 'There is a season for competition, which is March to September. I don't give up cycling [outside] this time of the year, I just give up training. I really enjoy going out just for the pleasure of going out and cycling. If I want to go at 10 miles per hour, just pottering along… Just to keep ticking over [until] the next season.'

Burton repeated these sentiments in several other interviews; clearly, in spite of her intense drive to win as much as she could, she never lost sight of what drew her to cycling in her teens, when the main pleasure was in club outings to the countryside with family and friends. That is obvious in the footage from the 'Morley film unit' – sedate club runs, larks at youth hostels, the fun of a cyclo-cross race with nothing at stake. At the start of her competitive career in particular, winning was not the be all and end all. Indeed, in 1958 she was criticised for effectively losing the Best All Rounder by skipping a particular race which clashed with a family holiday in Ireland: the holiday was her top priority. That love of cycling for its own sake continued throughout her career alongside the competition.

It might seem unlikely that she could switch so readily between being an almost inhumanly driven athlete and a human being who loved cycling, but it is not out of the question. Burton was not competing for cash: she remained an amateur cyclist all her life, no matter how central racing on a bike was in her life. Continuing to compete was not a matter of squeezing out extra races in order to keep earning, as it would be for a professional cyclist.

Although the image of a monomaniacally driven athlete who rode herself into the ground seems simplistic, it is probably true that competing through her various illnesses contributed to Burton's premature death. 'She was still trying to achieve things when her health deteriorated in the last 10 years of her life,' Charlie Burton told the writer Hugh Gladstone. 'Her times were getting slower, so she was never happy or content with that,' Charlie said. 'She was always trying to thrash herself back into shape.' 'I think she'd just done it for most of her life,' said Denise Burton-Cole. 'She'd pushed her body so much she'd find it hard not to... Your body eventually says it's about time you should rest but she didn't... When she used to train she'd do more miles than was ever needed. That was her. She wouldn't have done anything else. Pushing her body was the way she did things.'

In fact, after a relatively poor season in 1985, Burton did have some successes, and at the end of the season, she managed to beat that year's BAR June Pitchford over 25 miles. In 1986 she took her 26th national championship at 25 miles, and her 24th at 50, and even at the age of 49 she still had her sights set on the Seoul Olympics and the Tour de France. That year, she said that her 'will to win' might sustain her for another 20 years; she was certainly still good enough to win a team medal in the 1989 '25' championships, her last medal at national level.

What of those closest to her? Charlie took early retirement in the expectation – hope? – that Beryl might stop racing and the pair of them would be able to enjoy activities that had been impossible while she was competing. That never happened. Denise, meanwhile, rebuilt her cycling career after anorexia and the breakdown of her first marriage; as previously noted, in the early 1980s her mother acquired a tandem for the pair of them to ride while she regained her strength. Eventually they raced on it, setting a British record at 10 miles. In 1985, Denise resumed her international career, finishing the women's Tour de France in 1986. She was all set for another go at it in 1987 when she had a serious crash, resulting in crushed vertebrae and severe facial injuries, which forced her to quit. She eventually remarried and had two children: Mark, born in 1989 and Anna, born four years later.

In 1992, Dennis Donovan wrote that Burton's face 'lit up when you ask about Denise and her baby, in a way that has been missing for far too long'. Her daughter qualifies this image of grandmotherly devotion: 'She wasn't one for looking after my children – [my parents] lived in Scar Beck, and on a Thursday I used to take [the children] so I could go out on my bike. I'm not sure whether it stopped when Anna was born. She and my dad took them for part of the day, in return for me making the dinner at night' – here she gives a wry laugh. 'If I didn't make the dinner they wouldn't take them. They were hard. That's the way they were.'

It was at this time that it emerged that Burton had suffered from breast cancer and undergone a mastectomy. As Dennis Donovan wrote, this was an open secret in the Yorkshire cycling world. Unsurprisingly, the cancer was both mentally and physically traumatic. 'I knew for some time that something was wrong, as all my strength had gone,' Burton told Donovan. 'It went on and on until I was finally told that it was a tumour.' There is little further information about the episode, other than this quote: 'There was a cyst on top of a lump on my breast. If I had been hit by a brick I couldn't have been more stunned.'

On the morning of Sunday 8 May 1996, Burton was riding her bike to Denise's house to deliver invitations for her 59th birthday picnic – to be held in four days' time – when she suffered heart failure and died. Denise was told the news by Charlie and a policeman. 'It was like a big stone that falls in your stomach. You're just numb.' Beryl's body was identified by Denise, Charlie and her brother Jeffrey. The previous day, the extended Burton-Charnock family had all been together for the wedding of Beryl's nephew Graham Charnock in Micklefield; for Jeffrey the shock was all the more marked coming as it did after joyful hours spent in a house packed with family members.

'Death of a cycling legend,' read the banner headline on the front page of the *Morley Advertiser* above David Beddows' report, which gave few details. Morley's 'most famous sporting personality' had been found beside her bike at 9.55am in Skipton Road, Harrogate. A week before she died, she and Denise had won the team prize in the Yorkshire Ladies CA '15' for Morley CC, and the day after her death she had been expected to line up in the Holme Valley Wheelers '25' along with other Morley club members, all of whom withdrew from the race as a mark of respect. She had also entered the following weekend's national '10' championship, although once again, there was little expectation that she could repeat her old form (she had been given number 3 on the start sheet). She had, in fact, told friends and family that she was planning to race all that season's national championships.

It fell to me to write Burton's obituary for both *Cycling Weekly* and the *Guardian*; 'The end of an era' was the only way to sum up the sense of what had finished with her passing. The following week, my colleague Dennis Donovan provided the long view of a man who had lived through the previous half century of bike racing in the UK. He was one of the many who remembered being overtaken in a time trial by Burton, who had, of course, told him he was not trying hard enough. 'As with so many who were caught and passed by the great "BB"' – Donovan noted that she was rarely referred to as anything else – 'the sense of loss is tremendous. It is akin to the loss we all felt when another hero of ours died – the great Tom Simpson, another who would never admit defeat.'

Prior to the arrival of social media, the letters page of *Cycling Weekly* was where the voice of the sport in the UK could be heard most clearly; the outpouring of grief after Burton's death matched that following the passing of Simpson, but without the questions over doping. The 1967 world champion Graham Webb – who won his title on the same day Burton took her second road World's in Holland – and Eileen Sheridan were among the writers. 'The greatest sportswoman of all time' was Sheridan's verdict as she highlighted Burton's 'immense courage'. John Turner of Newtown, Powys, expressed nostalgia for a past age, describing Burton as 'the best of "old-fashioned" club folk, riding all kinds of events and mixing with your mates without any "side".' He continued: 'You took on the world and won many times over… Best of all you still had time for a chat, retained that wonderful cheery, positive outlook… If ever there were a Superwoman you were she.'

The family gave Beryl a low-key funeral, with Charlie driving the coffin to the crematorium himself; it was carried in by family members. A memorial service was held on 5 June in Christ Church, Harrogate's oldest church, a 19th-century stone building in West Park. Within the church it was standing room only, and the crowd spilled onto the lawns outside. West Park has a strong cycling connection today: the road adjacent to it hosted stage finishes at the Tour de France and Tour de Yorkshire, and was the finish of the world road race championships in September 2019.

At the service the hymns included *Guide Me O Thou Great Redeemer* and *Praise My Soul the King of Heaven*. Denise Burton-Cole gave a reading that included these words, from *Philippians* verses 10–14: 'But one thing I do: Forgetting what is behind and straining toward what is ahead, I press on toward the goal to win the prize…' Another reading, from *Corinthians* chapter 9 verses 19–27, was by Yvonne McGregor, the Yorkshire rider who had been motivated to follow in Burton's footsteps as a world champion after reading her memoirs; the previous year, Burton had been present in Manchester to watch McGregor take one of the few prizes that had eluded her, the women's Hour record. That Bible passage is utterly appropriate for any sporting great: 'Run in such a way as to get the prize. Everyone who competes in the games goes into strict training. They do it to get a crown that will not last, but we do it to get a crown that will last forever. Therefore I do not run like someone running aimlessly; I do not fight like a boxer beating the air. No, I strike a blow to my body and make it my slave so that after I have preached to others I myself will not be disqualified for the prize.'

Eileen Sheridan delivered a eulogy: 'I remember saying that if Beryl had been French they would have treated her like Joan of Arc. I spoke about all the championships she won, about their grandchildren… Poor Charlie, he turned round and saw everyone there in the church and was upset that so many had turned out.' Over two decades later the former BAR remains distressed by the memory of seeing Burton in her final years and by her early death: 'It was dreadful. She was 58. It upsets me to think about it.'

There are many ways of measuring Burton's enduring impact on her sport and on those around her. At the time of her death, her women's competition records at 25, 50 and 100 miles all still stood, as did that epic 12-hour. The only mainstream record of Burton's that had been beaten by May 1996 was her 10-mile time; just the previous year McGregor had shaved 10 seconds off it as she began a bid to succeed Burton as world pursuit champion. Winning that rainbow jersey, incidentally, took her another seven years.

Burton's world championship career (1958-76) remains one of the longest in cycling history, and she is among the most prolific women's medal winners, with a tally of 15. For comparison, France's Jeannie Longo managed 17 world and Olympic medals over a quarter of a century; in 2019, Marianne Vos's running total stands at 23 medals over 17 years. Both Vos and Longo had more events to compete in than Burton, so the playing field is not entirely level. Few British men have managed to win medals on road and track; Sir Bradley Wiggins's total is 23 across Olympics and world championships. Among Burton's contemporaries, Yvonne Reynders managed 12 medals, 11 of them in her heyday between 1959 and 1966; Katie Hage took home 18 between 1966 and 1979.

Burton's records began to be updated in the years following her death. Three of them fell later in 1996: the 25-mile time – set in the dry, hot summer of 1976 – fell to McGregor; her 50-mile time, also 20 years old, was beaten by Jennie Derham of Twickenham CC; while the 28-year-old '100' record went to Sharon Lowther of VC York. Befitting its status as the definitive Burton record, her '12' distance lasted half a century before it was finally broken by Alice Lethbridge in 2017.

None of Burton's records were updated under the same conditions as those in which she set them. That is true of most time trial records, obviously, except for those set on the same day in the same race. However, there had been a major change since Burton's heyday, reflected in the fact that most of her records fell in the early to mid-1990s. All those who shaved off minutes and seconds – or, in the case of the '12', added on miles – did so using the aerodynamic equipment that came into vogue in the 1990s: triathlon handlebar extensions, skin-tight racing suits and disc wheels, all of which combined might conservatively be estimated to save around five seconds per kilometre. For 100 miles that equates to a saving of almost 12 minutes.

It was only once her health had begun to decline in the early 1980s that Burton was beaten regularly. The fact is that even the most talented British woman cyclist of that period, Mandy Jones, struggled to beat Burton in a time trial, in spite of the fact that Jones was 25 years younger and a world champion who was training and racing full-time. The duration of Burton's dominance and the enduring status of her records makes it clear that she was an outlier: a truly exceptional athlete. She is one of a number of exceptional women cyclists from Eileen Sheridan and Yvonne Reynders through to Jeannie Longo, Nicole Cooke and Marianne Vos. That does not mean, however, that she should be viewed as a physiological aberration: there is no reason to suppose that other women were not physically capable of doing what she did. Others who might have had the same physical potential may never have had the opportunity to race a bike, or may have fallen victim to social pressures.

Burton was an obvious first choice when British Cycling inducted the initial 50 nominees into its Hall of Fame in 2009. However, in terms of recognition of her legacy, the turning point came 18 years after her death, in 2014, when Yorkshire hosted the *Grand Départ* of the Tour de France;

that event gave all Yorkshire's cycling stars a renewed place in the limelight as the county celebrated its cycling heritage. It was in that year that the actor Maxine Peake forced Burton back into the wider national consciousness; having been given a copy of *Personal Best* by her boyfriend, Peake felt that the way Burton had been ignored was 'criminal'; her radio play *Beryl: a love story on two wheels*, broadcast in 2012, had set out to redress the balance.

In 2014, the radio play was transformed into a stage production, simply entitled *Beryl*. On the back of the London Olympics and the Tour's visit to Yorkshire, cycling in the UK was enjoying a collective 'moment', and Peake's play was a triumph, eventually touring to packed local venues across the country after an extended run at the West Yorkshire Playhouse. 'What surprised me was the intensity of warmth and affection which the show generated,' wrote the theatre's artistic director, James Brining, who described Burton as 'a metaphor for determination, modesty, loyalty, love and keeping your feet on the ground'.

The play appeared at an apposite moment. Since the London Olympic Games in 2012, Britain had begun to discover a new generation of women cycling champions – Lizzie Armitstead, Victoria Pendleton, Laura Trott, Emma Pooley, Dani King – all of them brought on by a national squad system that, while far from perfect, at least accords Olympic medals won by women the same value as those gained by men. At the same time, the issues raised during Burton's career – equality of racing opportunity, remuneration for women – have taken on greater resonance as the 21st century progresses, with campaigns for a women's Tour de France to be refounded, and pressure brought to bear on the UCI to give equality of opportunity.

Partly owing to the success of Peake's play, Burton was granted the posthumous Freedom of the City of Leeds, and there have been other tributes, including a lengthy video – featuring that footage from the 'Morley film unit' – by Ray Pascoe, whose other subjects include Tom Simpson and Brian Robinson; Burton was also listed alongside Eddy Merckx when *Rouleur* magazine launched its Cycling Hall of Fame in 2018. She is remembered each year at the Dave Rayner Fund gala dinner in Leeds, where money is raised to help young cyclists, male and female, gain racing experience abroad; Denise Burton-Cole is a patron of the fund.

Asked in 1986 if she enjoyed winning, Burton replied, 'Yes, I do.' It's an obvious question, and which athlete would not give that answer? Her contemporaries concur: 'she was addicted to winning,' said Bernadette Malvern. 'She couldn't get enough of it.' Two things stand out: the utter certainty with which Burton says those three words, and the way she takes the act of winning itself as a fact of life. For the bulk of the population, the thought of winning an athletic event of any kind is a mere dream; to Burton, it was the stuff of everyday life.

Getting increasingly animated, she explained to the Yorkshire TV interviewer, 'Not when I'm actually on the bike and I'm striving to win – I think, "What on earth am I doing here and why am I doing this?" And yet the bit's between my teeth and the eyeballs are hanging over the front wheel and I'm really giving it 100 per cent, and yet I think, "Why can't I just go home and be like other people and go out for a day in the car in the Dales or something?"'

Burton's penchant for saying a few words to every competitor that she overtook in a time trial has been widely documented, and it seems to be taken for granted. The liquorice allsort moment' with Mike McNamara during the Otley CC '12' remains the most celebrated of these episodes, but it was far from the only one. I have yet to find a cyclist who was passed by Burton in a time trial who does not recall something of this kind. They must have been legion, over 40 years. To the men, she would usually say something along the lines of 'You're not trying hard enough'; for a female victim in a '25' near Hemel Hempstead in the 1970s, it was 'C'mon, chuck'.

It is by no means the norm for a faster time triallist to say something to a slower rider when overtaking, unless it is a senior rider giving encouragement to a much younger one. It does reflect the fact that in the time trials Burton rode, particularly the women's events, many of the riders would have known each other, and the friendships might date back decades. Even so, I don't think that Burton was normal in doing this: most time triallists are so focused on their ride that they don't have time to spare for anyone who is overtaken.

Those little phrases of Burton's suggest that the moment when she caught another rider was an occasion that had to be marked in some way. Every time you catch another competitor in a time trial, that is a victory, even if you don't win the time trial outright. Time trial numbering runs from 1 (the first rider to start) to 120, with the fastest riders on the '10 marks' (the numbers ending in zero), so when a rider comes into sight with a number on their back that is lower than yours you have visible proof that you are faster than they are; unless they catch you again before the finish and put time into you, you have definitely beaten them.

If the fall guys were men, so much the better. Given the words Burton invariably seems to have directed at her male opponents – not in any malicious way, but to denote her success – a counsellor or psychologist might have asked her, 'Which man in your past told you that you were not trying hard enough?' Someone is bound to have said this, most likely a teacher or a male relative, quite possibly around the time that she took her 11-plus. She probably felt driven to keep exorcising those words until the end of her days.

Burton expressed her need to win in eloquent terms; that need helps to explain why she kept time trialling right up to the end of her life. It was about the act of winning, rather than anything she earned from it. With those little victories there for the taking every time you started a race, that would be an extraordinary incentive to keep competing. That would be especially true when – as you can in a time trial – you could look at a start list and know which of the other riders were likely to be slower. Even if Burton was nowhere near as good in her final years as she had once been there would always be people to be caught.

One of the last victims was Mary Horsnell. 'The last time I saw Beryl was the day of the 1992 women's 10-mile championship,' Horsnell recalled. The race was promoted by Essex's Hainault Road Club on the E3/10 course between Newmarket and Cambridge. 'They were anxious to point out that as a mark of respect they had placed Beryl last off, and me a minute in front of her, in order that we should not be passed by other riders. It was a kind thought, as I was over 60 and Beryl was past her best.'

She was indeed: the winner that day, Marie Purvis of the Isle of Man, finished in 23min 5sec – a time that would have been well within reach of the Beryl Burton of old – while the 55-year-old Burton posted 27min 36sec and finished 69th of the 96 starters. 'It was not a good day,' recalled Horsnell, 'and after the turn I thought there was an even chance of keeping in front [of Beryl], but I should have known better. It must have been a headwind finish, for as I faltered in top gear on the flyover bridge, Beryl briefly drew alongside. A quick word and she was gone.

'Rock steady in her own inimitable style she made up [another] minute in the short distance to the finish… The lasting memory that I will have of "BB" is of her riding away into the distance, leaving us all behind as she always did.'

Postscript

Beryl and her Bike
Ooh here comes Beryl such a sight
for sore cyclists' eyes
trim ankles turning blazing thighs
burning up the road
and miles ahead she shows
a clean pair of wheels
to all her trailing rivals
perfect on her perfect bike
Beryl always beats the clock
pure pleasure unalloyed is Beryl
for Beryl is the best yes
Beryl is the best
Beryl passes in a flash
chromey spokes Italian alloy gleam
lovely clean machine flown by
in a dazzling blink
yes in the pink is Beryl
for Beryl is the best
and evermore shall
be so

Jeff Cloves.

Beryl Burton Race Record

Author's note: this listing is complete for Burton's many individual championship wins, but to the best of my knowledge there is no full record available for her many other victories, so this is an indicative rather than completely comprehensive list. In a few places it is not clear what race an RTTC competition record was set in, so I have limited that entry to the record time on its own. All championships are women-only unless stated otherwise.

Prior to 1970 Burton was restricted to riding women-only time trials, often in conjunction with a men's race run on the same course on the same morning or afternoon; from 1957-70, I have denoted time trials where she finished faster than the men in the corresponding men's event with an asterisk.

Born: 12 May 1937, Halton, Leeds. Died: 5 May 1996, Harrogate.

1956: Winner: White Rose Ladies '25'.

1957: silver medal, RTTC 100-mile national championship.

Winner: Morley RC 25-mile time trial; Yorkshire Cycling Federation 15-mile time trial (tied with Iris Miles).

Fifth overall, RTTC British Best All Rounder.

1958: gold medals, RTTC 25-mile national championship; RTTC 50-mile national championship (competition record: 2hr 9min 17sec); RTTC '100' championship (competition record: 4hr 29min 21sec).

Winner: Tees-side Cycling Association '100' (competition record: 4hr 33min 26sec); Herne Hill women's pursuit.

Second: RTTC British Best All Rounder.

1959: gold medal, world 3,000m pursuit championship, Rocourt, Belgium; 5th, world road race championship, Amsterdam.

Gold medals, RTTC '25' championship; RTTC '50' championship (competition record: 2hr 6min 38sec); RTTC '100' championship (competition record: 4hr 20min 4sec); RTTC British Best All Rounder, 23.724mph; BCF road race championship.

Winner: Goole Wh '25'; three stages and overall, stage race, Northamptonshire; Roanne kermesse; Yorkshire CF 12-hour time trial (competition record: 250.37 miles); Nottinghamshire '25' (competition record: 1hr 1min 27sec).

1960: gold medals, world pursuit championship, Leipzig, East Germany; world road race championship, Sachsenring, East Germany.

Gold medals: RTTC '25' championship; RTTC '50' championship (competition record: 2hr 5min 45sec); RTTC '100' championship (competition record: 4hr 18min 19sec); RTTC women's British Best All Rounder 23.714mph; BCF pursuit championship; BCF road race championship.

Winner: 2,000m pursuit, Berlin; pursuit and point to point, Fallowfield; Doncaster Wh '10' (competition record: 24min 35sec); '50', Midlands; two time trials, Ben-my-Chree road race and two track races, Isle of Man week; Amersham road race; pursuit, Welwyn.

1961: silver medals: world pursuit championship; world road race championship, both Isle of Man.

Gold medals: RTTC '25' championship; RTTC '50' championship; RTTC '100' championship; RTTC British Best All Rounder, 23.656mph; BCF pursuit championship.

Silver medal: BCF road race championship.

Winner: Beacon RCC '10' (competition record: 24min 27sec); pursuit Welwyn meeting (British best: 4min 10.1sec); WCRA road race championship; Goole Wheelers '25'; Ellen Vannin '25'; Isle of Man road race; pursuit, Herne Hill; Great Missenden road race; exhibition pursuit v Yvonne Reynders, Herne Hill.

Road Records Association record: 25 miles, 1hr 0min 31sec.

1962: Gold medal: world pursuit championship Milan (world record: 3min 59.4sec); eighth, world road race championship, Salò, Italy.

Gold medals: RTTC '25' championship; RTTC '100' championship; RTTC women's British Best All Rounder, 24.036mph.

Silver medals: RTTC '50' championship; BCF pursuit championship.

Winner: ladies' cyclo-cross, Tingley; pursuit, Doncaster; pursuit, Herne Hill; Hounslow & Dist RC '25'; WCRA road race championship; Long Eaton CC '25' (competition record: 1hr 1min 10sec); Dragon RC '100' (competition record: 4hr 14min 29sec); Nene Valley '25' (competition record: 1hr 0min 34sec); Yorkshire CF '12'.

1963: Gold medal, world 3,000m pursuit championship, Rocourt, Belgium; did not finish, world road race championship, Renaix, Belgium.

Gold medals: RTTC '25' championship; RTTC '50' championship (competition record: 2hr 4min 53sec); RTTC British Best All Rounder, 24.118mph; BCF pursuit championship; BCF road race championship.

Winner: Easterley RC '25' (competition record: 59min 25sec); WCRA championship road race; West London CA Ladies '50' (competition record: 2hr 5min 16sec); Isle of Man road race; Buckinghamshire road race; Rosslyn Ladies '100'; Nelson Wheelers '100'.

British records: one mile and 3,000m.

1964: silver medal: world pursuit championship, Parc des Princes, Paris; 10th, world road race championship, Sallanches, France.

Gold medals: RTTC '25' championship; RTTC '50' championship; RTTC '100' championship; RTTC British Best All Rounder, 24.716mph; BCF pursuit championship.

Fourth, BCF road race championship.

Winner: 3,000m pursuit, Berlin; Eastern Counties '50'* (competition record: 2hr 4min 29sec); WCRA championship road race; Roamer CC '25' (competition record: 59min 2sec); Morley CC '25' (competition record: 58min 39sec); Central District Ladies '25'; North Notts Olympic road race; Becontree Wh '25' (competition record: 58min 2sec); Dragon RC '100'; Viking RC '50' (competition record: 2hr 1min 12sec).

World records: 3,000m, at Nottingham and Newcastle-under-Lyme.

1965: Eliminated in qualifying, world pursuit championship, San Sebastian, Spain.

Gold medals: RTTC '50' championship; RTTC '100' championship; RTTC British Best All Rounder, 24.489mph; BCF pursuit championship; BCF road race championship.

Winner: Goole Wh '25'; Easterley RC '25'; Middleton CC '25'; WCRA championship road race; Sipelia road race; Newark Castle

'100' (competition record: 4hr 13min 4sec); Worcestershire CA '10' (competition record: 24min 23sec).

1966: Gold medal: world pursuit championship, Frankfurt; fifth, world championship road race, Nürburgring, West Germany.

Gold medals: RTTC '25' championship; RTTC '50' championship; RTTC '100' championship (competition record: 4hr 8min 22sec); RTTC British Best All Rounder, 24.812mph; BCF pursuit championship; BCF road race championship.

Winner: Notts and Derby Clarion 30-mile time trial (competition record: 1hr 13min 12sec); WCRA championship road race; Worcestershire 15-mile time trial (competition record: 34min 56sec); Tees-side RC '50'; Northampton & District '25'*; Ratae RC '25'; invitation omnium, Ghent, vs Yvonne Reynders.

Road Records Association record: 25 miles, 59min 32sec.

RTTC competition record: 10 miles, 23min 17sec.

1967: Gold medal, world road race championship, Heerlen, Holland; bronze medal, world pursuit championship, Amsterdam.

Gold medals: RTTC '25' championship; RTTC '50' championship; RTTC '100' championship* (competition record: 4hr 4min 50sec); RTTC British Best All Rounder, 25.696mph; BCF pursuit championship; BCF road race championship.

Winner: WCRA handicap road race; 10-mile team time trial (with Margaret Allen); Norlond Combine '10' (competition record: 23min 5sec); Middleton CC '25'*; Huddersfield Star Wh '15'; Havering CC '25'; Notts and Derby Clarion '30* (competition record: 1hr 12min 43sec); Newark Castle CC '25'; Goole Wh '25'; Wales road race; Morley CC '25'; Isle of Man '10'; Isle of Man '25'; Nunbrook Wh '50' (competition record: 1hr 56min 0sec); Beacon RCC '10' (competition record: 22min 43sec); Becontree Wh Ladies '25' (competition record: 56min 7sec); WCRA championship pursuit; Yorkshire Century '100'; Otley CC '12'* (men and women's competition record: 277.25 miles); Southend & County Wh '25'.

1968: silver medal: world 3,000m pursuit championship, Rome; 13th, world road race championship, Imola, Italy.

Gold medals: RTTC '25' championship; RTTC '50' championship; RTTC '100' championship (competition record: 3hr 55min 04sec);

RTTC British Best All Rounder, 25.942mph; BCF 3,000m championship; BCF road race championship.

Winner: Staffordshire '30'; Havering CC '25'; Norlond Combine '10'; Morley CC '25'; Nunbrook Wh '50'; Rutland CC '25'; Southend & District '25'; Becontree Wh '25'; Harold Hill '25'; Newark Castle '100' (competition record: 4hr 1min 41sec); Camberley Wh '50'.

British record: one-mile flying start (Herne Hill).

1969: gold medals: RTTC '25' championship; RTTC '50' championship; RTTC British Best All Rounder, 24.812mph; BCF 3,000m pursuit championship.

Winner: Norlond Combine '10'; Huddersfield Star 25-mile team time trial* (with Maureen Wroe); York '15'; Long Eaton Paragon '25'; Fenland Clarion '30' (competition record: 1hr 12min 20sec); Isle of Man '10'; Isle of Man '25'; Morley CC '10'; Morley CC '25'; Rutland CC '25'; track kilometre & pursuit, South Shields; Yorkshire Century '100'; Tees-side RC '50' (competition record: 1hr 55min 4sec); Worcestershire Cycling Association '10'; Easterley road race.

Second, Heatherbell '25' (event under Scottish rules, thus open to men as well as women).

**After 1970, the RTTC and BCF permitted women to race with men rather than restricting them to competing in separate events. As a result Burton increasingly tended to enter men's races, hence her domestic results now tend to be placings rather than victories. Where possible I have denoted these open events.*

1970: bronze medal, world 3,000m pursuit championship, Leicester.

Gold medals: RTTC '25' championship; RTTC '50' championship; RTTC '100' championship; RTTC British Best All Rounder, 25.729mph; BCF pursuit championship; BCF road race championship.

Winner: Concorde Women's '25'; WCRA championship road race; Yorkshire Century '100'.

Eighth, Sheffield Phoenix '25' (open); eighth, Clifton CC '25' (open team time trial, with Nim Carline); sixth, Hartlepool '25' (open; competition record: 54min 55sec.

1971: Bronze medal: world pursuit championship, Varese, Italy; ninth, world road race championship, Varese.

Gold medals: RTTC '25' championship; RTTC '50' championship; RTTC '100' championship; RTTC British Best All Rounder, 25.463mph; BCF pursuit championship; BCF road race championship.

Winner: Nottingham '25'; Morley CC '25' (open); Essex CRA '100'; third, Morley 25-mile team time trial (teams of three, with Roy Caspell and Nim Carline).

1972: fourth place, world 3,000m pursuit championship, Marseille; fifth, world road race championship, Gap, France.

Gold medals: RTTC '25' championship; RTTC '50' championship; RTTC British Best All Rounder, 26.112mph; BCF pursuit championship; BCF road race championship.

Winner Glade CC '50' (open); WRCA road race championship; Barnet CC '10' (open; competition record: 22min 6sec); Middleton RC '25' (open); second, Meanwood Wh '25' (open; competition record: 54min 44sec); Yorkshire Ladies CA '100'; Colchester Rovers '25'*; Brighton Mitre '25'.

Third, Huddersfield Star Campagnolo Trophy '25' (open); sixth, Harrogate Nova CC '50' (open).

1973: bronze medal: world pursuit championship, San Sebastian, Spain; eighth, world road race championship, Barcelona.

Gold medals: RTTC '25' championship; RTTC '50' championship; RTTC '100' championship; RTTC British Best All Rounder, 24.812mph; BCF pursuit championship; BCF road race championship.

Winner: Yorkshire Ladies CA '10'; Spartan Wh '25'; Yorkshire Ladies '15'; Sharrow CC '50' (open, competition record: 1hr 54min 7sec); Rockingham CC '25' (open).

Fifth, Nunbrook Wh '25' (open); second, Don Valley Wh '10' (open, competition record: 21min 25sec); fifth, St Neots CC '10' (open).

1974: Eliminated, quarter-final world pursuit championship; fifth, world road race championship, Montreal.

Gold medals: RTTC '25' championship; RTTC '50' championship; RTTC '100' championship; RTTC British Best All Rounder, 25.302mph; BCF pursuit championship; BCF road race championship.

Winner: three stages and overall, WCRA International weekend; two stages and overall, Four Days at Le Havre.

Fifth, Yorkshire Century '100' (open).

1975: Gold medals: RTTC '25' championship; RTTC '50' championship; RTTC 100 championship; RTTC British Best All Rounder, 26.047 mph.

Winner: two stages and overall, WCRA International weekend; Harrogate Women's '50' and '25'.

Third, Warwicks RC '50' (open); second, WCRA championship road race; sixth Yorkshire RC '50' (open).

1976: Gold medals: RTTC '25' championship; RTTC '50' championship; RTTC British Best All Rounder, 26.665mph.

Silver medal: BCF road race championship.

Winner: Otley CC '25' (open); two stages WCRA International weekend; Harrogate '50' (competition record: 1hr 51min 30sec); stage, Havro-Cauchois three-day (third overall).

Third, Richmond & Darlington '25' (open, competition record: 53min 21sec).

1977: Gold medals: RTTC '25' championship; RTTC Veterans '25' championship (open); RTTC '50' championship; RTTC British Best All Rounder, 25.069 mph.

Bronze medal: BCF national pursuit championship.

Winner: pursuit, Salford Park; Harrogate Festival '50'.

1978: Gold medals: RTTC '10 'championship; RTTC '25' championship; RTTC '50' championship; RTTC '100' championship; RTTC British Best All Rounder, 25.565mph.

Winner: Nunbrook Wh '50' (open).

Competition record: 15 miles, 34min 43sec.

1979: Gold medals: RTTC '10' championship; RTTC '25' championship; RTTC '50' championship; RTTC British Best All Rounder, 25.228mph.

1980: Gold medals: RTTC '10' championship; RTTC '25' championship; RTTC '50' championship; RTTC '100' championship; RTTC women's British Best All Rounder 25.732mph.

Competition record: 30 miles, 1hr 9min 16sec.

1981: Gold medals: RTTC '10' championship; RTTC '25' championship; RTTC '100' championship; RTTC British Best All Rounder, 25.219mph.

Winner: Icknield '10'; Becontree Wh '25'; Southend & County Wh '25'; Yorkshire Ladies '15' (competition record: 32min 56sec); Braintree '30' (competition record: 1hr 8min 36sec).

1982: Gold medals: RTTC '25' championship; RTTC British Best All Rounder, 25.006mph.

Silver medals: RTTC '10' championship; RTTC '50' championship;

Winner: Southend & County Wh '25'; Yorkshire Ladies '50'; Leeds Wellington '25'; East Bradford '25'.

Record: tandem 10-mile (with Denise Burton) 21min 25sec.

1983: Gold medals: RTTC '50' championship; RTTC British Best All Rounder, 25.219mph.

Silver medal: RTTC '25' championship.

Bronze medal: RTTC '10' championship.

Winner: Yorkshire LCA '50'; Otley CC '50'.

1984: Gold medal: RTTC '25' championship; silver medal, RTTC '10' championship.

1986: Gold medals, RTTC '25' championship; RTTC '50' championship.

Acknowledgements

Sincere thanks are due to:

Denise Burton-Cole for her boundless patience, cups of tea, and kind help in sharing memories of her parents.

Jeffrey Charnock for sharing memories of his family and showing me places where the Charnock and Burton families lived.

The current *Cycling Weekly* editor Simon Richardson for making it possible for me to go through the magazine's photo archive for this book's plate section, and to Simon Swarbrick at the magazine for scanning the images and advising on picture credits.

For sharing memories of Beryl Burton and her times: Charlie Burton, Alf Engers, Mary Horsnell – with further thanks for help with contacts, with press cuttings and for drawing my attention to the Jeff Cloves poem – Eileen Cropper, Mike and Barbara Penrice, Eileen Sheridan, Pam Hodson, Bernadette Malvern (née Swinnerton), Mike McNamara, Keith Lambert, Ernie Feargrieve, Phil Liggett, Mike Breckon, Yvonne Reynders (with thanks to my colleague Joeri De Knop for translating), Graham Snowdon, Maggie Gordon-Thompson (née Gordon-Smith), Shirley Robinson, Alan Sturgess, Ann Battersby (née Pallister), Martyn Roach (with particular thanks for connecting me with Mike McNamara), Ken Workman, Janet Salmon, Sue Sill (née Wright).

Jos Ryan for seeking out *Sporting Cyclist* magazines, and for connecting me with the Dave Rayner fund; Cath Leahy for sourcing archive footage from the BBC; Sheila Hardy at *Cycling Time Trials* for making Bernard Thompson's archive available to me, and other archive material.

Jeff Cloves for permission to reproduce his poem *Beryl and her Bike.*

Rupert Guinness for supplying the pages from his book *Power of the Pedal, the Story of Australian Cycling*, relating to the Melbourne-Warrnambool Classic.

To David Higham for locating issue No2 of *International Cycle Sport* with feature and pictures of Beryl Burton.

For invaluable editing at the manuscript stage, Caroline Arthur. For cover design, Matt Morris; for internal design, Steve Edwards. For sustained support and inspiration with the whole project from start to finish, Isla Rowntree. For helping to make it happen, Lee Garrington at Islabikes. Richard Hawkins for the copy edit, and Bob Fowke and Robert Branton at YouCaxton.

For their support and tolerance of the many hours spent absent either at the computer or on various trips to Yorkshire, I am indebted as so often in the past to Caroline, Patrick and Miranda.

Bibliography

Personal Best, Beryl Burton, Springfield Books 1986, reprinted 2009, Mercian Manuals

The Benny Foster Story... By himself, Benny Foster, Kennedy Brothers, 1971

A Wheel in Two Worlds: the Ron Kitching Story Ron Kitching and Mike Breckon; Ron Kitching 1993

Scientific Training for Cycling, Dr CR Woodard, Temple Press 1952

This Island Race, Inside 135 years of British Bike Racing, Les Woodland, Mousehold Press 2005

I Like Alf, 14 Lessons from the Life of Alf Engers, by Paul Jones, Mousehold, 2018

12 Champions, Peter Whitfield, Wychwood Publishing 2007

Time Speed and Truth, A History of Time Trialling 1890-2010, Peter Whitfield, Wychwood Editions 2013.

Kings of the Road, Robert Dineen, Aurum Press, 2015

Cycle Yorkshire, Jonathan Brown, Great Northern 2015.

Alpaca to Skinsuit, Bernard Thompson, Geerings of Ashford, 1988

Cycling Yearbook 1970, NG Henderson, Pelham

Of other publications consulted, *Cycling* in its various incarnations (*Cycling and Mopeds*, *Cycling Weekly*) was most valuable as a work of record, and thus is frequently cited.

Anna Kessel's *Eat Sweat Play* (Pan McMillan 2016) and Sarah Shepherd's *Kicking Off, How women in sport are changing the game* (Bloomsbury, 2016) both offered valuable insights into the history of sexual politics within sport.

Ray Pascoe's DVD *Racing is Life* (2012) offered unforgettable images of cycling between 1960 and 1980; the film features extracts from the

Yorkshire TV feature on Burton from 1986, Calendar Summer Sport Special.

The following specific articles were of particular value: Arthur Wright, *Sporting Cyclist,* 1960; Mike Daniell, *International Cycle Sport*, 1968; Colin Willcock, *Cycling*, May 1970; Bernard Thompson, *Cycling* January 1974; Liz Jackson, *Cycling* January 1985; Hugh Gladstone, *Cycling Weekly* 2009; *Yorkshire Post* obituary of Nim Carline, 15 June 2007.

List of Illustrations

18. **The crowds throng, but Burton will fall short: Mersey RCC 24-hour, 1969.**
    Allan Cash Picture Library/Alamy Stock Photo.

19. **With a young Denise.**
    Cycling Weekly archive, photographer unknown.

20. **Mother punctures, daughter waits, two-up time trial, Bedford, mid-70s.**
    Cycling Weekly archive, Jeff Katz.

21. **With Denise and Carol Barton on the podium after the national championship finish in 1976.**
    Cycling Weekly archive, photographer unknown.

22. **The sparsely furnished Burton kitchen.**
    Cycling Weekly archive, John Drysdale/Camera press.

23. **Burton and Eileen Gray meet at 1985 RTTC '10' championship.**
    Phil O'Connor.

24. **Selecting images from *Cycling* magazine's archive for her autobiography.**
    Cycling Weekly archive, photographer unknown.

25. **Remembered in the Morley town-centre mural.**
    Photograph: author's own.

26. **In a time trial, mid 1960's.**
    Allan Cash Picture Library/Alamy Stock Photo.

27. **"BB" signing autographs with the Sunday morning time trial safely behind her.**
    Cycling Weekly archive, photographer unknown.

Also by William Fotheringham

Put Me Back on My Bike: In Search of Tom Simpson

Roule Britannia: Great Britain and the Tour de France

Fallen Angel: The Passion of Fausto Coppi

Cyclopedia: It's All About the Bike

Merckx: Half-Man, Half-Bike

The Badger: Bernard Hinault and the Fall and Rise of French Cycling

Sunday in Hell: Behind the Lens of the Greatest Cycling Film of All Time

These titles are all available via www.williamfotheringham.com

Index